FLEET AIR ARM

D1380659

By the Same Author

H.M. SUBMARINES
NINE VANGUARDS
PRIZE MONEY
RACING FOR AMERICA'S CUP
SAILING :
  Vol. I, Cruising
  Vol. II, Racing
ETC., ETC.

(*Charles Brown*)

H.M.S. *Eagle*

FLEET AIR ARM

By

LIEUT.-COMMANDER P. K. KEMP

R.N., F.R.Hist.S.

HERTFORD
61002
355
PUBLIC LIBRARY

LONDON: HERBERT JENKINS

First Published by
Herbert Jenkins Ltd.,
3 Duke of York Street,
London, S.W.1
1954

COPYRIGHT   ALL RIGHTS RESERVED

BS4-15724

358-4

Printed in Great Britain by Butler & Tanner Ltd., Frome and London

Foreword

BY *Admiral of the Fleet* SIR PHILIP L. VIAN,
G.C.B., K.B.E., D.S.O.

THE AUTHOR OF THIS BOOK BEARS THE FORMIDABLE letters F.R.Hist.S. after his name, but the potential reader need have no fear; there is neither dryness nor dust anywhere in its too few pages.

The title, in fact, had it not been ill-descriptive of the book's purpose—and perhaps because the word is lately overworked—might have read " The Epic (or Epics) of the Fleet Air Arm ", since hardly, if ever, in so little a volume can so many tales of stirring adventure and of heroism have been told. The stories are relative to, and part of, the writer's design, which is not to present a detailed study of Fleet Air Arm operations, but to show the place occupied by air in the exercise of sea power, and the essential relation between the two.

This is done by recounting a selection of actions and encounters of the two wars in which the air power of the Fleet Air Arm exercised a preponderating influence on results, sometimes on history.

Because too often the calibre of the machines and equipment with which the pilots were provided fell woefully short of the minimum standard needed to execute the assignments given, success demanded undue risks—and got them, but at a grievous price of admiralty.

Written in this way, the book not only achieves the author's aim, but makes a story of absorbing interest, sure in its appeal to all who would read of high adventure, great issues in suspense, and gallantry and sacrifice.

There is much beside of which we all should know, and the book is laid aside with a welter of impressions and conclusions in the mind.

No conclusions, perhaps, are stronger than that in attack and in defence the navies of today have forged their principal weapon in the air ; that the exercise of sea power, even under water, has indeed ceased to be a practical proposition for a navy without a balanced air component ; and the inevitability of the carrier in any navy whose exercise of sea power must be worldwide and not confined to the narrow seas.

The most vivid of the impressions left with me are the vital part played in the development of naval aviation by the intrepid pioneers of the Royal Naval Air Service ; the wonderful luck the Navy had in the two wars in the courage and quality of its far too few regular naval pilots ; and in their hands how surely the volunteer pilots, who manned the great proportion of our order of battle, overcame the inherent and particular problems of naval aviation and sea fighting to become quickly knit into air squadrons, who showed time and again the capacity and tenacity to carry through the exacting and hazardous operations with which they were constantly confronted.

These men and their kind were described long ago :

> The best men are inspired by marks of distinction which drive them forward like ships in a brisk gale ; they seek no reward and would blush to fall short of public expectation, and therefore seek to surpass it.

Contents

Contents

List of Illustrations

FLEET AIR ARM

This book is published by permission of the Admiralty.
Any opinions expressed in it are those of the author and do not necessarily reflect official Admiralty policy.

First Thoughts on Naval Flying

It took some centuries of endeavour, and a considerable loss of life, for man to learn to fly. A far-sighted observer during the 1890's might, perhaps, have foretold something of the future of aviation had he been able to assess accurately the achievements of Sir Hiram Maxim, who was the first man actually to become airborne in an aeroplane fitted with an engine. Maxim's efforts, however, were dismissed as the antics of a crank, especially as his " hops " through the air rarely measured more than two or three hundred yards.

Nevertheless, Maxim was on the right lines and it was only a matter of increased engine power and cleaner design that, some ten years later, enabled the Wright brothers to make a flight at Kitty Hawk that startled the world. On that 17th of December, 1903, they remained in the air for over an hour, and most men's eyes were at last opened to the possibilities that lay ahead.

Perhaps one could say that the first tenuous link between the Navy that floats and the Navy that flies came a little over three years after that historic flight at Kitty Hawk. In March, 1907, a communication was received at the Admiralty from the Wright brothers, offering to sell all their patents to the British Navy. The offer was refused. But even with its refusal there must have been an early glimmer of appreciation of what the conquest of the air could usefully add to the mastership of the sea. At the very least it brought before the Lords of the Admiralty, startlingly, vividly, the actual fact of sustained flight.

It is difficult to criticize the Admiralty for its decision. Throughout the nineteenth century the Navy, by the exercise of undisputed sea power, had guaranteed the peace of the world. It had established itself into an instrument that held in its hands not only the destiny, but also the actual existence of the nation. By a policy based on the experience of centuries, it had steered a safe and steady course through storms that had swept other nations to their doom. In the profound peace of 1907 there was no reason to suspect that the Navy, as then constituted, could not continue to discharge its responsibilities with its existing means of fighting. It could hardly commit itself to an entirely new and still untried weapon until the proof of its value rested on a sounder foundation than that of a few successful flights over the land.

Nevertheless, even though the offer of the Wright brothers was politely refused, the Admiralty was by no means prepared to turn a completely blind eye to the antics of the flying men. In 1908 Captain R. H. Bacon (later Admiral Sir Reginald Bacon) was sent to France to observe and report on the first international air races at Rheims, and a year later the Admiralty appointed him as the naval member of the Government's Advisory Committee for Aeronautics, which held its initial meeting in 1909. In that same year Louis Blériot flew the Channel from Calais to Dover, and to all intents and purposes Great Britain ceased to be an island inviolably guarded by the might of the Royal Navy.

It was hardly surprising that, when the Admiralty did at last seriously consider the addition to the fleet of some sort of air service, it should turn its attention to craft lighter than air. The only naval task that was immediately evident in man's conquest of the air was that of scouting over the water ahead of the fleet. Naval eyes at that period were firmly focussed on Germany, where the Kaiser, aided and abetted by his naval adviser, Admiral von Tirpitz, was creating a new fleet that was already challenging the maritime might of Britain. And it was in Germany that the rigid airship, known by the name of its designer, Count Zeppelin, had reached the highest pitch of development. As yet the German airships were not entirely successful, but the very fact that they were being built there focussed naval attention on their possibilities.

The airship, at first sight, looked to be the ideal machine for naval reconnaissance. It was stable in the air and could fly if need be at a suitably low speed to enable a detailed observation to be made of enemy squadrons that might be in the offing. But a still more potent argument in its favour was that it was large enough to carry a wireless transmitter and so could communicate its observations instantaneously to the Commander-in-Chief.

The first step was taken by Captain Bacon who, on July 21st, 1908, put forward a paper to the First Sea Lord, Admiral Sir John Fisher, containing three main proposals. The first was that a Naval Air Assistant be added to the naval staff in the Admiralty, the second that the War Office be asked to allow their Superintendent of Ballooning to be consulted by the Admiralty, and the third that a rigid type airship be built for the Navy by the firm of Vickers Sons & Maxim. These proposals received Fisher's support, were accepted by the Board of Admiralty, and were submitted to the Committee of Imperial Defence. In due course that committee, on January 28th, 1909, reported in favour of the proposals and recommended that the sum of £35,000 be included in the Naval Estimates for 1909–10 for the express purpose of building a rigid-type airship. In the meantime, Vickers Sons & Maxim had been asked to tender for such an airship, and on May 7th, 1909, the order was firmly placed.

Within a few days of the acceptance by the Admiralty of the tender from Vickers Sons & Maxim, the next proposal in Bacon's memorandum was put into effect. Captain Murray F. Sueter was added to the naval staff as Inspecting Captain of Aircraft, with Commander Oliver Schwann as his assistant and, a few months later, Lieutenant G. P. Talbot as an additional assistant. A fourth member of the team, Chief Artificer-Engineer A. Sharpe, was sent to Barrow-in-Furness to superintend the actual construction of the new airship.

It took exactly two years to build No. 1 Rigid Naval Airship, as she was officially called. Unofficially she was given the somewhat equivocal name of *Mayfly*, a name that, not unnaturally, gave rise to many jokes about her. As built, she was a large ship, 5.2 feet long and 48 feet in diameter, with a blunt bow and pointed stern. Her framework was constructed of duralumin and she was filled with 700,000 cubic feet of hydrogen, contained in 17 gas bags. It took 46,000 square yards of watertight silk fabric, treated with aluminium dust and rubber to cover her.

The *Mayfly* had an unhappy history. When, in May 1911, she first emerged from her building shed, her graceful lines gave a promise of a good speed in the air, and as she lay at her mooring mast she behaved wonderfully well, riding out several hard gusts of wind without the slightest trouble. It was discovered during these mooring trials, however, that she had not been given sufficient lift, and four days later she returned to her shed for additional buoyancy to be built into her. On September 29th, 1911, she was ready once more, and the great doors of her shed opened. As she came out, a strong cross wind caught her, swung her bows away, and broke her back. Within a few minutes she had become a total wreck.

It was an unhappy start to naval flying, and as a result of the accident the Admiralty abandoned for a time its interest in airships. At the same time the air section at the Admiralty was disbanded and Captain Sueter and his assistants returned to general service. What little naval flying that took place was left to those amateur enthusiasts who could scrape together enough money to buy a machine of their own, or interest some pioneering spirit in the provision of an aeroplane on which to carry out their ideas of the sort of aircraft that the Navy might need.

To the rescue of naval flying came the Royal Aero Club which, in 1911, had reported to the Admiralty that one of its members was prepared to lend two of his aeroplanes, free of charge, for the purpose of enabling naval officers to learn to fly. This was Mr. Francis McLean, to whom the Navy owes a special debt of gratitude. Another member, Mr. C. B. Cockburn, volunteered to teach them, and to him, too, the Navy owes much of its early skill in the air. The offer of the Royal Aero Club was accepted and the Admiralty called for volunteers who were prepared to undergo a course of tuition in flying.

Over two hundred names were sent in and from them the Admiralty selected four, Lieutenant C. R. Samson, of H.M.S *Foresight*, Lieutenant R. Gregory of H.M.S. *Antrim*, Lieutenant A. M. Longmore of H.M. Torpedo Boat 24, and Lieutenant G Wildman-Lushington, R.M.A., of H.M.S. *Bulwark*. Wildman-Lushington fell sick just before the course started and Lieutenan E. L. Gerrard, R.M.L.I., of H.M.S. *Hermione* was appointed i his place. Later, on his recovery, Wildman-Lushington joine the other four and successfully completed the course.

The first four officers reported at the Royal Aero Club aerodrome at Eastchurch on the island of Sheppey on March 2n 1911, and placed themselves in the accomplished hands of M Cockburn. He was a brilliant instructor, and so keen were th four pupils that, in less than six weeks, they had all qualified f the Aviator's Certificate of the Royal Aero Club. The cour of instruction also included a thorough technical grounding in aircraft engineering, given by Mr. Horace Short, of the firm of Short Brothers.

The course ended in September, and so enthusiastic were the five officers who had qualified, and so convinced were they that the aeroplane had a large part to play in future naval warfare, that Samson succeeded in persuading the Admiralty not only to buy the two machines at Eastchurch, but also to send there twelve naval ratings to form the nucleus of a naval flying school. The two machines purchased by the Admiralty were both of the Farman type, each being fitted with a 50-h.p. Gnome rotary engine of the " pusher " type. As the new school developed, further machines were bought, including a monoplane of the Blériot type, and two Short twin-engined biplanes, of which one had three propellers. It was with this motley collection that the naval flying school at Eastchurch started to train the new naval pilots.

In the meantime Commander Schwann, who had spent much time at Barrow-in-Furness supervising the building of the *Mayfly*, had been making his own experiments. With his own money and other funds contributed by his brother officers and their wives, he bought an Avro machine on which to test out his own ideas. His ambition was to take off and land on the water, and during the summer of 1911 he carried out many experiments with different types of floats and gas bags. At last, in November of that year, he succeeded in devising a float that would support the machine on the water, and on the 18th of the month he succeeded in getting the machine into the air after taking off from the sea. He was the first man to make such an ascent, and although he crashed when attempting to land on the sea, his experiment saw, in effect, the birth pangs of the seaplane.

The next evolutionary step was taken by Samson. Flushed with his success in getting the Admiralty to continue with the Eastchurch experiment, he once again used his powers of persuasion to obtain permission to construct a landing platform that could be fitted to a warship. Such a platform was built at Chatham Dockyard and was erected over the bows of H.M.S. *Africa*. In December, 1911, using a Short " pusher " biplane, Samson made a successful ascent while the ship was at anchor. The machine was fitted with flotation bags lashed alongside the

B

landing wheels, and Samson brought it down safely after a short flight to land on the sea alongside the ship.

With Schwann demonstrating that he could take off from the water, and Samson proving that he could land on it, there was little to stop the actual building of a proper seaplane. With the able assistance of Mr. Horace Short, Lieutenant Longmore designed such a machine and by March of the following year (1912) the first real seaplane, fitted with mahogany floats of satisfactory design, made its appearance. Samson carried out the test flights at Portland, taking off and landing on the water without the slightest difficulty.

With the seaplane came the flying boat, designed and built by another pioneer of the air, Mr. T. O. M. Sopwith. It proved to be yet a further spur to the official establishment of naval aviation, for now the enthusiasts in the Navy could justifiably point out that they had the machines that were needed, machines that could fly independently of aerodromes and landing fields ashore.

The impetus given to naval flying by the successful achievements mentioned above brought to the Admiralty a further realization of the importance of the new arm. Naval officers began to formulate the duties of a naval air service, and by the end of 1911 the following list had been drawn up of aerial requirements in the event of war. It was to be expected that naval aircraft should be able to :

(1) Ascertain what vessels were in enemy ports if they were invisible from a blockading squadron.

(2) Ascend from a floating base (i.e. from over the bows of a battleship or hoisted out on to the water from a seaplane carrier) and ascertain if any enemy ships were in the vicinity.

(3) Fly above the fleet and locate submarines.

(4) Detect minefields.

(5) Direct the fire of the guns of the fleet.

Later, a further requirement was added to those already enumerated, that of bombing enemy harbours and installations. At the same time Lieutenant H. A. Williamson, a submarine officer who had learned to fly, wrote a paper advocating the aerial bombing of submarines at sea, using 50-pound bombs designed to burst 20 feet below the surface of the water.

Although it was as yet too early to appreciate the importance of his paper, the submarine still being very much of an unknown quantity in war, to him must go the credit for producing the first idea of the depth-charge.

The year of 1911 was an important one in the history of naval flying, quite apart from the successful seaplane experiments, for it was in November of 1911 that the Government took the first positive step towards the official establishment of a properly constituted flying corps. Mr. H. H. Asquith, the Prime Minister, sent a memorandum to the Committee of Imperial Defence, asking it

> to consider the future of aerial navigation for both naval and military purposes, the means which might be taken to secure to this country an efficient air service, and also whether steps should be taken to form a corps of aviators for naval or military purposes, or otherwise to co-ordinate the study of aviation in the Navy and Army.

The problem was studied by a technical sub-committee, on which the naval members were Lieutenant Samson and Lieutenant Gregory. Mr. Mervyn O'Gorman, who had had much to do with the early design and building of naval aircraft, was also a member, and Rear-Admiral Sir C. L. Ottley, a former Director of Naval Intelligence, and Captain M. P. A. Hankey, R.M.A., later to become Secretary of the Committee of Imperial Defence, were appointed as joint secretaries. Three months later, on February 27th, 1912, the sub-committee reported its findings to the Committee of Imperial Defence, which in its turn, on April 25th, accepted its recommendations. The main provisions of the sub-committee's report were the formation of a single Service, to be known as the Flying Corps and divided into two wings, naval and military ; the setting up of a central flying school to be administered by the War Office ; the formation of a permanent consultative committee of twelve members, to be known as the Air Committee ; and the establishment of several flying grounds in various parts of the country. It also envisaged a central pool of pilots, drawn from Navy and Army, trained at the central school, and available for work with either Service.

Most of the recommendations were presented to Parliament in a White Paper, dated May 11th, 1912, and were accepted by the Government. Accordingly, the Royal Flying Corps was constituted by Royal Warrant on May 13th, and the first official step had been taken.

The White Paper was never fully accepted by the Admiralty, which throughout had been reluctant to allow the development of naval flying to pass out of its own individual control. Although, in accordance with the White Paper, a central flying school was set up at Upavon, in Wiltshire, the Navy still retained its own flying school at Eastchurch and, in fact, all naval pilots continued to receive their first instruction there. In the Admiralty's view it was essential that the naval wing, recommended in the report, should be composed exclusively of naval officers who could fly, rather than of pilots from another Service allocated to naval work as and when required.

Following the acceptance by the Government of the report of the Committee of Imperial Defence, the Admiralty once more set up an Air Department of the naval staff, and again appointed Captain Sueter as its director. As his assistants he had Commander Schwann, Lieutenant C. J. L'Estrange-Malone, and Engineer-Lieutenant G. W. S. Aldwell. Samson, now promoted to the rank of commander, was appointed to the command of the naval flying school at Eastchurch.

The unofficial breakaway by the Admiralty from the Royal Flying Corps was accentuated by a change of name. The Royal Flying Corps, Naval Wing, which was the official title of the Navy's side of the new organization, was only used for a month or two, and in its place the name Royal Naval Air Service made its appearance. Completely unofficial at first, it found its way into general use in all official documents and, as a result, was soon adopted as a permanent title. Naval aviation was to fight under that title in the conflict that was so shortly coming, until finally it was merged into the new Royal Air Force a few months before the end of the war.

While this basic organization was being set up, the naval flying men were busier than ever. The next experiment carried out was that of bomb-dropping. In the early days of flying many pilots had made attempts to hit targets on the ground with dummy bombs, but as yet no one had tried to construct a bomb sight or to develop any type of release gear. The Air Department of the Admiralty concentrated for a time on this aspect of naval flying and many experiments were carried out at Eastchurch. Quite early in 1912 Samson dropped a dummy 100-pound bomb from a Short pusher biplane and was surprised to discover that the sudden release of so much weight had no effect on his machine. At the same time he started to work out mathematically the path of a bomb released by a moving aeroplane and devised, with the subsequent aid of Lieutenant R. H. Clark Hall, a gunnery specialist, a bomb sight that proved to be reasonably accurate.

With the solution of, at any rate, some of the problems of bombing, the next requirement was to discover the minimum height at which a bomb could be dropped without damage to the aeroplane by the blast of the subsequent explosion. For this purpose a destroyer was moored out at sea with an electric cable attached to a float, on which explosive charges of various sizes were fired. Attendant seaplanes were then flown above the explosion at differing heights. Once again pilots were surprised at the results, and it was worked out that an aircraft could drop a 100-pound bomb from as low as 350 feet without danger to itself from the blast.

While these experiments were being carried out, the new Air Department was going ahead with a plan of rapid development. With the enthusiastic support of the First Lord of the Admiralty, at that time Mr. Winston Churchill, himself a firm believer in the new weapon of air warfare, it decided to establish a chain of seaplane stations along the south and east coasts. Plans were completed in October, 1912, and the first of the new stations, on the Isle of Grain, was opened two months later. Others followed rapidly at Calshot, Felixstowe, Yarmouth, and Cromarty. At the same time the old cruiser, H.M.S. *Hermes*, was commissioned as the parent ship of the Royal Naval Air Service and fitted to carry two seaplanes, which could be launched on trolleys from a short flying deck built out over her bows.

It is necessary now to go back a few months in time and to take a look at airship policy again. It will be remembered that, after the disaster to the *Mayfly*, the Admiralty had turned its back on airships and had concentrated instead on the development of the seaplane. But recent events in Europe, and especially in Germany, made necessary a re-examination of the question. Captain Sueter and Mr. O'Gorman were sent by the

Committee of Imperial Defence on a tour of Europe to study the state of development of airships in various countries, and returned to present an enthusiastic report, especially of the German Zeppelins and Parsevals. The Committee of Imperial Defence, equally impressed, advised that immediate measures be undertaken to provide the Navy with airships, especially of the rigid kind. The naval members of the Board of Admiralty were less enthusiastic, only one of them coming down heavily in favour of the Zeppelin type. This was the Second Sea Lord, Vice-Admiral Sir John Jellicoe. During 1911 he had paid a visit to Berlin and had been for a trip in a naval Zeppelin, arranged for him by the Naval Attaché there, Captain Watson.

But it was now too late. Although Mr. Churchill acted with impressive speed and ordered eight to be built, the " know-how " was lacking and not one was ready by the time war had come. A small Astra-Torres type was bought in France during 1913, and a small Willows airship, which happened to be on the market, was purchased for training purposes, even though it was known to have no military value. These two airships passed into the naval Service under the names of Naval Airships Nos. 2 and 3. Later, the five airships owned by the Army were transferred to the Royal Naval Air Service, to do valuable work in the early days of the war.

The years of 1912 and 1913 saw remarkable progress in the further development of naval flying, progress in which the name of Commander Samson was always outstanding. In the naval review at Weymouth in 1912 he successfully flew a machine off the forecastle of H.M.S. *Hibernia* while she was proceeding at a speed of 10½ knots, and two months later repeated the feat from the forecastle of H.M.S. *London*. In the following year he tested a machine fitted with folding wings, which was launched from the special platform built over the bows of H.M.S. *Hermes*. The design of this machine sprang from the fertile brain of Mr. Churchill, who foresaw, with uncanny accuracy, the problems of aircraft stowage on board ship that were to make their appearance some years later.

So it was, during these two short years, that naval aviation fitted itself for the war that was only just beyond the horizon. A shaky and hesitant start had been followed by a swift reversal of policy and a spirit of experiment that had led to a vital advance in technique. It was naval pilots who practised and evolved a workable method of bombing, who experimented with wireless transmitters in aircraft, who first attempted to fit machine-guns in aeroplanes. It was their zeal and enthusiasm, backed up by an adventurous and far-seeing First Lord, which had produced the finest aerial fighting force in the world by the time the war clouds burst over Europe in 1914. When the time came the Royal Naval Air Service, whose separate existence was at last officially recognized on July 1st, 1914, possessed fifty-two sea-planes, thirty-nine aeroplanes, and seven airships, of which one, the little Willows bought in 1913, was used for training only. The strength in men was 128 officers and approximately 700 petty officers and ratings. It was on these that the main burden of naval flying in war was first to fall.

It was a motley collection of aircraft that took to the skies in those early days of war, Sopwith, Farman, and Short biplanes, Blériot-type monoplanes, and a miscellaneous assortment of odd machines converted into seaplanes. The first flying boats, designed and built by Sopwith, were beginning to make their appearance, and new airships, ordered in 1913 and 1914, came along in increasing numbers as the war wound its weary way through the years.

Shortly before the start of hostilities, the Royal Naval Air Service adopted its own ranks, suitable to the new medium in which it was to fight. These were :

Wing-Captain,	ranking with a	Captain, R.N.
Wing-Commander,	,, ,,	Commander, R.N.
Squadron-Commander,	,, ,,	Lieutenant-Commander, R.N.
Flight-Commander,	,, ,,	Senior Lieutenant, R.N
Flight-Lieutenant,	,, ,,	Junior Lieutenant, R.N.
Flight-Sub-Lieutenant	,, ,,	Sub-Lieutenant, R.N.
Warrant Officer, 1st Grade,	,, ,,	Commissioned Warrant Officer, R.N.
Warrant Officer, 2nd Grade,	,, ,,	Warrant Officer, R.N.

As the clouds of war moved slowly westwards over Europe during those hot summer days of 1914, the great fleet of Britain was massed at Spithead for a review by the King, lasting from the 18th to the 22nd of July. On the 20th, with a roar of engines, a large flight of naval aeroplanes flew over the assembled fleet in a " V " formation, the first public exhibition of formation flying. With them came seventeen seaplanes, while high above the aircraft four naval airships flew their White Ensigns in the sky as they droned across the review area. This was the greatest display of fighting aircraft yet seen in Britain, and in the precision of its formation flying there was ready evidence of the enthusiasm and skill which had, in so short a time, turned a miscellaneous band of adventurous men and crazy machines into a disciplined and cohesive force trained for the new job of fighting above the seas.

After the review the naval machines set out on an aerial tour of Britain. From Spithead they flew to Dorchester, and from there to the Central Flying School at Upavon. As they came in to land, urgent orders were waiting for them to return to Eastchurch. They took off again within the hour, and by the evening of July 27th were back at their home station. The rest of the naval aircraft were concentrating there, too, and machines kept arriving until the daylight failed.

On the 29th the Cabinet informed the Admiralty that since the Royal Flying Corps, as the military wing was now called, would inevitably accompany the Army when it fought abroad, the Royal Naval Air Service would have to take over responsibility for the air defence of Great Britain, and that these duties must take precedence over the purely naval requirements of scouting and patrol. These orders had been foreseen, and during the early months of 1914, the R.N.A.S. had been practising air fighting over Chatham, with two aircraft attacking the dockyard and neighbouring installations, and six defending. On August 1st, orders reached Eastchurch that all machines were to be kept tuned up day and night, ready for instant action. The day for which the Royal Naval Air Service had been training had arrived, and from now on the flights and manœuvres were to be in deadly earnest.

The R.N.A.S. in Action

HOSTILITIES OPENED QUIETLY ENOUGH IN THOSE AUGUST days of 1914 and there was little work for the Royal Naval Air Service to do. Early German minelaying off the Suffolk coast resulted in a system of coastal air patrols along the east coast, and the passage of the Expeditionary Force across the Channel to France brought seaplanes and airships into the air to search the seas for enemy vessels. But as yet the enemy made no move at sea, and all the patrols were negative.

Already, however, one lesson had been learned. Naval seaplanes, still in the early stage of development, lacked the range to accompany the fleet to sea and were therefore unable to perform their primary duty, that of scouting ahead of battlefleet and signalling early information of the position and movements of enemy squadrons. The answer had lain in the *Hermes*, with her two seaplanes which she could launch on trolleys from her short flying deck. So successful had the experiment been that, late in 1913, the Admiralty had taken over a merchant ship which was still lying in frame on her building slip. She was completed as a second seaplane carrier, with a large launching platform built over her bows. When completed she had accommodation for ten seaplanes, which could be flown off on trolleys, as in the *Hermes*. She was launched in September, 1914, and was given the name of *Ark Royal*.

Without waiting for the *Ark Royal* to be completed, the Admiralty also took up three cross-Channel passenger steamers, the *Empress*, *Engadine*, and *Riviera*. Sent to Chatham Dockyard, they were adapted to carry four seaplanes each. But these small carriers, useful as they proved to be in coastal work, had not the endurance necessary to accompany the fleet for long periods at sea. An old Cunarder, the *Campania*, was therefore purchased and fitted with a flying deck over her forecastle 120 feet long. Like the *Ark Royal* she carried ten seaplanes, which she could launch on trolleys.

It will be remembered that, at the start of the war, the Royal Naval Air Service had been made responsible for the air defence of Britain. Although there was, as yet, no idea of when the enemy would attack, there was lively discussion as to the form, and the weight, of the attack. It seemed inconceivable that the great Zeppelins, which Germany had been building in large numbers, would not be used for bombing British towns, and there was much discussion in the newspapers as to the weight and number of bombs they could carry. Some much exaggerated statements were published, which caused considerable apprehension in many quarters.

Although the R.N.A.S., in its pre-war experiments, had worked out methods of attack against Zeppelins in the air, and had introduced incendiary bullets and bombs and tracer ammunition into the naval armoury, it had no intention of waiting for the Zeppelins to cross the sea before engaging them. Once again plans had been made on the assumption that the correct method of dealing with the threat was to attack the Zeppelins in their sheds. Before the month of August was out, the three Eastchurch squadrons, with Samson in command, were established in Belgium at Ostend. They consisted of three B.E. biplanes, two Sopwith biplanes, two Blériot monoplanes, one Farman biplane, one Bristol biplane, and a Short seaplane with wheels in place of its floats. At first the Astra Torres airship was also stationed at Ostend with the squadrons, but returned to England after a brief stay.

The squadrons moved to Antwerp on August 30th and soon began the first raids on the airship sheds at Cologne and Dusseldorf. While the original planning was in operation, the aircraft themselves were busy, flying over enemy positions on reconnaissance, while the ground crews manned their armoured cars—taken over to France by the squadrons to salvage machines forced to land outside the aerodrome and to establish subsidiary air bases inland—and harried the German communications. As yet, no aerodrome was available for the naval machines at Antwerp, and the aircraft took off from the open fields in the vicinity.

The first raid was planned for September 12th. Three aircraft were to be used and were flown out to a flat stretch of beach. They were pegged down in the shelter of some sand dunes while Samson opened negotiations with the Belgian authorities for the use of their military aerodrome for the raid. But before the negotiations could be completed, a sudden squall sprang up, tore out the pegs holding down the three machines, and carried the aircraft along the sands, turning them over in huge "cartwheels" as they went. All three of them were completely wrecked.

Nothing daunted by this mishap, another raid was planned. This time four machines were to be used, each carrying three 20-pound bombs. On September 22nd they set out, two aircraft to bomb the sheds at Cologne, and two those at Dusseldorf. It was the first British air raid into German territory.

As the four aircraft flew across the Rhine and Roer rivers, they ran into fog. Aerial navigation in those days being still in the elementary stage of development, it was hardly surprising that three of the four aeroplanes turned back. The fourth, however, piloted by Flight-Lieutenant C. H. Collett, kept on and came out of the fog to find his target, Dusseldorf, below him.

He was flying at 6,000 feet, and at once came down to 600 to locate the aircraft sheds. After flying round for a few minutes he saw them and set a course to pass above them. As his bomb sight came on he dropped his three bombs and made a steep climbing turn to observe the result. One of the bombs fell a few yards short and exploded, causing no damage, the others hit the sheds, but failed to explode. Collett then set a course home to Antwerp, to find the other three aircraft safely there on his arrival.

The advance of the German Army along the Belgian coast was by now beginning to threaten Antwerp. One of the three squadrons was flown back to Hazebrouck, to form a new headquarters of the unit, and the remaining two remained at Antwerp, attempting to delay the enemy's advance by continuous attacks from the air on his lines of communication.

While the German advance was continuing, another raid into Germany was planned. Once again the target was to be the Zeppelin sheds at Cologne and Dusseldorf, but only two aircraft were available now, one directed on each target. The date selected was October 8th.

It was touch and go whether the enemy would not reach Antwerp before the aircraft could take off, so close had their advance brought them to the town. On the morning of the 8th the weather was considered too bad for flying and the raid was postponed for a few hours. But later in the morning the flying field came under enemy fire and it was now or never. The ground crews worked at the two machines under continuous fire and the pilots, Squadron-Commander S. D. A. Grey and Flight-Lieutenant R. L. G. Marix, took their machines up through the gunfire. Both were flying Sopwith Tabloids. The weather was still considered unfit for flying.

Once in the air the two pilots separated, Grey bound for Cologne, Marix for Dusseldorf. Grey's target was obscured by mist, and he came down to 600 feet and flew for 12 minutes under a heavy rifle and shell fire, in a vain search for the Zeppelin shed. Finally, failing to locate his target, he made for the main railway station and unloaded his bombs there. He then returned safely to Antwerp, to find that the enemy had been driven back by the squadron's armoured cars and the field safe for landing.

Marix had no difficulty either in finding Dusseldorf or in locating the shed. He dived from 5,000 feet and released his three bombs at 600 feet. As he pulled out of his dive he looked back to see the shed crumple under the force of the explosion and flames shoot up to a height of 500 feet.

Although the full result of the raid was not accurately known until later, it was fairly obvious that a Zeppelin was in the shed at the time the bombs dropped. In fact it was Z.9, a new airship just delivered and yet to make her maiden flight. With the Zeppelin were destroyed also the machine shop and the erecting shed alongside the hangar.

Marix's adventures were not yet over. He had spent some time over Dusseldorf evading the heavy anti-aircraft fire and on his way home his petrol became exhausted. He landed in a field about 20 miles short of Antwerp but managed to borrow a bicycle from a Belgian farm worker, and it was on this machine, instead of in his Sopwith, that he finally reached his destination.

Even this was not the full extent of the day's adventures, though Marix was no longer alone concerned in them. At 8.30 p.m. the sound of bursting shells indicated that the airfield was again under attack. Pilots and ground crew dashed out and began moving the aircraft in an attempt to save them from undue damage. The task, however, was hopeless, for no matter where the machines were moved, the bursting shells riddled them. By 11.30 p.m. the shells were supplemented by rifle fire, an indication that enemy patrols had reached the edge of the field. There was nothing to be done now but to abandon the aircraft and to withdraw in the armoured cars. They reached Ostend in the morning of October 9th, and a day or two later Antwerp was abandoned to the enemy.

The unit was now split up, one half under Samson working with the Army at Ypres, the other stationed on the coast at Ostend. This was the period of the great German thrust for the Channel ports, and the naval aircraft co-operated with monitors and destroyers in an attempt to bring the enemy advance to a stop. Their main task was the location of targets and spotting for the guns of the ships, though in addition every opportunity was taken to attack German forces on every possible occasion. Slowly, however, the enemy forced his way forward, capturing Zeebrugge and Ostend before the line could be stabilized. On the loss of the Ostend aerodrome the R.N.A.S. squadrons concentrated at Dunkirk, there to build up a new base.

As 1914 began to draw to its close, the U-boats started to reveal their power. Operating from German North Sea ports, they crept across to the English coast and penetrated through the Straits of Dover into the Channel. H.M.S. *Pathfinder* was sunk off May Island, at the mouth of the Firth of Forth, and the cruiser *Attentive* was attacked in the Dover Straits, in both cases the U-boat escaping undetected. It seemed the sort of warfare in which aircraft could well take an active and valuable part, locating enemy submarines at sea and reporting their positions to surface forces engaged in the hunt. And the loss of Zeebrugge made the matter more urgent, for this was an ideal base for the small coastal submarines which Germany was known to be building in large numbers, saving some hundreds of miles of sea in a U-boat's cruise to the British coast.

It was decided, therefore, to reinforce the R.N.A.S. squadrons at Dunkirk, and on October 30th H.M.S. *Hermes* arrived at the port to disembark the ground staff for the establishment of a large flying base. She set out for home on the following day and, 8 miles north-west of Calais, was torpedoed and sunk.

This further evidence of the growing power of the U-boat intensified the work of the Dunkirk squadrons. Added now to the daily task of assisting the coastal ships in their bombardment of the German right flank by spotting and target location was the need to keep Ostend and Zeebrugge under constant watch and attack to hinder their use as submarine bases. An attempt to use the Astra Torres airship for the reconnaissance and photography of these two ports was found to be too great a risk, and seaplanes and aeroplanes had to be used in her place. A large number of raids were carried out, and the size of bomb dropped rose from 20 pounds to 100 pounds.

While these new tasks were being laid at the door of the R.N.A.S., the old one was still very much of a priority. The loss of Antwerp had placed the Zeppelin sheds at Cologne and Dusseldorf beyond the range of naval aircraft, but there were other targets of a similar nature still within reach. The Zeppelin factory at Friedrichshafen, on the shores of Lake Constance, was not beyond the range of aeroplanes flying from Belfort. Similar sheds on the German North Sea coast could also be attacked by seaplanes from the carriers, provided that these were taken right into the enemy's jaws and the aircraft launched in the Heligoland Bight.

A raid on Friedrichshafen was planned to take place towards the end of November, and a month before it was due Lieutenant N. Pemberton-Billing arrived to arrange with the French general at Belfort for the use of the military aerodrome there. Plans were quickly agreed. Four Avro biplanes were taken to pieces, packed in crates, and sent by rail to Belfort, it being thought that German spies might get wind of the operation should they see the arrival of British aeroplanes at a French aerodrome so far to the south. The biplanes were fitted with 80-h.p. Gnome engines instead of the usual 50-h.p. Gnomes, to enable them to make the long journey, which involved a round flight of 250 miles over the mountainous country of the Black Forest.

Less than sixteen hours after the arrival of the train the four machines were assembled and drawn up on the aerodrome ready to take off. A full week of bad weather, however, prevented any flying, and it was not until the morning of November 21st that they were able to take to the air. Each Avro carried four 20-pound bombs. At the last moment the fourth machine, piloted by Flight-Sub-Lieutenant R. P. Cannon, developed engine trouble and failed to take off. The raid was now reduced to three aircraft.

The claim made after the raid, that very severe damage was caused would, perhaps, make a modern reader smile. Between them the three aircraft dropped eleven small bombs in the face of fairly heavy small arms and anti-aircraft fire. In fact, however, the damage was severe, for two bombs fell on a Zeppelin shed, wrecking it and greatly damaging a new airship under construction, and a third hit the gasworks, which exploded in flames and was totally destroyed. It was a most satisfactory dividend for a comparatively tiny investment.

The leader of the raid, Squadron-Commander E. F. Briggs, was forced to land in enemy territory when his petrol tank was riddled with bullets. He was taken prisoner. The other two pilots, Flight-Commander J. T. Babington and Flight-Lieutenant S. V. Sippe, returned safely to Belfort. There the three remaining aircraft were dismantled, repacked in their crates, and sent back to England.

Lord Fisher, once again First Sea Lord, sent his congratulations.

Lord Fisher desires [he wrote] to express to all concerned his high appreciation of the services rendered by those who carried out the recent daring raid on Lake Constance. He considers that the flight mentioned, made over 250 miles of enemy country of the worst description, is a fine feat of endurance, courage, and skill, and reflects great credit on all who took part in the raid, and through them on the Air Service to which they belong.

A more difficult target was the Zeppelin shed which had been constructed at Cuxhaven. The raid, which was to be carried out by seaplanes from the carriers *Riviera*, *Empress*, and *Engadine*, was planned in co-operation with a surface force consisting of two light cruisers, ten destroyers, and ten submarines. The main force of two light cruisers and eight destroyers were to escort the carriers, the other two destroyers and the submarines being stationed further inshore off the enemy coast to intercept any German ships and to pick up pilots and observers should they be forced down short of the carriers.

The squadron sailed from Harwich on December 24th, 1914, and early on Christmas morning had reached the flying off position 12 miles north of Heligoland. Each carrier had on board three seaplanes, but of these nine only seven were able to get up into the air. Although it was very cold, the morning was clear as these seven machines sped away to the southward. The ships settled down to await their return.

Evidence that the seaplanes had found their target came about an hour later with a sudden increase in the enemy's wireless traffic. With it, too, came a Zeppelin, which flew above the squadron and dropped bombs harmlessly until driven off by anti-aircraft fire from the ships. A German seaplane also flew over and dropped bombs, with equal lack of results.

By mid-morning three of the raiding seaplanes reached the supporting squadron, landed on the water, and were hoisted on board the carriers. The remaining four failed to put in an appearance, and after searching the Frisian coast for them in vain the ships set a course for home. The submarines, however, remained in position and E.11, stationed off Norderney Gat, sighted a British seaplane in the sky and came to the surface. The seaplane alighted in the water alongside, her pilot reporting that his petrol was almost exhausted. He was hauled on board the submarine and the seaplane taken in tow in an attempt to find the carriers. Almost at once two more seaplanes landed near E.11, while overhead a Zeppelin approached. The captain of E.11, casting off his tow, came up alongside the second seaplane and took off the pilot and mechanic, at the same time shouting across to the crew of the third seaplane to abandon their machine and swim across. Simultaneously, the submarine opened fire on the floats of the three seaplanes with her machine-gun, hoping to puncture the floats and sink the machines.

Meanwhile the Zeppelin was closing rapidly and another un-identified submarine, which had been closing rapidly, dived. Her action gave the impression that she might be German and E.11, hauling the last of the aviators on board, herself dived. As she went down two bombs from the Zeppelin exploded in her wake but did no damage.

The second submarine, in fact, was British. As she reached the scene of action she surfaced in case there might be a seaplane crew still to be picked up. After making sure that all three machines were empty and sinking, she dived again under heavy machine-gun fire from the Zeppelin, which was no more than 50 feet above her. The fourth seaplane, having lost touch with the other three, had meanwhile alighted alongside a Dutch trawler. The pilot and mechanic were taken aboard and later interned in Holland.

Although all the seaplanes had now been accounted for and

The first *Ark Royal* fitted as a seaplane carrier

The aircraft carrier *Vindictive*, with her two separate flying decks.

(*Imperial War Museum*

(Imperial War Museum)

Volunteers for the R.N.A.S. A first inspection of recruits at the Crystal Palace, the
great training centre for the R.N.A.S.

One of the R.N.A.S. coastal-type airships being hauled down.

(Imperial War Museum)

all their crews safe, the raid itself had been a failure. The clear weather at sea had changed to low cloud and thick fog inshore. As the pilots came in over Cuxhaven, they had been forced to fly at only 300 feet in order to see anything of the town itself. They were under constant fire, suffered fairly severe damage, and had all been unable to locate the Zeppelin sheds, which in fact were well to the southward of the town. Bombs were dropped on the port installations and ships in harbour, but the damage was negligible, although an indirect result was the removal of part of the German Fleet from Cuxhaven, through the Kiel Canal, into the Baltic, where they could do little harm.

The Cuxhaven raid was the last major operation of 1914, and as the year ended it was possible to assess, in some measure, the value of the new arm in naval fighting. It had, as yet, had little opportunity of demonstrating its value to the fleet at sea, but already it had proved its worth in its ability to observe enemy ports and harbours and report on the disposition of the German Fleet. On the credit side, too, was the destruction of one Zeppelin and severe damage to another, but these could hardly be classed as naval objectives. Nevertheless, these five months had largely vindicated the faith of the original enthusiasts, and the Admiralty had no hesitation in placing orders for large numbers of aircraft of all descriptions and in opening several new flying schools to train the many new civilian pilots who had volunteered for wartime service in the R.N.A.S.

So it was that 1915 opened with high hopes, only to receive a rude setback in the first hours of the new year. This was the sinking of H.M.S. *Formidable*, a battleship, off the Isle of Wight by a German U-boat. So great a loss focussed attention on the growing menace of the submarine and caused, to some extent, a revaluation of the primary task of naval aviation. More important now than the destruction of Zeppelins was the curbing of the U-boat, and plans were at once prepared for a greater naval air effort against the known submarine bases.

It was, however, no easy task, for very soon there were conflicting claims on the limited number of naval machines available. In February, the first shots in the Dardanelles campaign were fired, while a week or two earlier the first Zeppelin raid on Great Britain had taken place, bombs being dropped by the airships on King's Lynn, Sheringham, and Yarmouth. It seemed that it could only be a matter of time before London itself became the target of the Zeppelins. All those three were naval commitments, the anti-U-boat campaign, the air defence of Great Britain, and the campaign against Turkey in the Dardanelles, and the strength of the R.N.A.S. was to be stretched to the utmost to meet them.

The most dangerous and the most pressing was the German submarine campaign, for even in those early days of its development there were not lacking signs of its future severity. On February 4th, 1915, the German Admiralty declared that all the waters round the British Isles were to be considered a war zone in which all British merchant shipping would be sunk at sight and in which neutral vessels could penetrate only at their peril. That this was no empty threat was revealed when the German U.21 bombarded Barrow-in-Furness, the first indication that U-boats had reached the west coast of Britain.

The aerial war against the U-boats began with raids on Zeebrugge and Ostend on February 11th and 12th. In the light of modern knowledge, those raids would now appear laughable, but then the whole world could marvel at their size and ferocity. The first, on the 11th, was a failure because of adverse weather, but in the second twelve aeroplanes and one seaplane reached the target and between them dropped thirty-seven 20-pound bombs. Four aircraft were lost, of which one landed in Holland.

Although much was hoped from these raids, it did not take long for the Admiralty to become aware that they were no answer to the problem. Even when the raiding aircraft dropped 100-pound bombs, the damage was negligible and no U-boats were hit. New submarines were making their appearance in increasing numbers, the small coastal " U.B." class and the larger minelaying " U.C." class apparently being produced on some sort of mass production lines. Although the raids were continued, new plans had to be devised and put into operation in an attempt to bring the growing peril under control. Lord Fisher, the First Sea Lord, appreciated that, until some more definite way of destroying a U-boat was found, other than trying to hit it with an aerial bomb, the only alternative method of keeping the danger in check was to close the coastal waters of Britain to the submarine, partly by extensive minefields, partly by the coastal patrol of narrow waters. At the best this could be but a partial control, but at least it offered some small respite until more effective methods could be discovered.

With the minelaying policy the R.N.A.S. was not concerned, but the patrol of narrow waters was something it could do more economically and more efficiently than surface ships. Fisher, sending for Commodore Sueter, told him that he required a large number of small airships, and wanted them at once. Within three weeks the first had made its appearance, being no other than the old Willows airship with the body of an aeroplane slung under its envelope. This had been devised by Commander Masterman and Lieutenant Usborne. As such she was the first of the famous S.S., or submarine scout, airships, and it was found that this adaptation gave the Willows an endurance of eight hours at a maximum speed of 40 knots. The type was at once put into full production and, being simple to manufacture, soon began to come forward in encouraging numbers.

The narrow waters across which they were to carry out their anti-submarine patrols were the Straits of Dover, and the northern and southern entrances of the Irish Sea. Airship stations were set up at Capel, near Folkestone, Polegate, near Eastbourne, and Marquise, in France, for the Channel patrol, and at Luce Bay, Larne, and Anglesey, for the Irish Sea patrols. If the airships achieved nothing of an offensive nature against the U-boats, at least they made the entry into these waters a more hazardous matter, for a U-boat sighted and reported on passage could be hunted by surface craft called to the scene by signal from the airships.

With the growth of the U-boat campaign came also the reality of Zeppelin attacks on this country, first against east coast towns, and later directed on London. There were as yet no clues to the probable reaction of the civil population against repeated bombing, and fears were widely expressed that they might result in panic. The Government began to press the Admiralty for an increased effort against the unknown menace.

First efforts were not encouraging. It was thought that the destruction of the enemy wireless station at Norddeich, from which the Zeppelins received their wireless bearings, would possibly bring the attacks to a halt, albeit a temporary one, and so a carefully planned series of operations was put into effect. On March 20th the carrier *Empress*, with an escort of light cruisers and destroyers, sailed from Harwich, but the weather was too rough for seaplanes to be launched. Three days later the operation was repeated, this time to run into thick fog over the German coast. Two more attempts, each time with three carriers, the *Engadine*, *Riviera*, and the newly commissioned *Ben-My-Chree*, were equally unsuccessful through similar causes. A fifth attempt was also a failure, one machine crashing on take-off and three others running into thick fog with disastrous results. There seemed to be some malignant fate which protected Norddeich from attack, and the raids were at last called off.

This setback forced the Admiralty to return to its original plan of attacking the Zeppelins in their sheds and, where possible, in the air. Nor was success long in coming.

Air reconnaissance had discovered the erection of new Zeppelin sheds at Evere and Berchem St. Agathe, in Belgium, and shortly after midnight on June 6th four naval pilots took off from Dunkirk for an attack on them. As it happened, the three occupants of the sheds had, that night, left for a raid on England but had run into trouble. LZ.38 developed an engine failure soon after starting, had at once returned to Evere, and had been quickly housed in her shed. The other two lost their bearings in the thick mist and also turned back.

One of these two, LZ.37, was sighted in the air over Ostend by Flight-Sub-Lieutenant R. A. J. Warneford, one of the four raiding pilots, who was flying a Morane. He at once turned in pursuit and at last caught up with his giant opponent, only to come under very heavy machine-gun fire from the Zeppelin. He broke away in order to gain height, but was chased by the Zeppelin and again subjected to very accurate fire. Nevertheless, disregarding the fire, he climbed steadily and at 11,000 feet found himself well above the airship. Switching off his engine, he turned and dived towards the Zeppelin, flattening out when 150 feet above her and dropping his six 20-pound incendiary bombs. As they hit there was a tremendous explosion, a vivid sheet of flame, and Warneford's machine was turned upside down.

He managed to right it, and was about to set a course for home when he discovered that his petrol pipe had been shot through. Coming down, he managed to make a good landing in a field behind the enemy lines, where he succeeded in repairing the damaged pipe. He found that he had still got enough petrol left to get back to his base and, after several attempts, succeeded in getting his machine into the air. Before long, however, he ran into fog and lost his way, but just as his petrol was at last running out he reached a French aerodrome at Cap Griz-Nez. Here he refilled his tank and returned safely to Dunkirk.

Warneford was awarded the Victoria Cross for his achievement, the first member of the R.N.A.S. to receive the honour. Ten days later he was dead, killed when a Farman biplane he was testing broke up in the air over Paris.

While Warneford was dealing so successfully with LZ.37, two other pilots of the raid, Flight-Lieutenant J. P. Wilson and Flight-Sub-Lieutenant J. S. Mills, both flying Farman biplanes, were still on their way to the airship sheds at Evere. Wilson arrived before there was sufficient light to distinguish objects on the ground, to be met by signals flashed up at him from a search-light. He replied with flashes from his pocket torch, which not only seemed to satisfy the signallers but also those who manned the anti-aircraft defences. He was left in peace to fly around in the dark and half an hour later, as the first light of dawn broke across the sky, dived down on the Zeppelin shed which was dimly visible below him. He was carrying three 65-pound bombs, and all these landed squarely on the shed.

The resultant explosion sent up a pillar of dense smoke, sufficient to act as a target for Mills, whose Farman arrived on the scene just as Wilson completed his attack. By now the guns were in action and Mills had to take drastic evading action to avoid being hit. Nevertheless, his four 20-pound bombs all hit the target, and a moment or two later a vivid sheet of flame lit up the countryside. It was LZ.38, which burned fiercely until nothing remained but a twisted mass of aluminium.

The year of 1915 ended in home waters with experiments that were to bring yet nearer the aircraft carrier as we know her today. The experiments were still bound up with operations against Zeppelins and were made in an attempt to adapt the seaplane into a machine suitable for these attacks. The normal seaplane as supplied at this time to the R.N.A.S. was not fast enough, nor had it a sufficient rate of climb, to tackle a Zeppelin with much hope of success, but Mr. Sopwith had by now developed his " Schneider Cup " seaplane into a machine with the necessary attributes for such work.

The first headache arose when these " Schneider Cup " aircraft broke up when being launched normally on trolleys on the deck of the small carriers. It was quickly obvious that the cause was lack of space in which to develop proper flying speed before take-off. The larger *Campania* was therefore used, but even her flying deck was not long enough with the normal launching methods. At last, however, constant experiment provided the answer. It was found that, if wheels were fitted under the floats, the fast seaplane could just get into the air with the *Campania* steaming into the wind at a speed of 17 knots, although even then the safety margin was small.

Concurrently with this problem another arose. An urgent requirement of the Commander-in-Chief, Sir John Jellicoe, was for a seaborne aircraft that could ascend from a carrier and search ahead of the fleet for the enemy. Something larger than a " Schneider Cup " seaplane was needed, an aircraft that had considerable endurance in the air and could also carry a reliable wireless transmitting set. The *Campania's* experiments had shown the way, for what could be done with a light seaplane could also be done with a larger machine, provided that additional flying space was made available. The *Campania*, therefore, was put in hand for the necessary reconstruction to incorporate a longer flying deck.

These flying-off experiments, operationally urgent as they were at the time, were destined to have a profound effect on the development of naval flying. It was but a step from the seaplane with wheels beneath the floats to the normal aeroplane, which was both faster and more manoeuvrable than the seaplane. The problem of landing on had still to be solved, and two years later it was solved, but it was these early *Campania* experiments which sounded the death knell of the seaplane as a naval combatant machine.

By mid-1915 the R.N.A.S. had grown into so large a service that its administration was taxing the powers of the Air Department at the Admiralty. There was, too, a lack of liaison between the air stations and the various naval squadrons, so that the flying branch ashore rarely knew of the requirements of the surface ships, with whom they were to operate. There was, also, a real danger developing of a new and separate Service being formed within the Navy itself, fostered to a certain extent by the youth and exuberance of most of the naval pilots and observers who, coming mainly from the volunteer reserve, had not been brought up under the rigid discipline of the regular Navy. It was a situation that called for a radical reorganization of the Air Department, a step which was taken by the Admiralty shortly before the end of 1915.

Mediterranean and Middle East

WHILE THE MAIN OPERATIONS AT HOME IN 1915 WERE directed against the twin menace of U-boats and Zeppelins, a new campaign had been opened in the Middle East. This was the attack on Gallipoli, and it was in these waters that another major development of naval flying was to be staged.

The small carrier *Ark Royal* was sent out before the campaign opened, bringing with her one Short and two Wight seaplanes, each with 200-h.p. engines, three Sopwith seaplanes with 100-h.p. engines, and two Sopwith Tabloid aeroplanes with 80-h.p. Gnomes. The *Ark Royal* arrived at Tenedos on February 17th, and within two hours of reaching there one of her seaplanes was airborne and carrying out a reconnaissance of the outer defences of the peninsula to a depth of 4 miles.

The first tasks of the *Ark Royal*'s aircraft were reconnaissance and spotting during the naval bombardments. From the first they carried out these duties almost non-stop and it was not until it was decided to land a military force that any real opportunities came for more offensive operations. There were one or two small raids on Turkish installations and ships, but none was made in any strength and in only one did any real damage occur, when a 100-pound bomb hit the main hangar of an enemy aerodrome at Chanak and destroyed a German aeroplane inside it. Perhaps the most important work during this early period was that carried out by Flight-Lieutenant C. H. Butler, who made daily photographic flights over the peninsula and took over 700 photographs which, pieced together, revealed every defensive position in the area.

The first landing on Cape Helles took place in the morning of April 25th, and from then on the naval aircraft were in constant demand for support of the infantry. Wing-Commander Samson, who was in command of the naval aircraft in the *Ark Royal*, was later reinforced with a second wing of aircraft, under

Wing-Commander E. L. Gerrard, and between them they put up a magnificent performance in close support of the forward troops, in spotting for the heavy naval bombardments, and in bombing attacks on Turkish strongpoints.

Samson, in fact, did far more with the aircraft under his command than his orders strictly entailed. He was, above all, an adventurer in the air, a man who found in flying the great excitement of his life. So, in addition to the normal duties of spotting and reconnaissance, he ranged over the peninsula in search of adventure, carrying bombs for unauthorized raids, fitting a machine-gun into his aircraft and engaging the enemy from the air, swooping down on bodies of troops to fire his pistol at them. He was thus a difficult man to fit into the pattern of a planned campaign and it was hardly surprising that adverse reports on his private war should be sent back to the Admiralty. There was only one thing that the Admiralty could do in such a case and, perhaps a little reluctantly, a relief was sent out to take over his command, although he remained in the area as the senior pilot.

In spite of all that the aircraft could do, progress on the peninsula was slow and painful. The enemy positions were laid out in great depth, and the rocky scrub made concealment easy. But constant supervision from the air, if it could not greatly influence forward movement on the ground, could at least give advance information of enemy concentrations and preparations to attack. Such a case was the Turkish attack on the night of May 18th–19th, an attack that failed because of prior information. This had been gained on the 17th, when Flight-Commander Marix, patrolling in a Breguet biplane, noticed unusual activity in the port of Ak Bashi Uiman, with a large military camp set up alongside. This could only point to the arrival of fresh reinforcements and the probability of an enemy attack. Marix, with Samson as his observer, took off again with the Breguet loaded with bombs, and their unauthorized attack caused something like a panic in the enemy camp.

News of the concentration, and details of the numbers of men seen from the air, enabled the Army Commander to meet the threatened attack with confidence. When it was launched on the night of May 18th, all was ready for it. It was driven back with tremendous losses, so great that the Turks were forced to ask for a temporary armistice in order to bury their dead.

During June the *Ark Royal* was withdrawn, the reason being that enemy submarines had made their appearance in those waters and the *Ark Royal* was not fast enough to avoid torpedo attacks. She was replaced by the *Ben-My-Chree*, and with her came Samson's relief, Colonel F. H. Sykes, R.M.L.I., sent by the Admiralty to reorganize the naval air effort and to take over command of the R.N.A.S. in the eastern Mediterranean. As well as additional machines, he asked for eight of the small S.S. airships for anti-submarine work. Two R.N.A.S. balloon ships, the *Manica* and *Hector*, were also sent as reinforcements to assist in the work of spotting from the air.

If the Turk, by the tenacity of his defence, seemed immovable on land, there was still one point in which he was vulnerable. His lines of communication were long, stretching back to Constantinople, and they were widely open to attack. British submarines had been playing havoc with Turkish shipping in the Sea of Marmora, and had also succeeded in cutting the only railway line where it ran along the shore within reach of their guns. There was no reason why the R.N.A.S. should not reinforce this attack and add their quota to the toll of enemy supply ships sunk.

Torpedo attacks on ships from the air was something new, though it had for long been in the mind of the R.N.A.S. as a distinct possibility. That a seaplane could rise from the water with a torpedo slung between its floats had been demonstrated in the Solent before the war ; all that was required now to turn it into a weapon of attack was a reliable method of release that would, at the same time, start the torpedo's engine so that it could run after launching. There was no difficulty in that, and the engine-room artificers in the *Ben-My-Chree* soon produced a workable scheme.

All was set, then, for the first attempt to torpedo a ship from the air. On the morning of August 12th, 1915, the *Ben-My-Chree*, lying in the Gulf of Xeros, hoisted out on to the water a Short seaplane with a 14-inch torpedo slung under its fuselage. The pilot was Flight-Commander C. H. K. Edmonds and, after a short run, he got the machine safely into the air. Flying over the isthmus at the top of Gallipoli, he sighted a 5,000-ton supply ship off Injen Burnu. He cut off his engine and glided down towards the target, releasing his torpedo at a height of 15 feet above the water and at a range of 300 yards. As he cut in the engine again and began to climb, he saw the torpedo explode opposite the mainmast and the supply ship settle in the water. The first attempt had been crowned with success and a new weapon at sea had been forged.

Five days later, the same method of attack was tried again, and once again it was successful. Two seaplanes were used, piloted respectively by Edmonds and Flight-Lieutenant G. B. Dacre. Edmonds's torpedo hit a steamer that was bringing supplies to Ak Bashi Uiman, set her on fire, and left her a complete wreck. Dacre, however, was hindered in his attack by an engine failure, which forced him to land on the water, near Galata. In a short time he got his engine running again, and seeing a ship across the bay, taxied over and fired his torpedo. Once again it was a hit, and the steamer was sunk by the explosion. Turning, Dacre taxied out of the bay, managed to get his seaplane into the air, and finally just reached the *Ben-My-Chree* before his engine gave out again.

As the campaign progressed, the tasks imposed on the R.N.A.S. became more ambitious. That there were losses from time to time was inevitable, but generally speaking the machines had stood up magnificently to every demand made on their endurance and capabilities. Now they were to be tested even more severely than ever.

The entry of Bulgaria into the war had brought into strategic prominence the railway that connected that country with Turkey, and one obvious point of attack, that might do incalculable harm to the Central Powers, was the bridge that carried the railway across the Maritza River, just southward of Kuleli Burgas. Its destruction would hold up the passage of supplies not only to Constantinople, but also to Salonika, for the railway branches off to that city eastward of the bridge. The R.N.A.S. was asked to organize a series of air raids in an attempt to put it out of action.

The first raid, on November 8th, was made by one aeroplane from Imbros and two seaplanes from the *Ben-My-Chree*, each carrying two 112-pound bombs. The range, for those days, was extreme, involving a flight of 200 miles for the land-based machine, of which 60 were over the sea, and of 120 miles for the seaplanes, of which nearly all were over the land.

This raid, and the six others which followed it, were failures, although on each occasion the bridge was reached and the bombs fell accurately on the track and alongside the piers supporting the main arch. The cause of the failure, of course, was that the bombs were not nearly large enough for the tasks. Even direct hits did little more than tear up the track for a few yards, damage which was easily repaired in a few hours. The only point of importance in these raids was that they demonstrated the growing reliability of naval aircraft and their power to carry comparatively heavy bombs over long distances.

The lack of success in the attacks on the bridge caused the switching of the raids to the important junction of Feresjik, where a branch line connects the main line with Dedeagatch. Here a more immediate success was achieved with the complete destruction of the main station buildings and considerable damage to rolling stock and the permanent way. Here, too, was the scene of the winning of the second Victoria Cross to be awarded to a member of the Royal Naval Air Service.

This was won by Squadron-Commander R. Bell Davies after a raid on November 19th. One of the Farman aircraft, piloted by Flight-Sub-Lieutenant G. F. Smylie, was damaged during the attack by rifle fire and was forced to land in enemy territory with one bomb still in the rack. As Turkish soldiers ran up, Smylie set his machine on fire, expecting the heat to explode the bomb and blow the aircraft up. Bell Davies, however, flying a single-seater Nieuport, had seen the forced landing and decided to make an attempt to save the pilot. He came down and landed close to the burning machine. Smylie, seeing that a chance of escape had come, exploded his bomb with a shot from his pistol and, running across to the other aircraft, jumped on board and crouched beneath the petrol tank, hanging on to the struts. Opening up his engine, Bell Davies successfully took off and brought his passenger and himself safely back to Imbros, where he made a perfect landing.

Meanwhile Commander Samson was taking the opportunity, presented by this Gallipoli fighting, of carrying out further experiments. He was still very much a law to himself and all efforts to curb his impetuosity were in vain. He constructed the first incendiary bomb to be used from the air and dropped it behind the Turkish lines in an effort to set fire to the scrub which covered the barren hills. The bomb, which consisted of a 20-gallon drum of petrol with an explosive charge fitted to it, burst successfully when dropped, but the petrol was scattered over too wide an area and, although it caught fire, was not sufficiently concentrated to start a worthwhile blaze.

Samson's next " stunt " was to fly over Gallipoli with a 500-pound bomb, the biggest ever constructed, strapped to his fuselage. In spite of the great weight, he reached the Turkish lines and flew around for some time searching for a target. Finally he dropped it on a large shed and had the satisfaction of seeing it disintegrate. Nothing like this had ever been carried in an aircraft before, and the general ease of flight and manœuvre with it slung underneath opened the way to the heavier raids carried out later in the war.

The decision to abandon the Gallipoli campaign and to evacuate the peninsula came as a distinct blow to the Royal Naval Air Service in the eastern Mediterranean. It was true enough that the naval air warfare carried out in that theatre had been largely un-co-ordinated with the military campaign and that the opportunity had been seized to use the war there more as a means of private adventure and experiment than of attempting to solve problems of naval and military co-operation. Yet they had not been barren months, for the experience gained had given a firm foundation to further development of the R.N.A.S., both in the construction of higher performance machines and in flying technique.

While naval aircraft had been blazing something of a trail over Gallipoli, another task in the air was being carried out some thousands of miles away in German East Africa. There, far up in the swamps of the Rufiji River delta, lay the German cruiser *Königsberg*, who had slipped away from Dar-es-Salaam on the eve of hostilities to engage in a raiding cruise in the Indian Ocean. She had already sunk the light cruiser *Pegasus* before seeking refuge in the tortuous channels of the Rufiji, and her total destruction was necessary if she were not again to become a threat to British shipping.

It was one thing to require her destruction, quite another to achieve it. Before she could be engaged her exact position had to be known, and only aircraft could discover that with any accuracy, for the Rufiji delta extended for many miles inland. It happened that, shortly after the outbreak of war, a civilian pilot, Mr. H. D. Cutler, was giving exhibition flights in South Africa in two ancient 90-h.p. Curtiss flying boats. The Admiralty took over one of the boats, gave Mr. Cutler a commission in the R.N.A.S., and sent him up to the Rufiji.

Cutler's first effort to find the *Königsberg* was hardly successful. His flying boat, after being patched up by the engine-room staff of H.M.S. *Chatham*, who was watching the mouth of the river, was forced down in a fierce storm of rain and beached on an uninhabited island. Quite by chance Cutler was found by a search-party from the *Chatham* and brought back. Two days later, with the flying boat again made tolerably airworthy, he made another attempt to find the *Königsberg*. This time he was successful and discovered her some 12 miles up the river, moored up against the bank under overhanging trees, and well beyond the range of the *Chatham*'s guns. On a further reconnaissance flight, Cutler again ran into trouble, his engine breaking down. This time he landed in the river and was taken prisoner, but the flying boat was saved by the gallant action of a motor-boat which, under covering machine-gun fire from an armed tug, dashed up the river, made a line fast, and towed the machine safely back to the base on Niororo Island.

Out from England to destroy the *Königsberg* were sent two shallow-draught monitors, the *Mersey* and the *Severn*, and down from Bombay, to replace Cutler and his flying boat, came a small seaplane unit of two Sopwith machines under the command of Flight-Lieutenant J. T. Cull. On arrival, however, the aircraft were found to be unsuitable for tropical flying. Two Short seaplanes were sent out to replace them and, since the monitors could not arrive before June at the earliest, the time was spent in the construction of a small aerodrome on the island of Niororo. As soon as it was ready a reinforcement of two Farmans and two Caudrons was sent, only to be almost immediately reduced by one-half through the wrecking of one Farman and one Caudron in practice flights.

The two monitors arrived during June and at dawn on July 6th entered the estuary. Above flew one of the two available aeroplanes to spot the fall of shot. The *Königsberg* fired back with such accuracy that the *Mersey* was hit twice and had to retire for repairs, while the *Severn* only escaped by frequent changes of position. The *Königsberg* was repeatedly hit, but fought back so fiercely throughout the day that in the end the *Severn* had to leave in the gathering darkness with the task still unfinished. The two aeroplanes from Niororo had, between them, been in the air for fifteen hours and the accuracy of their spotting reports had enabled the *Severn* to score several direct hits.

Five days later the monitors again entered the river and Cull, with Sub-Lieutenant H. J. Arnold as his observer, was above the German cruiser when they opened fire. Spotting only for the *Severn*, he corrected range and elevation so that her third salvo hit the *Königsberg* on the forecastle. At that moment the aircraft herself was hit by shrapnel and her engine put out of action. As Cull was planing down towards the water he passed the information to the *Severn* that her salvoes were hitting the enemy's forecastle. A small correction for deflection brought her next salvo amidships, and the *Königsberg* was engulfed in a great explosion and set on fire. The two monitors continued to hit her, ranging on the two pillars of smoke that marked her position, and after an action lasting less than two hours, withdrew with their task accomplished. The *Königsberg* was no more than a burning wreck and would never again threaten British shipping on the high seas.

Cull and Arnold both had narrow escapes when their machine crashed. As it hit the water it turned over. Arnold was thrown clear, and was reached by a motor-boat just in time and dragged out of the water. Cull, whose safety-belt was still fastened, went down with his machine as it sank. After a tremendous struggle under water he managed to free the belt and kick himself clear of the sinking aircraft. Reaching the surface, he too was hauled into the motor-boat. Each was decorated for their coolness, accuracy, and gallantry during the operation, Cull receiving the D.S.O., and Arnold the D.S.C.

This year was also one which saw considerable technical development in the R.N.A.S. The prime cause of this was failure, the stimulus that so often precedes achievement. In spite of a strong naval flying contingent in Gallipoli, the campaign there had ended in stalemate, so soon to be turned by evacuation into a technical defeat. Equally strong R.N.A.S. contingents in France had failed to stop the Germans as they swept along the Belgian and French coast. Perhaps the most alarming failure—

certainly the one which caused the most despondency at home
—was the total lack of success against the Zeppelins as they flew
over England and dropped their bombs at leisure. During 1915
many raids were carried out, ranging from Hull in the north to
Southend and London in the south, and although naval aircraft
were flown off on each occasion, not one even caught sight of
a Zeppelin over the home coasts.

It was this lack of success that brought home to the Admiralty
the need to concentrate on design and, if possible, to limit the
large numbers of different types of aircraft which were still
finding their way into the naval air service. A start was made
with a reorganization of the Air Department at the Admiralty,
Commodore Sueter being placed in charge of the construction
branch with the title of Superintendent of Aircraft Construction, and Rear-Admiral C. L. Vaughan-Lee being appointed as
Director of Air Services. Discipline was tightened up, the
various air stations coming under the disciplinary control of the
Commander-in-Chief of the area in which they were situated
instead of under the Air Department, as formerly. New construction was mainly concentrated into three general types, a large
bombing plane capable of carrying 500 pounds of explosives for
a radius of 150 miles, a small single-seater fighter with great
speed, a high rate of climb, and a machine-gun firing through
the rotating propeller, and torpedo-carrying seaplanes. At the
same time, more powerful engines were designed, Sunbeam and
Rolls Royce being the leaders in this field, with horsepowers
ranging up to 260 b.h.p. Wireless, too, came in for considerable
research, and light, reliable transmitting sets were designed
especially to fit into the various types of aircraft.

It was, naturally, some time before the results of these technical
decisions came into service, and in many cases it was not until
1917 that the R.N.A.S. received the machines it needed for its
specialized work. But by 1915, flying in the Navy was passing
out of the stage when pilots were looked upon as irresponsible
madmen and approaching that in which many senior officers
realized that it had come to stay as an integral, and essential,
part of the Navy. More and more thought was being given to
its proper development and to the tactical and strategic tasks
which it should undertake. As yet these were still a bit vague
in the minds of most naval officers, even though they were now

(*Imperial War Museum*)

The first deck landing. Squadron Commander Dunning bringing his Sopwith Pup
down on the foredeck of the *Furious*.

The second attempt. The Sopwith plunging over the side.

(*Imperial War Museum*)

The first naval air V.C., Flight Sub.-Lieutenant R. A. F. Warneford, who destroyed a Zeppelin over Belgium in 1915.

(Imperial War Museum)

Lieut.-Commander W. Esmonde, who won the Victoria Cross when leading the F.A.A. attack on the *Scharnhorst, Gneisenau* and *Prinz Eugen.*

(Imperial War Museum

accepting the air service as a new weapon of immense potential value. It was to this end, in 1915 and 1916, that some of the best brains in the Navy were devoting their energy.

Any history of the R.N.A.S. in 1915 would be incomplete without at least a passing reference to the volume of advice that poured into the Air Department at the Admiralty from the public at large. Some, perhaps, was prophetic, such as that which suggested the use of artificial moonlight, or the setting up of lights in open spaces to simulate dummy towns. Others were less helpful. One of the most fantastic perhaps, came from a lady who was concerned with the anti-Zeppelin campaign.

It is well known [she wrote] that ice is water and that ice floats on water. The clouds, if made into ice, would of course still float in the sky. Why not, therefore, freeze the clouds and carry anti-aircraft guns, ammunition, gun crews, and stores on them, letting them roam about looking for enemy airships.

She went on to confess that she herself was not a scientist, and was quite prepared to leave the technical problems associated with her suggestion to the scientific members of the Government.

Another suggestion was almost equally fantastic. This was to construct an immense floating island as large as, and in the shape of, England, Scotland, and Wales. This island was then to be moored in the North Sea. Zeppelins, flying over to attack England, would be misled into thinking that they had reached their destination on sighting this island and would waste their bombs on it. If they became suspicious and, flying on further, sighted the real England, they would mistake it for Ireland and turn back!

These and similar suggestions, may well have caused a smile at the Admiralty when they were read and passed round the directorate, but they did little to help the main problem of air defence at home. It was, in fact, an insoluble problem, for it entailed the use of machines designed for naval purposes in a purely shore role. It was not until the middle of 1916 that sanity, in this particular requirement, prevailed, and the Royal Naval Air Service was released from its responsibility for the air defence of the home country.

D

The First Carrier Trials

IF THE VARIED EVENTS OF 1915 HAD STRETCHED THE capacity and ingenuity of the Royal Naval Air Service almost to its limits, those of 1916 gave it a much better chance of consolidating the knowledge gained and of producing a more coherent pattern of naval air responsibilities. Various favourable factors worked to this end, and the Navy was not slow to take full advantage of them.

The ending of the campaign in Gallipoli was the first of these, releasing a large number of aircraft for other duties. During 1916, too, the Royal Flying Corps took over the responsibility for the air defence, first, of London, and a month or two later, of the whole of Great Britain. Once again that released more aircraft for their purely naval duties, so that for the first time since the start of the war it was possible to concentrate naval strength into the channels where it could do most good.

A broad pattern of 1916 would show increased activity on the Belgian coast, where aircraft were invaluable in spotting for the monitors engaged there, a larger concentration in the east coast stations for dealing with Zeppelins over the sea as they approached or left the shore of England, and a vigorous effort to relate air power to the growing menace of the U-boat. These were the major tasks which faced the R.N.A.S. in 1916. The year, too, saw the first tentative attempts to work aircraft from carriers with the fleet, though as yet not entirely in an offensive role. The new service was too young yet, and its machines not sufficiently developed, to carry the Gallipoli lessons in torpedo attack to their logical conclusion.

The naval war against the German Zeppelins reached its highest pitch of intensity during 1916. Frequent raids by the enemy were made on a variety of targets, as many as nine or ten airships being employed at a time, though on the whole the damage was remarkably slight and the loss of life proportionately small. What the raids lacked in military and material damage, however, was probably more than made up by the drop in morale that they caused in the civilian population, so that every possible effort was made to intercept these giants of the air out at sea and drive them off before they could cross the coast.

It was not an easy task, for the raiding Zeppelins only flew in the dark. Night flying had been practised by the R.N.A.S. ever since the start of the war, but in those days there were no aids to navigation and an interception was almost entirely a matter of fortunate encounter. Another great handicap was the lack of any effective weapon against such craft, for the normal armament of intercepting machines was nothing more than a Lewis gun mounted on the upper plane so as to fire clear of the propeller. Incendiary darts, invented by Engineer-Commander F. Ranken, were also carried, but the use of these entailed reaching a position above the Zeppelins, and almost invariably these airships had a higher rate of climb than the attacking aircraft.

In the face of these difficulties, it is not surprising that most of the raiding airships got through to their objectives unscathed. There was no form of location from a distance and often enough the first warning of the presence of a Zeppelin came with the dropping of its bombs. Although machines could be flown off from the air stations without any loss of time, they could, once in the air, do no more than grope about in the dark for their opponents.

Yet, in spite of this, there were some successes. Quite a number of Zeppelins were hit and damaged, but though several were brought down, R.N.A.S. pilots could only claim one of them as entirely theirs. This was L.21, shot down at sea off Lowestoft on November 28th. She had been raiding in the north, dropping bombs at Wakefield, Barnsley, and Hanley. Returning home over Lowestoft she was attacked by three naval BE 2C machines, piloted by Flight-Lieutenant Cadbury, Flight-Sub-Lieutenant Pulling, and Flight-Sub-Lieutenant Fane. Each attacked in turn under a galling fire from the Zeppelin, firing their Lewis guns into her tail at a range that was at times as little as 30 feet. She eventually caught fire in her stern as a result of these attacks and the flames soon spread along her whole length. Burning fiercely, she plunged into the sea and sank almost immediately. For their gallantry during this attack

Pulling was awarded the D.S.O., while Cadbury and Fane each received the D.S.C.

Across the water, other machines of the R.N.A.S. were strenuously engaged on the Belgian coast. The main base was still Dunkirk, with subsidiary airfields at St. Pol, Coudekerque, and Petite Synthe. In addition to the normal work of fleet co-operation and spotting, a considerable bombing force was built up under the command of Squadron-Commander S. D. A. Grey. It carried out several raids, mainly on German aerodromes in Belgium, on aircraft sheds and shipbuilding yards in Germany itself, and occasionally on targets deep into enemy country. Some of these raids were in considerable force compared with the earlier efforts of 1914 and 1915, on one occasion as many as twenty-nine machines being engaged. Raids by fifteen or twenty bombers were frequent, but although a great many bombs were dropped on a wide variety of targets during the course of them, the damage caused was, on the whole, very small. Bombs were still not large enough to cause any appreciable damage in the area in which they were dropped, and the bomb sights used were too rudimentary to permit of any great accuracy in aiming.

But by far the most important work on this coast was that of spotting for the monitors and for attacks carried out from time to time by ships of the Dover Patrol. The main objectives of these bombardments were the many batteries which the enemy had installed within reach of the big guns of the monitors. The work, often uninspiring and often tedious, was carried out day after day, so that the unrelenting pressure exerted by the ships tied down a large number of enemy troops who could have been far more usefully employed elsewhere. So important did this work become that, during 1916, the Admiralty opened a special school for training observers and instituted a new rank of Observer Officer. There were never enough of them to fill the numbers required.

Typical of this work was the systematic shelling of the notorious " Tirpitz " battery, set up by the enemy in the neighbourhood of Adinkerke. In addition to a bombardment by monitors off the coast, a naval 12-inch gun was set up ashore to add to the weight of metal falling on the battery. In order, too, to achieve surprise and prevent retaliation, it was essential to keep enemy aircraft away from the vicinity of the gun.

The systematic shelling of the battery was begun on July 8th, and the R.N.A.S. laid on not only a continuous relay of spotting machines but also a continuous fighter escort for the spotting aircraft, photographic reconnaissance aeroplanes to record the result of the firing, and a naval balloon to assist in observation, flown from the balloon ship *City of Oxford* moored just off the coast.

Corrections for range and deflection were made by the spotting aircraft by wireless signal direct to the guns of the monitors and to the 12-inch gun ashore. When the shelling was begun in the morning the first four rounds fired from ashore were not seen from the aeroplane above the battery. The bursting of the fifth, however, was plainly visible, and a deflection correction brought the sixth right for line. A range correction was then passed and the seventh round fired scored a direct hit. Once found, the 12-inch gun continued to hit with complete regularity until the Tirpitz battery was no more than a heap of twisted metal.

Towards the end of the year the fighter wing at Dunkirk was called upon to provide a squadron of eighteen machines for duty with the Army on the Somme. Under the command of Squadron-Commander G. R. Bromet, this unit was based on Vert Galand aerodrome and was soon engaged in flying operations over the front. It consisted of one flight (six aircraft) of Nieuports, one flight of Sopwith Pups, one of the most successful types of aircraft produced throughout the whole of the war, and six other miscellaneous machines. In two months of fighting on the Western Front, the squadron shot down twenty-four enemy aircraft for the loss of only two pilots killed.

While all these shore-based operations of the R.N.A.S. were going on, the main problem still facing the Admiralty was that of countering the U-boat. Under Mr. Churchill as First Lord, the Admiralty had in 1915 ordered fifty of the small " S.S." airships to be used for anti-submarine patrol duties. On Mr. Churchill's relief by Mr. Balfour, the " S.S." programme was brought to a halt, and it was decided to order thirty of a larger type, known as " Coastal " airships. These had a considerably greater range and endurance than the small " S.S." ships and as a result could carry out much more protracted patrols. As this year progressed, new areas were brought under observation from these airships, with new bases established at Pembroke, Dulham, Howden, Longside, Mullion, East Fortune, and finally at Cranwell. In addition to becoming an operational airship base, Cranwell was developed as a great R.N.A.S. training centre for aeroplanes and airships.

The new Coastal type airship was made up of an Astra Torres envelope, to which was attached a car made by joining two Avro fuselages together end to end with their tails cut off. They were thus quick and cheap to manufacture and they did excellent service in the anti-submarine role until the end of the war.

The next development was the Zero, an improved "S.S." airship designed for towing by ships. Here the object was not anti-submarine work, but spotting and reconnaissance. It was found that these airships could be towed perfectly satisfactorily by all types of ships and even at maximum speed, but a great drawback was their vulnerability to attacks by gunfire and by hostile aircraft. After a few trials off the Belgian coast with the airships towed by monitors, the experiment was abandoned.

All these airships were of the non-rigid type, and it was during 1916 that the Admiralty re-started their original programme of building rigid ships. Four, based on the pre-war design of Naval Airship No. 9, were ordered early in the year, and orders for a further four, to an improved design, followed later. While they were being built, however, a German Zeppelin was forced down just north of Mersea Island, in Essex, and landed relatively undamaged. She was L.33, and the design was quickly seized upon by the Admiralty for a new class of rigids. They were known as the " 33 " class, but with the prefix R, and they were the ships that were to achieve some fame immediately after the war, the second of them, R.34, flying the Atlantic in both directions in July, 1919.

Of most interest, however, during this year of 1916, was the development of naval aircraft and carriers to operate with the fleet. The *Campania* had been taken in hand in 1915 for considerable structural alterations, and came back into service in March, 1916, with a much larger flying deck. An Isle of Man passenger steamer, the *Viking*, was taken up and converted, appearing in the fleet as H.M.S. *Vindex*, with a flying-off deck and hanger forward, and stowage for five seaplanes aft.

It was an operation planned for the *Vindex* which, in 1916, almost led to the first major fleet action of the war. The immediate object was a seaplane raid on the Zeppelin sheds thought to be at Hoyer, on the Schleswig coast. H.M.S. *Vindex*, escorted by the Harwich force under Commodore Tyrwhitt, and supported by the battle-cruiser force under Admiral Beatty, sailed on March 24th. The weather was stormy, with frequent squalls of snow and sleet, but by 4.30 a.m. on the 25th the Harwich force was in position off the enemy coast. The *Vindex* proceeded farther in and successfully launched her five seaplanes.

Two of the raiding machines returned a couple of hours later. The pilot of the first reported that there were no Zeppelin sheds at Hoyer but that he had successfully bombed a huge factory and set it on fire. The second pilot, returning some minutes later, had flown further inland and had discovered the sheds at Tondern. He had, however, been unable to release his bombs, as the rack was choked with ice and snow. Of the three other seaplanes there was no sign.

Commodore Tyrwhitt ordered the *Vindex*, her task completed, to return to Harwich and with his destroyers carried out a sweep towards the enemy shore to search for the missing airmen. In doing so, he came across two armed trawlers and promptly sank them. This action was followed by an attack on the destroyers by German seaplanes and by the sailing of the High Seas Fleet.

Admiral Beatty, realizing that the Harwich force could be no match for the combined might of the German battleships and cruisers, moved south from his position off the Horns Riff to cover Tyrwhitt's withdrawal and the Admiralty ordered Admiral Jellicoe to put to sea with the Grand Fleet. During the night the light cruiser *Cleopatra* rammed and sank an enemy destroyer, but in doing so collided with the destroyer *Undaunted*, damaging her so much that she could steam at no more than 6 knots. With the speed of the Harwich force now reduced to this figure, it looked almost certain that a major action was inevitable. During the night the two main forces closed rapidly, the Grand Fleet under Jellicoe steaming down from the north, the High Seas Fleet approaching from the south. But the heavy weather was too much for the Germans and, as dawn broke on the 26th, the enemy ships turned for home and the shelter of their bases.

The action of the enemy seemed to show an undue sensitivity

to raids on Zeppelin sheds and it was thought by the Commander-in-Chief that a repetition of the operation might well produce another sortie of the main enemy fleet. And so a further raid on the Tondern airship sheds was planned. Two carriers were involved this time, the *Vindex* and the *Engadine*, and on May 3rd they sailed, escorted once again by the Harwich force, with the battle-cruisers covering from Horns Riff and the Grand Fleet in position in the approaches to the Skagerrak. The stage was set for what was hoped would develop into a drama of the first magnitude.

But alas, the result was an anti-climax. In the early hours of May 4th the *Vindex* and *Engadine* were lying off the island of Sylt and the eleven Sopwith seaplanes carried were being hoisted out. Eight of them failed to get into the air at all, the rough sea causing several broken propellers and flooded magnetos. Of the three which succeeded in rising into the air, one immediately flew into the wireless aerial of one of the escorting destroyers and crashed and a second was forced to return after two or three minutes with engine failure. Only one of the original eleven reached Tondern—to find the airship sheds completely hidden in the morning mist. The two 65-pound bombs that it carried did no damage.

Although the German Fleet did not emerge from its harbours, the operation was not entirely without a dividend. The Zeppelin L.7 left Tondern and flew over the Harwich force, being engaged at long range by the guns of the *Galatea* and *Phaeton*. She was fairly heavily damaged and turned for home, losing height. As she approached the coast she was sighted by a British submarine, E.11, which surfaced and engaged her with her one gun, forcing her down on to the water and setting her afire.

If the enemy fleet made no appearance on May 4th, the hoped-for meeting was not to be long delayed. Admiral Scheer was as keen for action as Admiral Jellicoe and on the morning of May 31st the German battlefleet sailed from its bases in the Jade. Scheer had planned an elaborate operation in conjunction with U-boats and Zeppelins, designed to lead Beatty's battle-cruisers within reach of his battleships. When the weather at the end of May precluded the use of Zeppelins the operation became no more than a sortie and Scheer's hopes of action faded.

The Admiralty, however, had other opinions. As early as May 30th the unusual volume of wireless activity on the enemy's side indicated that something big was in the air and the Grand Fleet, together with Beatty's battle-cruiser force, were ordered to sea. The dramatic meeting of the cruiser screens and the subsequent battle fought off Jutland are matters of history and only slightly touch the story of the R.N.A.S.

This, in fact, was by accident, not by design, for the R.N.A.S. should have played a large part in the battle. The *Campania* had been attached to the Grand Fleet and the *Engadine* to the battle-cruisers for reconnaissance purposes for just such an action as this. By some mischance the signal to sail was not read by the *Campania* and the Grand Fleet went to sea without her. When she discovered her mistake, it was too late.

The *Engadine*, however, went to sea with Beatty's battle-cruisers. On the afternoon of the 31st, after the *Galatea* had made contact with Admiral Hipper's screen, Beatty ordered the *Engadine* to fly off a seaplane and investigate a large amount of smoke sighted away to the north-east. Flight-Lieutenant F. J. Rutland, with Assistant Paymaster G. S. Trewin as his observer, was quickly in the air and reported the smoke as three cruisers and five destroyers. Rutland proceeded to shadow this force and was able to report a large alteration of course before being forced down with a broken petrol pipe. He landed safely and repaired the break with a length of rubber tubing, but by now Beatty had realized the situation and did not require any further reconnaissance for the moment. He set off in pursuit of Hipper's scouting group, only to be led a few minutes later into the jaws of the High Seas Fleet coming up from the south. It is idle to speculate on what might have happened had he continued to use the *Engadine*'s seaplane for reconnaissance, but earlier information of Scheer's presence, which an air search would almost certainly have provided, might well have altered the whole course of the battle.

This single flight of the *Engadine*'s aircraft was the first use of the air as a new component of traditional naval warfare. Indecisive as it was, it pointed the way towards a closer naval co-operation and laid stress on the added value which proper air reconnaissance could contribute to tactical problems at sea. Further experiments in this direction were put in hand at once, mainly directed to the problem of flying off a two-seater aircraft from a flying deck instead of having to hoist her out to use the sea as her take-off platform. The first of such flights was made only three days after the battle of Jutland when, on June 3rd, a two-seater Short seaplane, carrying pilot and observer, was successfully launched from the flight deck of the *Campania*.

While these events were taking place in the western European theatre, No. 2 Wing of the R.N.A.S. was fully occupied in the eastern Mediterranean. Wing-Captain F. R. Scarlett had been sent out in command of the R.N.A.S. units there and, although the Gallipoli campaign had ended in failure, there was still plenty of work for the naval aircraft to do. Turkey and Bulgaria were still in the war, and a policy of maximum disturbance of lines of communication was adopted in order, by pinning down large defence forces and denying the passage of essential supplies, to assist the main campaign which was so soon to open in Palestine.

One of the more obvious targets in this policy of attack on communication lines was the railway connecting Bulgaria with Turkey. In the rugged country of the eastern Balkans, it was forced to run over many bridges, and the destruction of some of these might well bring all traffic to a halt for a period of several months. The easiest to attack was the big bridge which crossed the Nester River at Buk, as this was well within range of the new naval aerodrome constructed at Thasos.

The Buk bridge was bombed on October 15th by three Farmans with a fighter escort of two Bristol Scouts. The first bomb, dropped from 1,200 feet, hit the railway on the middle span of the bridge and two more exploded within 15 feet of the supporting piers. In the face of very heavy defensive fire it was not possible for the attacking aircraft to wait and see the result of this attack, but a reconnaissance flown over the area a week later showed the whole of the middle span lying in the river bed, while several trains were drawn up on each side of the severed line, unable to proceed.

If that was the first success, an almost exactly similar one was achieved on the Shimshirli bridge on the western side of Buk. It was attacked on October 30th by two R.N.A.S. bombers from Thasos, using 112-pound bombs, and when the aircraft had finished their attack the two central spans were lying in the river bed.

More ambitious, but with not so startling a success, was a long-distance raid carried out during this year. Operating from the R.N.A.S. field on Imbros, two machines set off for Constantinople on April 15th, involving a round flight of 360 miles, something of an achievement for the aeroplanes of 1916. Sixteen small incendiary bombs were dropped on the city, starting one or two small fires, but the distance was too great for the aircraft to carry the normal high-explosive bombs. One of the pilots made the whole flight successfully, the other came down exhausted in the Gulf of Xeros where he was picked up by a trawler.

Another notable flight was made in October of 1916, when the Admiralty decided, at the request of Roumania, to send a flight of naval aircraft to Bucharest, a straight flight of 310 miles from Imbros. One of the five pilots, who failed to arrive at Bucharest, made an even more notable, if involuntary, flight. He ran into a severe thunder-storm over the Balkan mountains, lost his way, and eventually finished up at Ismail, in Russia, after making a non-stop flight of 400 miles.

Finally, in this part of the world, the activities of ship-borne aircraft must be noticed. Flight-Commander Samson, on the termination of the Gallipoli campaign, had been appointed to command the *Ben-My-Chree*, based at Port Said under the operational command of the Commander-in-Chief, East Indies. She was joined during the year by the carrier *Empress*, and by two French steamers, the *Anne* and *Raven II*, each designed to carry two seaplanes.

The four ships were formed into one squadron with instructions to operate against the Turks in Palestine, the Sinai Peninsula, and the Yemen, where the Turkish general, Said Pasha, had attacked the southernmost province of Arabia, which was under British protection. In these areas the seaplanes from the ships flew many sorties, both offensive and reconnaissance. They were especially effective in the Yemen, where the great heat of midsummer made infantry operations against Said Pasha impossible. An almost continuous attack on the main Turkish positions was carried out over six days, with the *Ben-My-Chree* using Aden as her base. On the following day she proceeded to Perim to carry out raids on Jebel Malu and Jebel Akran, and a day later was off Jidda for further bombing attacks. The ceaseless hammering from the air was too much for the Turks and with their surrender the threat to southern Arabia was removed.

From the Red Sea the attention of the R.N.A.S. was directed to the Sinai Peninsula, where the first movements of the advance into Palestine were being staged. Reconnaissance was carried out for the Army and several bombing sorties were flown, particularly round El Arish and Levisi. Moving farther north along the coast of Palestine, further attacks were made at Tul Karm and Ramleh in attempts to dislocate the Turkish supply lines. While the naval aircraft were thus engaged, a great army was gathering along the Suez Canal, in preparation for the campaign that was destined to drive the Turks out of Sinai, up the length of Palestine, and finally to bring the Turkish Empire crumbling down into utter defeat at Damascus. It was towards the furtherance of that great enterprise that the R.N.A.S. in the eastern Mediterranean directed their attacks in 1916.

Integration into the Navy

By THE END OF 1916, THE ROYAL NAVAL AIR SERVICE CAN be said to have emerged at last from the experimental stage and to have become a reasonably coherent force with fairly clearly defined duties and responsibilities.   Trial and experiment had indicated the types of machines most worthy of development, and the aircraft industry in Britain had responded in a magnificent fashion. Aircraft were being delivered in increasing numbers and, as new requirements became apparent with the development of air fighting, the various firms in the industry spared no effort to design and produce machines which could perform the task required.

With the broad patterns of naval flying thus settled, 1917 became something of a year of decision.   The lessons of two and a half years of war had been well absorbed ; they were now to be put fully into practice.   Naval aviation had become, on its own merits, a vital and integral part of the fleet, recognized by many naval officers as a maritime weapon of steadily increasing value and power.   In order to place it on a more solid footing, a change in administration was made at the Admiralty, with direct representation on the Board of Admiralty.   On January 31st, a Fifth Sea Lord was created, responsible for all naval air matters, the first holder of the post being Commodore G. M. Paine, who had relieved Rear-Admiral Vaughan-Lee, the Director of Air Services.

Perhaps the development for which 1917 is most likely to be remembered is that of the aircraft carrier.   Hitherto they had consisted of ships, most of them with a short flying deck forward, carrying a few seaplanes on board.   Although it had been demonstrated more than once that a seaplane could take off from the flying deck, rolling down on a trolley on a pair of metal rails, or with detachable wheels attached to the floats, the normal method of launching was to hoist the seaplane over the side and let her ascend from the water.   It was at once slow, unhandy, and dependent on the state of the sea.

Something more reliable was needed, some method of launching an aircraft, and preferably not a seaplane, from a ship at sea with the fleet. So urgent was the problem that the Commander-in-Chief set up a Grand Fleet Aircraft Committee to deal with the matter. Primarily, the main object was to discover a method of dealing with Zeppelins, which were proving to be a thorough nuisance by the regularity with which they were reporting every movement of the Grand Fleet. The seaplane, with its slow rate of climb and comparatively slow speed, had shown itself unable to catch the modern Zeppelin of 1916 and 1917; any new method would have to embody the aeroplane.

The first step taken by the Committee was to fit up a temporary platform on the weather deck of H.M.S. *Yarmouth*, a light cruiser, and in June, 1917, Flight-Commander F. J. Rutland successfully flew off a Sopwith Pup. Further trials were carried out during July and in each case the Pup took the air perfectly.

The next step was to test the platform in action and to make sure that what could be done in practice could also be done during an operation. The chance came on August 21st, when the 1st Light Cruiser Squadron, including H.M.S. *Yarmouth*, was carrying out a sweep off the Danish coast. When the squadron was off Lyngvig, the inevitable Zeppelin made her appearance and began to shadow the squadron from a safe range of 12 miles. The ships altered course to the north to draw the airship farther from her base, and when they were off the Lodbjerg Light, with the Zeppelin still shadowing, they turned into the wind and orders were given for the *Yarmouth* to fly off her aircraft.

The Sopwith Pup was successfully launched by Flight-Sub-Lieutenant B. A. Smart, who climbed steadily to 7,000 feet before turning to engage the airship. He was well above her as he came within range and, diving down on to her tail, sprayed her with incendiary bullets. His first attack was unsuccessful, as he was firing from too great a range, but in a second dive he got within 20 yards of her stern and his incendiary bullets set her afire. In a matter of seconds she became a roaring furnace, crumpled up, and plunged into the sea. Smart, landing in the water alongside the ships of the squadron, was picked up by a boat from H.M.S. *Prince*.

So far, so good, and as a result of the successful attack twenty-two light cruisers were taken in hand for the fitting of aircraft platforms on their weather deck. But this was still not the full answer, because in order to launch the aircraft the ship had to turn into the wind and steam at full speed against it. Such a thing would be impossible in a fleet action without, perhaps, imperilling the Commander-in-Chief's tactical dispositions. Some other method of launching had to be found.

The next step of the Committee, therefore, was to fit a flying-off platform to the turret guns of a battleship. The platform was designed not to interfere with the normal sighting and firing of the guns, and it had the great advantage that the turret itself could be trained into the wind without the ship herself altering course. The first of these platforms was erected on " B " turret of H.M.S. *Repulse*, and on October 1st Flight-Commander Rutland made a successful ascent, again in a Sopwith Pup. Eight days later he showed that the feat could be carried out from one of the after turrets as well, using " Y " turret for the purpose. With the successful demonstrations, all the battle-cruisers were fitted with turret platforms and each carried two Sopwith Pups on board.

But still the Commander-in-Chief was not satisfied. The Pup was a single-seater machine, and consequently unsatisfactory for reconnaissance work. A further disadvantage was that, after a flight, the aircraft had to land in the sea and the pilot be picked up by boat. To do this a ship must stop while she sent her boat away, and in a fleet action such a procedure might be fatal.

But the experiments, if they had not yet produced the full answer, had at least shown the Committee that an ordinary land-plane could be used at sea, and was in fact the best type of aircraft, because of her speed and rate of climb, for many naval requirements. What was needed now was some reliable method of launching a two-seater aircraft at sea, so that the fleet's requirements for aerial reconnaissance could be adequately met.

There were two schools of thought about the problem. One, looking at the success achieved with H.M.S. *Repulse*, concentrated on the provision of longer take-off platforms and eventually managed to get a two-seater into the air from the top of the mid-ship turret of H.M.S. *Australia*. The other school turned their eyes back to the carrier, believing that in her development lay the real key to the problem. As a start in this direction, a passenger and cargo steamer, which was being built for Italy, was taken up.

She was the *Conte Rosso* and, on her adoption into the Navy, was renamed *Argus*. Her completion as a carrier gave her two flying decks, one forward designed for launching aeroplanes, and one aft for seaplanes. The decks were divided by the bridge structure, which was carried on a girder construction about 20 feet above the flying deck.

At the same time the fast battle-cruiser *Furious*, which had been laid down by Lord Fisher shortly after the start of the war, was taken in hand for completion as a carrier. She had a large hangar built on her forecastle, with its roof forming the flying deck. This flying deck was 228 feet long by 50 feet wide, a large enough space to ensure the safe take-off of any two-seater aircraft.

But there was still one more problem to be solved before the carrier could come fully into her own. When the *Furious* was commissioned, the only method of an aircraft's return was to land in the sea alongside and be hoisted in, or to carry out a similar procedure alongside one of the smaller carriers which usually accompanied the *Furious*. But on August 3rd, 1917, Squadron-Commander E. H. Dunning, D.S.C., flying a Sopwith Pup, made the first landing ever to be made on the flight deck of a ship at sea. Flying parallel to the ship's side, he made a sharp turn as soon as he was level with the funnel and just managed to get his wheels down on the flight deck. A deck party of officers standing by, hung on to the struts and wings and brought the machine to a stop. In a second attempt two days later, he was drowned when one of his tyres burst, throwing the machine over the side.

Dunning's death was a tragedy for the R.N.A.S., for he was an outstanding pilot and had already contributed much to the technique of naval flying. But even as he died he established the possibility of landing-on at sea, the final requirement of naval aviation to make it a completely self-supporting force with a tremendous future.

The way was now open and the R.N.A.S. was quick to seize it. The after deck of H.M.S. *Argus* was adapted for flying-on, with a large crash barrier of rope hawsers rigged at the forward end to prevent machines from overrunning the deck and crashing into the bridge supports. At the same time H.M.S. *Furious* was again taken in hand for the construction of an after flying-on deck. And to complete the pattern, a battleship building for Chile, the *Almirante Cochrane*, was taken over for completion as a carrier, while a contract was placed with Messrs. Armstrong-Whitworth for a new ship of this type, the first to be designed, from her original conception, as a carrier. Neither of these two ships was ready before the end of the war, but both of them marked an immense step forward in carrier design, and both became extremely well known under their new names of *Eagle* and *Hermes* respectively.

As with carriers, so with aircraft, and 1917 produced some notable additions to the R.N.A.S. range. Perhaps the most important was the flying boat, developed in the main by Wing-Commander J. C. Porte from a design he had brought back from the United States at the start of the war. Their advantage over the seaplane lay in the fact that they carried a crew of four and that their range and endurance were immensely superior. They proved their value as an attack weapon during the vital year of 1917.

Another machine which arrived during 1917 was the Sopwith Cuckoo, a most successful torpedo-carrying aircraft. The original torpedo used in air attacks had been the 14-inch, but this was not considered to be sufficiently powerful against warships. Mr. Sopwith was, therefore, asked to design an aircraft that could carry an 18-inch torpedo and at the same time take off from a flying deck at sea. He produced the Cuckoo, and its trials showed it to be an excellent machine for the purpose. Other aircraft that came into service during the year were the de Havilland 4, a bombing and reconnaissance plane, the Handley Page, a heavy bomber allocated to R.N.A.S. shore squadrons, the Sopwith Camel, a single-seater fighter or light bomber, and various types of Blackburn aircraft. Engines were beginning to develop much more horsepower, ranging up to 350 or 400 horsepower in comparison with the 80 or 100 horsepower of 1914 and 1915.

One other development of 1917 deserves some mention, the invention of the towing float designed by Commander Porte. These floats were 58 feet long and 16 feet wide, with a special hull form capable of being towed at 32 knots without throwing up sheets of spray. The original intention was to use them, towed by a destroyer, to transport flying boats into the Heligoland Bight in order to increase their radius of action against enemy installations ashore. Commander Samson, however, suggested that they could equally well be used for launching fighter aeroplanes

E

and in fact made a first attempt from one that nearly ended in disaster, his machine twisting sideways as it accelerated along the float and diving into the sea. A second attempt a few days later, however, was a success and, as a result of the trials, an order was placed for fifty of the floats. It was not until 1918 that they were ready for operational service, but when they were eventually used operationally at sea, they provided at least one startling success.

But it was against the U-boats that the R.N.A.S. concentrated most during 1917. In February of that year the enemy opened his unrestricted submarine campaign and the rate of merchant ship sinkings rose alarmingly. When the convoy system was developed as a reply, there came a demand for low-speed air escort, which was answered partly by the provision of airships for coastal convoy work and partly by kite balloons towed by ships as observation platforms. This, however, was but a negative answer to the problem, for what was required was some method of location and attack before the U-boats could reach the shipping lanes, and for this work the flying boat seemed to be the ideal weapon.

Careful plotting in the Admiralty had brought out the fact that most of the U-boats proceeding to their patrol areas passed through an area near the North Hinder Light Vessel. In order to conserve their batteries, they were usually on the surface as they crossed that area. An elaborate reconnaissance programme was worked out, centred on the Light Vessel, in which a wide area could be covered by a searching flying boat, the more likely sectors being decided from intercepted signals from the U-boats themselves fixed by wireless direction-finding.

The system of reconnaissance was known as the "Spider's web", and it bore fruit almost as soon as it was instituted. The first searches were carried out on April 13th, and in the first three weeks eight U-boats had been sighted and three bombed.

The first confirmed success came on May 20th when a flying boat, piloted by Flight-Sub-Lieutenants C. R. Morrish and H. G. Boswell, and with Air-Mechanics Caston and Shooter as crew, sighted a U-boat fully surfaced at a range of 5 miles. The flying boat made straight for her, firing recognition signals, and as these were ignored, attacked with bombs. Two were released as the submarine was in the act of diving and both hit with the boat just below the surface. Beyond a large patch of oil on the surface, there was no indication of the success or otherwise of the attack, and it was not until after the war that it could be confirmed that the U-boat had, in fact, been sunk. She was U.C.36 and was the first submarine to fall victim to an attack from the air.

The next U-boats to be caught in the " Spider's web " were U.C.1, attacked by a flight of five flying boats led by Commander Porte, and U.B.20, which fell to two flying boats piloted by Flight-Sub-Lieutenants W. R. Mackenzie and S. E. Ball, and Flight-Sub-Lieutenants C. L. Young and A. T. Parker respectively. Another victim was U.C.72, bombed and sunk by a flying boat operating from Dunkirk and piloted by Flight-Sub-Lieutenants N. A. Magor and C. E. S. Lusk, while a fifth was U.C.6, which went down after a particularly gallant attack carried out by Flight-Lieutenant B. D. Hobbs and Flight-Sub-Lieutenant R. F. L. Dickey. The U-boat was sighted a mile ahead and, when she ignored the recognition signal, a 250-pound bomb was dropped which burst on her stern. At this moment three more U-boats, escorted by three destroyers, were sighted approaching through the mist, and they put up a tremendous barrage in an attempt to drive off the attacking flying boat.

Undeterred by the heavy fire, Hobbs and Dickey came in for a second attack on their victims and dropped another 250-pound bomb which burst on the bows of the stricken U-boat. She rolled over and sank almost immediately, the fifth U-boat to be sent to the bottom by the bombs of the flying boats.

This was, however, not the full measure of the success of these aircraft. On May 14th, a flying boat from the Yarmouth air station, manned by Flight-Lieutenant C. J. Galpin, Flight-Sub-Lieutenant R. Leckie, Chief Petty Officer V. F. Whatling, and Air-Mechanic J. R. Laycock, sighted a Zeppelin near the Terschelling Light Vessel. The airship was cruising slowly at a height of 3,000 feet. A quick attack at a range of 50 yards set the giant airship ablaze and, 45 seconds later, Zeppelin L.22, now no more than a twisted skeleton, plunged into the sea. Exactly one month later, L.43 met a similar fate when she was found by Hobbs and Dickey in their flying boat. With them were H. M. Davis and A. W. Goody as W/T operator and engineer. Two bursts of gunfire were sufficient to reduce her to a mass of flames, and she, too, plunged into the sea to become a total loss.

No account of naval flying boats during this year would be complete without telling the story of two remarkable rescues in the North Sea. They show another facet of the men who flew these unwieldy machines against the enemy, another kind of courage that made them face great risk and hardship to save their comrades. When a flying boat crashed at sea there was always a reasonable chance of rescue if an accompanying aircraft returned to base to report the position of the crash so that ships might be sent out to search the area for the survivors. But in the close comradeship of the R.N.A.S. a reasonable chance was not considered good enough. The accompanying flying boat invariably landed alongside and picked up the survivors knowing that, as often as not, the extra weight on board would prevent her from taking off again. At the least the crew could share the ordeal of their less-fortunate comrades.

The first notable case of a rescue at sea did not, in fact, concern a flying boat. It was that of Flight-Sub-Lieutenant H. M. Morris and his air-mechanic, G. O. Wright. They were flying a Short seaplane on May 24th when engine failure forced them to land on the water. They came down in a minefield south of the North Hinder Light Vessel and started to drift. Later that day the sea began to rise and, in order to lighten the seaplane, they released the bombs and emptied the petrol tanks. The fumes of the petrol made both men violently sick. While wrestling with this nausea the weather deteriorated into a gale and the seaplane began to break up. As night fell, it was smashed to pieces on the still rising sea, leaving only one of the floats to which the two men could cling. Even with that the only handholds were the two fittings which normally held the undercarriage struts.

Throughout the darkness the two men held on, battered by wild seas and drenched with spray driven by the gale. As the day came at last the sea around them was empty. Fortunately the gale blew itself out during the morning, but both men were now beginning to suffer from thirst and their hands and feet were torn and sore from the action of the sea-water, and also badly swollen. The day passed with an empty sea and still the two men clung to their precarious support.

May 26th and 27th saw the North Sea shrouded in thick fog with no hope of rescue. Morris and Wright clung grimly to heir float, keeping up their courage with snatches of song, with jokes remembered from wardroom guest nights and lower deck messes, with long stories of their lives, their hopes, their ambitions. With torn, aching fingers and numbed legs, they still held on to the frail thread of life.

The fog lifted on the 28th and the hope of rescue grew brighter All through the day their eyes turned upwards to an empty sky or searched an empty sea. The hot sun beat down on them, and for a time they drifted into delirium and semi-consciousness. Yet still they clung to their float, though with only faint hopes now.

At sunset, sky and sea were still empty. Throughout the night the derelict seaplane float drifted on the surface of the North Sea, the two men still alive and still holding on. During the morning of the 29th the sea began to rise again and to their natural exhaustion was now added the hazard of the waves, which could so easily loosen a handhold and sweep them away to what could now be only a quick and merciful death. Somehow, their fingers did not loosen and still they clung grimly on with a flickering hope.

On the 29th there took off from Felixstowe a flying boat, piloted by Flight-Commander Lindsay Gordon and Flight-Lieutenant G. Hodgson. In the course of their patrol they sighted an object which could have been the conning-tower of a U-boat. Ready to drop their bombs, Gordon dived down on the U-boat, to discover just in time what it was that had been sighted. He pulled out of the dive and landed in the rough sea, taxi-ing right up to the float. Morris and Wright were dragged on board almost at their last gasp.

There was no hope of the flying boat taking off again, for the weight on board was too great and the rough sea prevented a smooth run. Gordon decided to try and taxi to England. As he set his course for home the gale returned, heavy seas sweeping over the hull of the boat. She began to pound badly on the steep waves and the strain was so much that the hull started to leak. Soon so much water was coming in that the bilge pump could not cope with it. The tail flooded, but by good fortune the after bulkhead held. Water in the hull was kept down by constant baling.

The gale was followed by a belt of fog, but Gordon kept his engines running and way on the boat. Four hours later he came out of the fog, to find the Shipwash Light Vessel no more than

3 miles to the northward of him. Very lights soon attracted attention and within a matter of a few minutes the flying boat was in tow. An hour or two later all were safely ashore, though in the meantime Morris and Wright had been given too large a meal on board the rescuing ship and both were violently ill.

Two months later, both were flying again, though Morris's legs never fully recovered from their long exposure to sea water. Their terrible ordeal was enough to have discouraged most men from further adventures in the air, but their indomitable spirit, so typical in many ways of all R.N.A.S. pilots and observers, could not admit defeat. Morris was awarded the D.S.C. and Wright the D.S.M. for their great gallantry and endurance, while the whole of the flying boat's crew was decorated with the Albert Medal.

The second rescue was almost as miraculous. A flying boat, piloted by Squadron-Commander Nicholl and Flight-Lieutenant Leckie, accompanied by a D.H.4 land machine flown by Flight-Lieutenant A. H. H. Gilligan and Observer-Lieutenant G. S. Trewin, were out on an anti-Zeppelin patrol on September 5th. They sighted two airships, L.44 and L.46, and closed to the attack. Although their tracer bullets were seen hitting L.44 she was not set on fire and managed to climb above the ceiling height of the two machines, at the same time subjecting them to intense machine-gun fire and attempting to drop bombs on them. As the Zeppelin soared away out of danger, enemy light cruisers on the sea below opened fire with their anti-aircraft guns.

The D.H.4 was hit by a fragment of shell in her water tank and her engine seized up. She began to glide down towards a heavily breaking sea, accompanied by the flying boat, when another squadron of light cruisers was sighted. Their shooting was extremely accurate and the flying boat was hit by shrapnel in her starboard wing. The damage was not serious and she could still fly.

In the meantime Gilligan was faced with the problem of making a landing.

> Trewin and I had an argument [he wrote] as to which way the wind was blowing, so that we could land head on. I took my chance and about ten feet up "pan-caked", a horrid crash, and all I could see was blue water above. I couldn't free myself and after trying everything (for I had blown up my waistcoat before

crashing) I suddenly remembered my headphone attachment was still plugged in—this was all that was keeping me down. As soon as I disconnected it, up I shot, to find Trewin swimming towards the relics of the machine.

As soon as Nicholl and Leckie saw what had happened they had to come to a quick decision. In the sea that was running there was no hope of the flying boat taking off again once she landed. If they did land, both crews might be lost; if they returned to base and organized a search-party, one crew would at least be safe and the other might yet be found. But neither hesitated for a moment. Leckie, who was piloting, dived to the rescue, so steeply indeed that his machine went into a spin and was uncontrollable for a few moments. He pulled her out at last and made a superb landing in the heavy sea. Gilligan and Trewin started swimming towards the flying boat, but they got separated. Gilligan, a strong swimmer, reached it in safety, but Trewin soon got into difficulties and was only just reached in the nick of time.

Once again a flying boat began to taxi towards England, but this time in the knowledge that there was not sufficient petrol on board to reach the goal. Matters were made even worse by the following sea, for the waves kept lifting the tail high into the air so that the bows submerged, taking in hundreds of gallons of water. Even this was not all, for, with the hull resting on the water, it was discovered that the boat had been holed there as well as in the wing during the recent action, more water coming in through the hole.

There was nothing for it but to alter course so that the flying boat could ride more easily on the sea. At the same time all hands in the machine had to start baling for their lives, while Leckie, in the cockpit, sat up to his knees in water.

The flying boat carried no wireless, but on board were four carrier pigeons. Two were released with identical messages that evening : (" We have landed to pick up D.H.4 crew, about 50 miles E by N of Yarmouth. Sea too rough to get off. Will you please send for us as soon as possible as boat is leaking. We are taxi-ing W by S.") One pigeon reached land, but its message was delayed and did not reach the Yarmouth air station until September 8th.

By evening the flying boat's petrol was exhausted and the

engines stopped. The six men on board, weakened by sea sickness, settled down to face the night with ceaseless baling. There was no food on board, and but 2 gallons of drinking water.

During the night the starboard wing-tip float, damaged in the action, fell off. In order to keep the wing out of the water, one of the men had to crawl out on the port wing so that his weight would keep that wing down. The six men took it in turns to lie out on the wing, their two hours there being their rest from baling. But it was little rest. It was impossible to sit or stand on the wing as the movement was too great, and they had to lie out there on their stomachs, holding on to the outer strut. " It was a terrible job," said one of the survivors later, " for one minute we would be at least 20 feet up in the air, the next minute down the wing would come with a hell of a crash, and we'd be buried under water, to be jerked out, spitting and gasping, half-drowned, to go up like a see-saw and then down again."

The 6th and 7th September passed with no sight of any rescuing craft, although the failure to return on the 5th had brought out a large search-party of aircraft and ships. But while they were searching the probable return route of the fliers, the flying boat itself, it will be remembered, had had to alter course because of the following sea, and had been taxi-ing away from the direct route.

Those two days on board passed almost mechanically with the crew working like automatons, baling and lying out on the wing. They began to lose count of time and lived in a kind of haze. They were still harrowed by sea sickness, Leckie becoming so bad that he started an internal haemorrhage, and Trewin still suffering from his immersion of the 5th when he was so nearly drowned. But both of them, in spite of their suffering, took their turns at the baling and the wing weighting, and their indomitable spirit set so fine an example to the remainder on board that there was no thought of despair.

On the 6th Nicholl set free the last two pigeons. One of them failed to reach land, but the other one arrived and its message reached Yarmouth at 10.45 a.m. on the 7th. " Very urgent," it ran. " We have sighted nothing. The wind has been drifting us west-north-west since we landed, so we may have missed Cromer. We are not far from the coast as we keep seeing small land birds. Sea is still rough. Machine intact still. We will fire Very's lights every 45 minutes tonight."

It was this message that led to their rescue on the 8th. The words " we may have missed Cromer " were the first indication received ashore that the flying boat was so far north of its return course. An old gunboat which had been based at Lowestoft for duty with the air station there —H.M.S. *Halycon*—set out to patrol the Wash area, her captain determined to find the missing men. He plotted as carefully as he could the possible effect of wind and tide and decided in his own mind that the machine must be in one of three areas. The first, which was the area of the Wash minefield, was drawn blank on the morning of the 8th, and the *Halycon* set a course for the second, an area north by east of Cromer. And it was here that success at last came. As the ship was proceeding to the new area :

At 12.45 p.m. we were at lunch when a seaman rushed into the wardroom. " The First Lieutenant reports he believes he has sighted the seaplane about 5 miles right ahead." Lunch was forgotten, and by the time we had got on deck the sun glistening on the planes removed any doubts that our search had not been rewarded, and we hoped that all would be well. As we drew near we manned ship and gave them a heartening cheer, to which those aboard the flying boat tried to answer. I can hardly describe the joy of meeting comrades one has feared as lost. . . . They were all bearing traces of their terrible experiences. It was the third day they had eaten no food. They had only 2 gallons of fresh water on board, and had had to tap the engine radiators and slake their thirst with the rusty water in them.

While all this activity was going on over the North Sea, the R.N.A.S. contingent on the Belgian coast continued their work of spotting for monitors and harassing the enemy. The big Handley Page bombers were now coming into full production and during 1917 the R.N.A.S. bombing squadrons at Dunkirk were largely re-equipped with these machines. As they came into service, the raids on enemy installations became more ambitious, and something of a record was set up on the night of September 25th when naval bombers dropped over 9½ tons of bombs on the railway junctions at Thourout, Lichtervelde, and Cortemarcke. A month previously Thourout had had 9 tons of bombs dropped on it, blowing up a large enemy ammunition dump.

The fighters at Dunkirk, mainly Sopwith Scouts, also had a busy year. The big daylight Gotha raids on London and the east coast ports had begun in May and it was to the naval fighters at Dunkirk that the task of interception was given. As a general rule, interception was only possible on the return of the raiders, after news of the attack had been wirelessed to the aircraft base there. Several of the bombers were caught and shot down.

Out in the Mediterranean, the R.N.A.S. were actively supporting the fighting on the Struma front and in Palestine. But the outstanding achievement of the year's work there was the bombing of Constantinople by a Handley Page which was flown out specially from England for the purpose. Taking off from Mudros in the evening of July 9th the bomber reached her target three hours later. Leaving Constantinople for another visit later in the day, the pilot flew to Stenia Bay, where the two German cruisers, *Goeben* and *Breslau*, were lying at anchor. After making three runs over the target to estimate dropping conditions, the pilot attacked down moon. The first four 112-pound bombs fell among some destroyers and submarines moored up alongside, setting one of them afire. The second salvo of four hit the *Goeben* just forward of her funnels, but did little damage against her armoured deck.

Leaving the German ships the Handley Page flew back to Constantinople and the pilot dropped his bombs on the S.S. *General*, lying up the Golden Horn. She housed the German Headquarters in the area and both bombs hit her and exploded on deck. The next target was the Turkish War Ministry in Constantinople itself, and the remaining two bombs were aimed at the building. Again two hits were claimed, although again the damage caused was relatively slight. Three hours later the Handley Page landed safely at Mudros after a round flight lasting seven hours.

A few months later the *Goeben* and *Breslau* were once again the targets of naval bombing aircraft. Early in 1918 the two German cruisers emerged from Turkish waters and on January 20th sank H.M.S. *Raglan* and a monitor off Kusu. Their presence at sea called for an all-out effort by the Royal Naval Air Service and they were continuously shadowed by seaplanes. Repeated bombing

attacks were carried out, gradually driving the two ships southward and nearer the British minefield off Rabbit Island.   The
non-stop attacks achieved their first success when the *Breslau* was
forced right into the minefield, hit a mine, and sank almost at once.

The *Goeben*, escaping the mines, headed for the Dardanelles,
still under attack from the air.   She was damaged by near-misses,
developed a large list to port, and was finally driven ashore at
Nagara Burnu.   For seven days the bombers from Mudros
continued to attack her, but the weather was against accurate
attacks and fierce anti-aircraft fire kept them at a respectable
height.   It was, unfortunately, impossible for torpedo carrying
aircraft to take off in the bad weather then prevailing, and ultim-
ately the Germans managed to get her afloat again.   She was
patched up and returned safely to Stenia Bay, not to leave her
anchorage again during the remainder of the war.

Further east still, the German raider *Wolf* was operating in the
Indian Ocean and once again the R.N.A.S. was called upon to deal
with her.   The seaplane carrier *Ben-My-Chree* had been sunk by
shore guns in January, but her place had been taken by the
Raven II and, later, H.M.S. *City of Oxford*.   It was the *Raven II*,
formerly French but by now taken over by the Admiralty, who
was sent to search for the *Wolf*, but although she never found
her, she was concerned in one of the most remarkable flying
adventures in the war.

One of her seaplanes, sent to search the area between Male
Atoll and Ari Atoll, failed to make contact with the carrier on
her return and was forced to land near one of the small islands,
inside the usual coral reef.   Attempting to taxi out to sea in order
to take off again, the machine stuck fast on the reef and was only
freed some five hours later as the tide began to rise.   The pilot
and observer decided to try and find a channel through the reef.
It was by now pitch dark and, with the observer lying on the
top plane and firing Very lights in an attempt to illuminate
the coral, the pilot taxied up and down.   No channel could be
found, however, and at last, exhausted, they decided to give up
the search and land on the island.   They tied their seaplane to a
coconut palm, tried to climb the palm to reach the nuts but failed,
and finally shot down some with their Lewis gun.   It was the only
food they had.

On the following day the seaplane was floated off by both pilot and observer swimming alongside and pushing. The pilot got aboard and started the engine and the observer kept her away from the coral by swimming with the machine until at last it got under way. He scrambled aboard and the seaplane took off. It was only when they were safely in the air that they remembered they had left all their clothes behind on the island.

As on the previous day, the search for the carrier failed and, since the petrol was beginning to run low, the two men returned towards the islands. The machine came down in a lagoon but an off-shore wind drifted it away from the land into deeper water. Once again it was a question of swimming, but no headway could be made against the wind.

On the beach ashore they made out, in the gathering gloom, the shape of a native boat. Although they were in shark-infested waters, they left the seaplane and swam ashore, meaning to row the boat out and tow the seaplane into safety. But when they reached the beach they found that the native boat had no oars, nor was there any sign of any in the neighbourhood. There was nothing for it but to abandon the seaplane, especially as darkness had by now fallen. The two men made a bed of palm leaves on the beach and, using others to cover themselves, fell asleep on the sand.

The pilot was wakened by a noise in the night and, springing up, found himself in the presence of three natives. Bowing deeply in his nudity, he greeted them with the word " Salaam ". This so terrified the natives that they fled in terror. The equally astonished pilot saw the boat disappear with considerable appre- hension, for with it went their last hope of communication with the outside world.

Word of the two naked white men must have travelled quickly round the islands for next morning quite a crowd of fishermen arrived in their boats to have a look at the wondrous sight. As they could not be enticed to bring their boats ashore, the pilot and observer swam out to them and managed to persuade one of them to take them aboard. They were rowed across the lagoon to Fiale Island where they were given food and drink and a native hut for shelter.

For three days they lived on Fiale, never quite knowing whether their hosts regarded them as gods or devils. On the fourth a fisherman took them over to Male Island, and brought

them to the Sultan.   He entertained them nobly and, to cover
their nakedness, dressed them both in the uniform of his Royal
bodyguard.   He arranged, too, for a native dhow to take them
to Colombo, and eventually they were able to rejoin the *Raven II*,
after having been given up for dead several days previously.

The End of the R.N.A.S.

IT WAS IN 1918 THAT THE ROYAL NAVAL AIR SERVICE lost its separate identity and became a part of the Royal Air Force. For some months past the necessity for some central control of flying had been growing ever more apparent, if only to bring to an end the competing claims of the two flying Services. Attempts to set up co-ordinating boards during 1916 and 1917 had ended in failure because of the lack of authority such boards were given. They were advisory, not executive, and they failed because neither Service was prepared to modify its ideas or its beliefs.

The public, too, was beginning to take a hand. There had been some grumbling at the ineffectiveness of the home defences in 1916, when Zeppelin raids came over with almost monotonous regularity, and the grumbles developed into an outcry with the daylight raids on London in June and July of 1917. It was this factor, more than any other, which forced the Government to take drastic action.

A further step in the direction of unified control came with the German production of the two new fighters, each fitted with two fixed machine-guns firing through their propellers. These were the Albatross and the Halberstadt, and they were more efficient than any British or French fighter either in service or on the drawing board. Their appearance on the Western Front caused Sir Douglas Haig to ask for a reinforcement of twenty fighting squadrons, a number far beyond the capacity of the Royal Flying Corps to produce. It could only be achieved by curtailing the production of machines for the R.N.A.S., a step which the Admiralty was reluctant to sanction. The Admiralty, too, had its problems, since the naval machines were playing an increasing part in the war against the U-boats.

It was to find an answer to these conflicting problems that, in 1916, the Government asked General Smuts to study the question and submit a report. It was ready by the end of October, 1917, and his recommendations were to form a new Air Ministry and to amalgamate the two flying Services. The report was accepted by the Government and in November the Air Force (Constitution) Act was passed in Parliament, the two Services coming under its control and being amalgamated as the Royal Air Force on April 1st, 1918.

The report of General Smuts, and its subsequent acceptance by the Prime Minister and Parliament, struck a grievous blow at the R.N.A.S. Although there were two naval officers appointed to the Air Staff, Rear-Admiral Mark Kerr as deputy chief and Commodore Godfrey Paine as master-general of personnel, there could be no doubt in naval minds that the overriding interest of the new ministry would be directed almost entirely towards the land plane. It was not so much the immediate future that worried the Sea Lords, for while the war remained in progress the stimulus on production would remain and the naval side of the R.A.F. could count of adequate supplies for operational requirements. But it was the post-war outlook that appeared most bleak, for it was then, with dwindling supplies and inevitable cries for economy, that starvation of the naval side was most likely to appear.

On April 1st, 1918, then, the Royal Naval Air Service disappeared. For the remainder of the war it fought as part of the Royal Air Force, even though its machines, its pilots and observers, its mechanics, and its air stations remained as before. On the amalgamation, the Navy lost 103 airships, 2,949 aeroplanes, seaplanes, and flying boats, 126 air stations, and some 67,000 officers and men. As an economy measure they were permitted to wear their naval uniforms until they were worn out ; subsequently they appeared in the light blue of the sister Service. On the absorption into the Royal Air Force all the naval wings and squadrons were renumbered, the wings starting from 61, instead of 1, and the squadrons from 200.

There were, of course, other reasons for regret at the passing of the R.N.A.S. than the strictly utilitarian ones. It meant the severing of old friendships and loyalties, the adoption of the new beliefs of a new Service. The naval ranks were changed, first for the equivalent rank in the Army and then for the new R.A.F. rank, and there were many naval men who deeply regretted the loss of their naval rank.   Perhaps they were little things, but they meant a lot to the men who, for three and a half years, had flown under the White Ensign.

The operations of 1918 in which the naval flyers took part were very largely a repetition of those of 1917.   Anti-U-boat patrols, offensive and reconnaissance patrols across the North Sea, naval co-operation work along the Belgian coast, attacks on Zeppelins and their sheds, the overall pattern remained much the same.   There were, however, one or two operations which called for a new departure in naval flying tactics, coupled with a good deal of development work in the technique of shipborne flying.

The most interesting operation of the year was one which vindicated the idea of launching an aircraft from a raft towed behind a destroyer.   It will be remembered that these had been tested out during 1917 and it had been proved then that aeroplanes could ascend from them, as well as the flying boats for which they had originally been designed.

The main operation was one in which coastal motor-boats, each carrying a torpedo, were taken across the North Sea on the decks of cruisers and launched in the Heligoland Bight with the object of torpedoing any enemy ship they might meet. Three flying boats were also towed across on rafts for reconnaissance and rescue work, while three more flew off from Lowestoft and accompanied the squadron to give air cover. For anti-Zeppelin work, a Sopwith Camel, piloted by Lieutenant S. D. Culley, was towed on a raft behind H.M.S. *Redoubt*.   In charge of the whole operation was Vice-Admiral Sir Reginald Tyrwhitt, who flew his flag in the light cruiser *Curacoa*.

The squadron put to sea on the evening of August 10th and early the following morning the coastal motor-boats were launched off Terschelling.   The three flying boats towed across on rafts were unable to take off in the long swell which was running, but the three from Lowestoft duly arrived and a few minutes later one of them, piloted by Major (formerly Squadron-Commander) Leckie, sighted a Zeppelin and reported it to the Admiral.   Leckie was told by signal to leave it to the Camel and Admiral Tyrwhitt turned to seawards and made a smoke screen in the hope of enticing the Zeppelin to follow him.

The Zeppelin, which was L.53, did so.   Her captain probably

(*Imperial War Museum*)

A Swordfish taking off for an anti-submarine sweep.

A German supply ship after a torpedo attack by Barracudas.   She broke in two and
sank a few seconds later.

(*Imperial War Museum*)

(*Imperial War Museum*)

A wartime inspection by the late King George VI of pilots and observers on board a carrier.

Carriers for a Malta convoy. H.M.S. *Indomitable* and H.M.S. *Eagle* seen from the deck of H.M.S. *Victorious*. The carriers have their crash barriers erected.

(*Imperial War Museum*)

felt quite safe from attack as she was flying at 19,000 feet, rather above what was thought to be the ceiling height of British aircraft at that time. As L.53 followed the squadron to sea, Culley took off from his raft, made a perfect ascent after a run of only 5 feet, and began his long climb towards the enemy.

After flying for exactly one hour he found himself some 200 feet lower than the Zeppelin and closing the range rapidly. At that height he found the aircraft had reached its ceiling height, for his Camel would not answer her controls. Pulling back his control stick and stalling, he opened fire with his two Lewis guns. Although he could see his incendiary bullets hitting, they appeared to have no effect, and he broke away as he reached the end of his ammunition. Reloading and returning for a second attack, he noticed several small spurts of flame all along the gasbag, and in a few seconds more L.53 was burning furiously. She fell rapidly, leaving in the sky a huge pillar of black smoke as she hit the sea and sank.

Culley was unable to see the squadron because of increasing cloud and, not quite sure of his position, flew off to the Dutch coast to fix his whereabouts. Reaching the Texel, he turned for the rendezvous off the Terschelling Bank, but still could see no ships on arrival. As his petrol was running low, he decided to land in the water alongside some Dutch fishing trawlers, but as he came down through the clouds he sighted the squadron. In his relief he looped the loop and rolled over the ships and Admiral Tyrwhitt, watching his antics, made a signal to the ships, " Attention is called to Hymn 224, verse 7." Turning it up in their prayer-books, they read :

> Oh happy band of pilgrims,
> Look upward to the skies,
> Where such a light affliction
> Shall win so great a prize.

Culley was recommended for the Victoria Cross for his action, but the award was not approved and instead he was decorated with the D.S.O.

The naval flying on the Belgian coast, for the first part of the year, was centred mainly on Zeebrugge and Ostend, in preparation for the operations planned to block the canal entrances. An extensive photographic survey was required, especially as the operation was to be carried out at night and depended largely for its success on the exact knowledge of the positions of the buoys marking the entrance. Several hundred photographs were required and they all had to be taken from the same height so as to present an even scale when developed. As the enemy had fortified these two towns with innumerable anti-aircraft guns, the work proved exceptionally hazardous, since evasive action was impossible in the interests of accurate photography. The task was carried out by No. 202 Squadron, based on St. Pol, and flying D.H.4 machines. It was from these photographs that scale models of the defences were prepared and the Navy briefed for the great exploit.

As the day for the blocking of Zeebrugge and Ostend approached, the fighter squadrons based on Dunkirk and Dover flew an almost ceaseless patrol over the route of the attacking squadron. In order to reach the target area just before midnight, the ships had to sail from England in daylight and success depended entirely on complete secrecy and surprise.

The first attempt, on April 11th, 1918, was cancelled because of the bad weather, but not before the bombers, who were to make a diversionary attack, had set out. These were Handley Pages, and their role was to drop bombs at intervals and generally so conduct themselves over the targets that they should draw towards themselves the attention of the fixed defences and the searchlights. Flying through mist and rain clouds, four of them, out of a total of seven, reached Zeebrugge and Ostend, and carried out their tasks. One of them, piloted by Captain (originally Flight-Commander) J. R. Allen, was hit and crashed at sea, Allen being lost, and a second one was damaged and had to land in Holland.

The attack on Zeebrugge was successfully accomplished eleven days later on the night on April 22nd-23rd. This time the weather stopped the aircraft, but not the ships. Nevertheless, the aftermath of the operation was the occasion of a gallant flight by Lieutenants R. Coulthard and J. D. Fysh who, flying a D.H.4, through atrocious weather, made an invaluable reconnaissance from 50 feet only four hours after the actual blocking.

Although the canal at Zeebrugge had been successfully blocked, that at Ostend was still open, as the last-minute shifting of a buoy had misled the block ships and they had run ashore. A second operation was necessary and on May 9th conditions of tide and darkness made it possible. As a necessary preliminary, a daily reconnaissance was asked for during the period immediately preceding the chosen night.

As luck would have it, the weather broke badly at the beginning of May and low cloud, rain, and mist made flying impossible. It was only just before sunset, on the actual evening of the operation, that an aircraft, piloted by Captain (Flight-Commander) R. Graham, managed to reach Ostend through broken cloud. The squadron, accompanied by H.M.S. *Vindictive*, the new blockship, were already on their way across the North Sea when Graham discovered that once again the enemy had removed the mark buoys. This time, however, early knowledge of the fact through the air reconnaissance enabled another buoy to be laid and it was safely in position for the *Vindictive* when she arrived.

As the *Vindictive* turned towards the mouth of the canal and the supporting squadron opened fire on the defences of Ostend, seven Handley Pages of No. 214 Squadron flew over to drop their bombs. Among the load carried that night were six of 550-pounds each, the biggest yet made. Most of the bombing had to be done through layers of fog, but in spite of this it was accurate and concentrated and created sufficient diversion for the *Vindictive* to reach her blocking position. As it turned out she was only partially successful, being unable to turn fully round between the piers of Ostend before sinking.

Another notable feat by the Dunkirk squadrons was the raid on Varssenaere aerodrome, one of the biggest operated by the enemy in the northern sector of the western front. It was fixed for dawn on August 13th, and fifty Camels, with a squadron of D.H.4s in support, set out to smash the place to bits. As they took off in the dark of early morning they flew out to sea and then turned parallel to the coast about 6 miles off the shore. The fifty aircraft flew in two long, parallel lines, led by Lieutenant W. E. Gray, and at a given signal from him they turned south, gaining height and crossing the coast at 5,000 feet. Speeding to the target through the grey half-light of dawn, they dived in succession on the aerodrome, finding on it three flights of Fokker fighters drawn up in preparation for the early morning patrol. Their engines were already warming up for take-off, pilots were clambering into cockpits, and ground crews were standing by ready to assist.

Out of the sky dived the fifty naval machines, while high above the squadron of D.H.4s circled the aerodrome to act as fighter cover for the bombers. In a few moments the scene below was chaos, with some enemy aircraft blown to fragments by the high-explosive bombs, others set on fire by the incendiaries which followed. Through the thick smoke the fifty Camels dived again and again, emptying their machine-guns into the tangled mass, spraying hangars with incendiary bullets and setting them on fire, and attacking the officers' quarters with concentrated gunfire.

In a few minutes the attack was over and the aircraft on their way home. One or two had been hit by fragments of anti-aircraft shells as they burst in the air, but the damage amounted to no more than a few holes in the fabric of the wings and fuselage. Not one of the British machines failed to return, indeed, the fighter escort shot down one enemy aircraft which was discovered flying over the sea.

In the meantime carrier-borne aircraft had also been active over the North Sea. H.M.S. *Furious*, escorted by light cruisers, had made many sorties into the Heligoland Bight in search of Zeppelins and other targets, though without much success. Finally, on the morning of July 19th, an attack on the Zeppelin sheds at Tondern brought the longed-for reward. Two flights of Camels, the first of three machines, the second of four, flew off at dawn. The first flight bombed and set on fire one of the large sheds, though after the attack two of the Camels were forced to land in Denmark, their crews being interned.

Of the second flight of four Camels, one came down at sea with engine failure, one crashed soon after taking off, and a third made a forced landing in Denmark. But the fourth, piloted by Captain B. A. Smart, reached Tondern. It was easy for him to see the results of the first raid, for the shed was still burning furiously, and it was equally easy for him to select the second Zeppelin shed as his target. He missed with his first bomb, but his second landed fair and square in the centre of the shed and soon it was blazing as fiercely as the first. It was a crushing blow to the German Zeppelin service, for each shed contained an airship, L.54 and L.60, and both were completely destroyed.

One more Zeppelin fell to naval machines in the course of what proved to be the last raid made by enemy airships on Great Britain. Taking off from Yarmouth, Major (Squadron-Commander) E. Cadbury, with Captain R. Leckie as his observer, intercepted two Zeppelins as they were crossing the Norfolk coast. The first to be attacked was L.70, and she was shot down in flames over the sea. Cadbury and Leckie then closed with the second, L.65, but just at the critical moment their machine-gun jammed. As the action was at night, it was too dark to discover the cause of the stoppage and the attack had to be broken off.

We can get a final view of the naval aircraft of the 1914–18 War on a grey, windy day of November, 1918. It was the 21st, and the war had been over for ten days. Across the cold wastes of the North Sea the light cruiser *Cardiff*, with a kite balloon aloft, led a long line of ships towards the Firth of Forth, on their way to Scapa Flow. It was the German High Seas Fleet. On either side of them steamed ships of the Grand Fleet, their guns trained on the erstwhile enemy. Above them flew airships, aeroplanes, seaplanes, and flying boats, all machines of the former Royal Naval Air Service which had waged such devastating war on the enemy ships below. It was the end of a chapter.

Birth of the Modern Carrier

IF THE WAR HAD TAUGHT ONE LESSON IN THE ART OF naval flying it was that, in the true exercise of air power at sea, the aircraft was married to the carrier. Naval shore-based machines had their uses, it is true, but it was a use limited by range, endurance, and the inability to act in time when wanted with the fleet.

For a good many years the seaplane had been considered as the ideal type of aircraft to fulfil the naval role. Superficially it had a great many advantages, an aerodrome as wide as the ocean, the fact that it required little space for stowage, and its ability to dispense with a runway for launching. Most of the early carriers, therefore, were no more than merchant ships adapted to carry a large hanger on the upper deck, and the accepted mode of operation was to hoist the seaplane out to take off from the sea at the start of its flight, and to hoist it in from the sea when it landed on the water after the conclusion of its task.

The first carrier, it is true, was fitted with a flying deck forward, but it was rarely used for take-off, and never for landing on. This was the old cruiser, H.M.S. *Hermes*. As has been written previously she was torpedoed and sunk in November, 1914, before any real experience could be gained from her use. She was followed by the *Ark Royal*, who again was given a flight deck forward. Being originally designed as a tramp steamer all her machinery and boilers were concentrated aft, so that it was possible to give her a comparatively large flying deck, some 130 feet long. She again carried, however, only seaplanes, and these were launched from the sea. In her case it was lack of speed that rendered her flying deck valueless, for she could steam at no more than 10 knots, insufficient to create the air speed over the deck for flying off in normal conditions.

With the outbreak of war, and in the lack of any precise knowledge or experience of air warfare at sea, it was hardly surprising that the call was, at first, for more seaplane carriers. Belief in the seaplane as the naval machine *par excellence* was still widespread and there were few who yet took seriously Samson's feat of flying aeroplanes off ships.   Quite apart from the scenic railway effect of the early flying-off platforms, which inevitably interfered with a normal ship's fighting capacity, there was as yet no answer to the problems of landing.   To land an ordinary aeroplane on the sea required the fitting of flotation bags beside the landing wheels and a quick recovery before the aircraft sank. It was too unwieldy a fitting to become a practical possibility.

So three cross-Channel steamers were taken up to be transformed into seaplane carriers, the *Empress*, *Engadine*, and *Riviera*. No attempt was made to give these three ships any sort of flight deck, and they were quickly converted by the building of a hanger aft, capable of accommodating four seaplanes.   As pure seaplane carriers they served their purpose well, and the *Empress* was later taken in hand for more extensive modifications, being given a short flight deck forward.   She still, however, carried only seaplanes and it is a matter of history that her flight deck was never used during her whole existence.

All these three early carriers have some claim to special remembrance, for, in a small degree, flying history was made in them. It was from them that the first offensive action ever made by ship-borne aircraft, the Christmas Day raid on Cuxhaven and Wilhelmshaven, was launched, and it was from the *Engadine* that the first step in naval co-operation with a fleet at sea was taken, when one of her seaplanes carried out a reconnaissance flight, and made an enemy report, at the Battle of Jutland.

Next in succession came the Isle of Man packet *Ben-My-Chree* who, as we have already seen, operated with considerable success in the Mediterranean.   Her complement of seaplanes, like those of the cross-Channel steamers, was four, housed in a deck hanger constructed aft.   She was also fitted with a portable launching trackway forward but, like the *Empress*, it was never used, her seaplanes, as before, being hoisted over the side to take off from the water.

A second Isle of Man packet, the *Vindex*, was acquired in 1915, and her conversion marked an important step forward. She was given a 64-foot flying deck forward with the express intention of launching fighter planes.   A Bristol Scout took off successfully from her deck shortly after her commissioning trials, and her official complement of aircraft was five seaplanes and two fighters. These were stowed in separate hangars, a large one aft for the seaplanes and a very small one under the flying deck forward for the two fighters. It was, indeed, so small that the two aeroplanes had to be partially dismantled before they could be stowed away. The *Vindex* could be considered, perhaps, to be the first approach towards the modern carrier, although as yet the landing-on problem had not been tackled.

A further step towards the orthodox carrier came with the conversion of the next three ships taken up for R.N.A.S. duties, the *Manxman* in 1916, and the *Nairana* and *Pegasus* in early 1917. The general layout was similar to that of the *Vindex*, with an after hanger for seaplanes and a forward one for aeroplanes. But in these ships the fore hanger, under the flight deck, was fitted with a " sliding roof", rather in the nature of a motor-car, so that the fighters could be brought up on deck direct from their hangar below. It was the start of the lift principle, adopted nowadays in the carriers of every nation.

But it was during 1917 that events really set the pattern for the future development of naval flying from carriers. There were several of them and their effect was cumulative.

The first was the conversion of the 20,000-ton Cunarder *Campania* as a carrier. Her flying-off deck was 200 feet long, designed to launch seaplanes mounted on trolleys. At first the trolleys were taken up by the seaplanes and dropped into the sea when the machine was air-borne ; later a buffer arrangement was fitted to the fore end of the flying deck so that the movement of the trolley was arrested and the seaplane left to become air-borne without the embarrassment of a pair of wheels attached to its floats. It was, however, not so much the launching arrangements of the *Campania* which made her noteworthy— her complement of seaplanes as the sole type of machine carried was in fact a slightly retrograde step—but the fact that she was the first carrier of any size to serve in the fleet. Her success, even in the seaplane role, was considerable, and so focussed attention on the value of a carrier as a definite part of the composition of any fleet. Also, the size of her flight decks gave to some pilots the vision of landing-on. There was very nearly sufficient room to do it in the *Campania*, and if the big carrier could only be developed a little further, the vision might well become reality.

The next event of importance in 1917 was the appearance of the Sopwith Cuckoo. This was the first aeroplane designed to carry an 18-inch torpedo, as opposed to a seaplane, and its preliminary trials were so successful that Sir David Beatty, Commander-in-Chief of the Grand Fleet, sent in a demand for 200 of the new Cuckoos to work with the fleet. To be of any value, these machines needed a carrier not only from which they could fly off, but also one on which they could land, for they had no floats, as had their predecessors as torpedo carrying aircraft, and so could not land on the sea.

As a result the *Conte Rosso*, a liner building for Italy, was purchased and converted into a real aircraft-carrier—that is, a carrier which could combine the functions of landing on and taking off. She became H.M.S. *Argus* and was the first ship to be given an unrestricted flight deck from bow to stern, 550 feet long and 68 feet wide. She was completed too late to be used operationally in the war, but after the armistice she carried out a long series of landing trials at sea which were most encouraging. Out of 500 landings, no more than 40 were crashes, while in 90 more cases the aircraft suffered minor damage. Considering the very early stage of these experiments, the record was impressive. In order to give her an unrestricted flight deck, her funnel smoke and gases were led aft through trunks and exhausted over her stern.

While the *Conte Rosso* was in the process of being turned into H.M.S. *Argus*, the Admiralty decided to complete H.M.S. *Furious* as a carrier. She was a fast battle-cruiser built on light cruiser lines, a design sponsored by Lord Fisher as an alleged answer to the lessons learned at the Battle of the Falkland Islands. She was taken in hand in March, 1917, her fore 18-inch turret removed, and a large hanger surmounted by a flying-off deck built over her forecastle. Her flight deck measured 228 feet by 50 feet, large enough to fly off any machine of the period, since the ship herself had a speed of 30 knots and could thus herself produce that wind speed over her flight deck. But she was not big enough to land on. In this first conversion the bridge superstructure amidships was left as originally planned, effectively preventing any approach to the flight deck from aft.

Yet it was on board the *Furious*, as has been described earlier, that Squadron-Commander Dunning made the first landing at sea, flying a Sopwith Pup. Although on this occasion the landing-on was a success, it was not practical politics in a carrier of this design and was, indeed, more of a " stunt " than a contribution to naval flying technique. But it showed the possibilities of carrier-borne aircraft, and the *Furious* was taken in hand for further alterations. These consisted of the removal of the after 18-inch turret and the construction in its place of a second flight deck above the quarter-deck. The bridge superstructure, in this conversion, remained amidships, being protected from damage by aircraft landing on by a rope buffer net erected at the forward end of the after flight deck.

This landing-on deck was fitted with rudimentary arrester gear, consisting of a series of wires running fore and aft some 6 inches above deck level and about 12 inches apart. At intervals across the top of these were laid ropes running athwartships, weighted with a sandbag at each end. Naval aircraft at that time were fitted with skids instead of wheels, and a lateral horn attached to the skid engaged itself under the fore and aft wires, preventing the machine rising again after landing, while an arrester hook aft engaged the transverse ropes, the sandbags at each end acting as a brake.

In spite of all these arrangements, the landing on deck was not a success. The fault lay not so much with the arrester gear or the rope buffer net, but with the position of the bridge super-structure and the funnel. The hot boiler gases affected the density of the air over the stern, while the bridge not only cut off the air streams over the deck but also created dangerous air eddies. Some other arrangement was obviously necessary, but it was thought better to delay further alterations until experience with the *Argus* gave a line as to what was really necessary.

In addition to the *Argus*, however, two more carriers were coming along. One of these was the Chilean battleship *Almirante Cochrane*, purchased while still building and re-named *Eagle*. The other was the *Hermes*, ordered in 1917 as a carrier and the first ship in the world to be built expressly for that purpose. Neither, however, was ready for launching before the war came to an end and it was decided to delay completion pending the *Argus* trials.

At the end of the war, and for the first few years after it, it was to the *Argus*, then, that the Navy looked for its answers to the problems of correct flight deck design. One feature of the *Argus*'s flight deck was a shallow pit at the after end, some 9 inches below the flight deck level, with the object of forcing an aircraft's " horns " on the skids to engage under the fore and aft wires. This pit was first formed by lowering the lift, in which aircraft were brought up on deck from the hangar, by this distance. This proved a failure, mainly because the lift was not in the centre line of the flight deck. The pit, therefore, was artificially constructed to extend the whole width of the deck. As the machine came out of the pit, with its " horns " engaged, it ran up a ramp and was brought to a stop by the fore and aft wires converging on the skids to act as a brake.

A great many landings were made with this gear, the majority successful, but some ending in bad crashes. The greatest drawback was that, once committed to a landing the machine had to complete it willy-nilly as the " horns " were engaged under the wires, firmly holding the machine down. There was no chance, if for some reason the last stage of the approach was faulty, of the aircraft revving up and flying round for a second attempt.

Another experiment in the *Argus* was the mock-up of several types of bridge superstructure to discover the most satisfactory form. It was through these experiments that the island type was developed, a form which finally became standard practice in every Navy in the world, except in some carriers of the Japanese fleet.

It was as a result of these trials that the *Furious* was reconstructed for a third time in 1925 and the *Eagle* and *Hermes* completed. In the case of the *Furious* she followed the original *Argus* design in the complete elimination of her bridge and funnel, leaving nothing but her flight deck. Smoke from the boilers, as with the *Argus*, was led aft through trunking below the flying deck and emitted through a vent on the side of the ship aft. Her deck was given a hump aft and a raised flying-off platform forward, so that she embodied the " pit " arrangement fitted in the *Argus*. Soon after her reappearance in 1925 in this new guise, her flying deck was fitted with palisades on each side to prevent aircraft ditching as they came in to land.

A new type of arrester gear was tried out in the *Eagle*, consisting of hinged wooden flaps running across the deck and supported by the fore and aft wires. When an aeroplane came in to land, it knocked down these flaps as it ran along the flight deck, the degree of resistance in the flaps acting as an additional brake. In the first landings tried with this gear the undercarriages of the aircraft were severely damaged ; when the undercarriages were specially strengthened to resist this harsh treatment they made the aircraft heavy and sluggish to handle.

With the *Furious*, in her new conversion, having eliminated most of the flight deck troubles of the past, her two sister ships, *Courageous* and *Glorious* were taken in hand for alteration into carriers. They did not follow exactly the *Furious* model, in that they were fitted with an island on the starboard side of the flight deck, with the normal funnel aft of the bridge. The after hump, too, was removed, giving a flat flying deck some 700 feet long by 80 feet wide. A more satisfactory type of arrester gear was eventually fitted, consisting of transverse wires on the after part of the deck which were picked up by a trailing hook on the aircraft. These wires terminated in a cushioning mechanism which acted as a cumulative brake. At first both these carriers had the hinged flaps as fitted in the *Eagle*, but it was not long before that unsatisfactory method was replaced by the transverse wires.

When the *Hermes*, ordered in 1917, was finally completed and commissioned in 1923, her displacement was a fraction under 11,000 tons, making her very small in comparison with the *Argus*, *Eagle*, and *Furious*. Yet she proved herself to be a splendid ship at sea, very steady for flying and with little roll except in the heaviest of weather. Her flight deck, extending the whole length of the ship, was 600 feet long and 90 feet wide, rather small for the effective handling of aircraft and making it a slower business to get aircraft into the air or landed on than if she had had another 100 feet of deck.

But she was, nevertheless, an interesting ship, being the first in the world built as a carrier from her original design up. All the remainder were conversions, and each suffered in one respect or another from being a " make-shift " job. In the *Hermes*, the genius of Sir Eustace Tennyson-d'Eyncourt, the chief naval designer, was allowed full sway within the limit of her displacement, and he was able to set a pattern for future ships of this nature. That he was able, in an unwieldly ship like a carrier, to provide one that combined a remarkably steady flying platform with a speed of 30 knots was a tremendous tribute to his genius.

The *Hermes* carried only three squadrons of aircraft, a fighter squadron of nine Flycatchers and two spotter-reconnaissance squadrons of six Fairey III F's each. She had one electric lift and special gear in her hangar to facilitate the handling of aircraft parked below. Being so small, there was a great need for meticulous design to save every inch of space below the flight deck.

By 1930, the Navy thus had six carriers, five of them conversions from other designs, one built as a carrier from the start. Under the limitations of the Washington Naval Treaty, there remained but 20,000 tons available for new carrier construction and the relative experiences of the *Hermes* and the *Furious* showed that this was none too much, especially in the light of normal improvements in design and performance of naval aircraft. For carrier work, a slow landing speed is essential, and the stalling speed of an aircraft depends entirely on its wing loading. Thus, with the early Sopwith Pups, Camels, and Cuckoos, the wing loading varied from 5 to 7 pounds per square foot, giving them an extremely low stalling speed and enabling them to fly off and land in a very restricted space. But as the aircraft improved, so their wing loading increased, partly by the reduction of wing surface to give a cleaner aerodynamic design, partly by the need to carry more and more technical equipment, so that the Hawker Osprey, for example, which made its appearance in 1930, had a wing loading of nearly three times as much as the Pup, giving it a correspondingly higher stalling speed and therefore requiring a longer space in which to land on and take off.

In the meantime, however, the difficult economic situation in which the country found itself after the war had been the cause of allowing the Navy to fall into a state of unbalance. Normal replacement of ships had been sacrificed to the political requirement of stringent economy, and each year saw the gap between modern and obsolescent ships growing wider. Even in the early 1930's, while the Washington Treaty was still in force, the Admiralty was alive to the danger that was being run, but its expostulations fell on deaf ears and nothing was done to alleviate a position that, with each delay, got more and more out of hand.

What the Admiralty asked for was the chance to build up a balanced fleet, giving due preponderance in it to each type of ship. Although to a certain extent it meant working in the dark, the Board of Admiralty of those days was fully alive to the value the carrier was likely to have in modern war, and their balanced fleet, which still existed only on paper, incorporated a considerable number of carriers, to provide not only fighter protection at sea but also to deliver heavy blows by airborne torpedo attacks. But these carriers, considered so essential during the early 1930's, remained but paper dreams, and as the years slipped away, the gap widened.

Thus it was that matters stood in 1935, when at last the decision was taken to build one new carrier. Her tonnage was announced as 22,000, and since under the Washington Treaty only 20,000 tons was still available for carriers, it was reasonable to suppose that she was going to replace the *Argus*.

In general line she followed the *Hermes* except that the whole width of her flight deck was extended right up to the bows instead of following the normal hull line. On her tonnage it was possible to provide a flight deck 800 feet long by 94 feet wide, a great improvement in view of the ever-increasing performance figures of naval aircraft. She was fitted with three large double-decker lifts from the flight deck to the hangar, and although she was designed initially to carry six squadrons of aircraft, a total of seventy-two, it was found that her efficiency was greatly increased by reducing this to five squadrons, sixty aircraft.

When she was launched on April 13th, 1937, she was named *Ark Royal*, to follow the tradition set up by that older seaplane carrier who, as we have seen, did startling service in the Mediterranean during the early part of the First World War. That old *Ark Royal* was, in fact, still in commission for experimental aircraft work and she had to be renamed to make way for the new ship. She thus became H.M.S. *Pegasus*.

While the new *Ark Royal* was still fitting out and long before she was ready for commissioning, the urgency of the problem became more acute and the long-delayed measure of increasing the carrier strength of the Royal Navy was at last faced. The cause was not far to seek, lying as it did in the sombre cloud of Nazi and Fascist tyranny that was spreading its shadow over Europe. As the shadow spread, so the forces of freedom had to look to their defences, partly to meet the growing threat of totalitarian domination, partly in the hope that an active policy of naval and military preparedness might discourage the dictators from taking the ultimate step of war.

So, in 1937, the great pre-war rearmament programme was born, and the three Services drew up their plans. In the Navy, the greatest single slice of the building " cake " was allotted to carrier construction, so firm by now had grown the Admiralty's faith in the new weapon. Four new aircraft carriers were ordered in 1937, and orders for two more followed in 1938. All of them were to be of 23,000 tons, each with a complement of six squadrons, comprising seventy-two aircraft.

The four ordered in 1937 were the *Illustrious*, *Victorious*, *Formidable*, and *Indomitable*, the two in 1938 the *Implacable* and *Indefatigable*. As the riveting hammers at the building yards clattered and the massive hulls grew apace, the clouds of war were gathering over Europe. The stage was being set for the great drama of 1939 and 1940 as the six carriers grew nearer to completion and the Fleet Air Arm, direct descendant of the Royal Naval Air Service, prepared for war.

How great, though, was the change that had taken place in the twenty-five years that had elapsed ! Let us try to measure it in a brief comparison of the *Ark Royal* of 1914 and the *Ark Royal* of 1939. The first was a converted tramp steamer, bought while still in frame and completed as a seaplane carrier. She had a flying deck 130 feet long which was never once used for flying-off. In the *Ark Royal* of 1939 the flight deck was six times as long and over twice as wide. The first *Ark* had a maximum speed of 10 knots, the second could steam at 32. The first carried ten seaplanes, which it launched by hoisting them out into the water so that they could use the sea as their flight deck. They landed in the same way, taxi-ing up to the ship to be hoisted in again. But in the new *Ark Royal* her aircraft were brought up on to the flight deck in electric lifts, and they took off and landed on without difficulty, completely independent of the sea. It was a dream come true, the vision of those early flyers like Samson, Longmore, and Dunning, and brought by infinite experiment, patience, and courage into a full reality. A new naval weapon had been forged and, by 1939, the curtain was being raised on a scene in which they were cast to play a leading role. The carrier, which alone made that role possible, was on the way to becoming the most important unit in the fleet.

(*Imperial War Museum*)

Down below.   A scene in the hangar of H.M.S. *Illustrious*.   The aircraft shown are Corsairs.

Ready for a strike.   Corsairs, with long-range tanks, ranged on the flight deck.

(*Imperial War Museum*)

(*Imperial War Museum*
The bombing of the *Tirpitz*.   She has been hit on her bridge superstructure.

Taken from an attacking Avenger.   The conning tower of a German U-boat, with an enemy gunner in action.

(*Imperial War Museum*)

The Inter-War Machines

FROM THE CARRIER, LET US TURN TO CONSIDERATION of the aircraft flown by naval pilots and trace its development in machines down the years. We have seen how at first naval thought turned towards the airship, and how disappointments in that sphere brought the seaplane into favour. In the light of present-day knowledge it is not difficult to understand the inevitable drawbacks of that type of machine, but in those days it appeared to be almost the complete answer to all naval requirements. Not only could it rise off and land on the sea, it could also be used for reconnaissance, for spotting, and, as was demonstrated in the Gallipoli campaign of 1915, it could carry a torpedo and launch it at enemy ships.

Various types of seaplane were built during the early days of that war, and they performed their task adequately in carrying out the various duties which the Navy demanded of them. In 1914 and 1915 air warfare was still much of a novelty and there were few who could appreciate and understand the possibilities that lay ahead. As each new task at sea appeared, so the seaplane, or some adaptation of it, seemed to provide the reply. That the seaplane performed most of them inefficiently was not yet apparent, for as yet there were no performance figures of more conventional aircraft against which to form a comparison.

They were bound to come, naturally enough, for the art of flying was a fast and continually developing technique and under the spur of war requirements the aircraft designers, and behind them the aircraft industry, surged with restless life. New engine designs, new machines, followed each other with an amazing rapidity, and the native genius of Britain developed this new dimension of war faster and more inventively than any other nation.

Against this background of swift development, of new techniques, of faster and more powerful aircraft, the seaplane began to fade into obscurity. As the potentialities of the new weapon were recognized, so the tasks demanded of it by the fleet became more exacting. Something even more versatile than the seaplane was needed, and by 1916 the cry was for fighters that would outfly and outmanoeuvre both Zeppelins and bombers, for torpedo-carrying machines that could lift and deliver a larger torpedo than that carried by seaplanes, for spotting and reconnaissance aircraft with more endurance than a seaplane could achieve. But above all was the requirement for aircraft that could proceed to sea with the fleet, that could be got up into the air more swiftly than a seaplane. By 1916, there was already a vision of an aircraft carrier that could not only launch aircraft from her deck, but also land them on again after the completion of their task. Well as the seaplane, till now, had done its job, it could no longer fill the bill in naval warfare. It was too slow in landing, too unwieldy, too dependent on the state of the sea to serve the growing needs of the fleet.

The seaplane did not disappear suddenly from the naval scene, and even in 1916 it was to have a few more years of useful life, mainly because the difficulties of landing on were as yet unsolved. But, increasingly, it was being edged out by the superiority of such machines as the Pup, the Camel, and the Cuckoo. As soon as these aircraft were properly adapted for ship flying the fate of the seaplane was sealed.

It was probably the Sopwith Cuckoo that drove the last nail into the seaplane's coffin. Designed expressly as a torpedo carrier, it was the only machine of its time capable of lifting the heavier torpedo and delivering it at a reasonable range. That alone made it an essential requirement for the fleet. Since it required a flight deck from which to take off at sea, its introduction into service made inevitable the production of the large carrier.

Once the carrier problem was solved, there was little limit to the development of new types of aircraft for work with the fleet, for here was the means of using land machines at sea, with all their superiorities in speed, power, and manoeuvrability. Fleet requirements began to crystallize into definite types, fighter, spotter, reconnaissance, and torpedo carrying, and performance figures rose as the more robust and flexible aeroplanes usurped completely the former precedence enjoyed by the seaplane.

The Sopwith Pups and Camels, which had shared the naval

fighter role during the First World War, gave way to the Fairey Flycatcher in 1924, a single-seated aircraft mounting two machine-guns, and fitted with a device for varying the camber of the main planes to reduce the stalling speed for landing on and flying off. This was the only difference between the Flycatcher and the standard shore fighter of the time, a startling commentary on the adaptability of the new carrier to operate high performance aircraft.

For spotting and reconnaissance, the Fairey III F came forward as a vast improvement on the older, tram-like machines. It was fast and very manœuvrable, and reasonably spacious to accommodate an observer and his instruments without being too cramped. The Fairey III F made its appearance in 1927 and served efficiently for several years. It was, at the same time, a precision bomber, though rarely used for this purpose, as there was little belief, at that time, in the efficacy of bombs against ships.

Rather than bombs, the Admiralty pinned its faith in the torpedo as the proper attack weapon for sea-borne aircraft. Like aircraft, the torpedo had been virtually a new weapon at the outbreak of war in 1914 but, again like aircraft, it had proved its value in emphatic terms. It had been responsible for more tonnage sunk during the war years than every other weapon combined.

It was not only this fact of past performance that influenced the Admiralty in its decision. That claims of the power of the bomb as a weapon against ships were extravagant had been borne out in trials, for the difficulty of accurate aim against a moving target had made the chance of a hit very remote. All these factors taken together indicated the torpedo as the most likely weapon for attack against ships, and so it was on torpedoes released from aircraft that current naval thought concentrated.

It was in the light of this requirement that the famous Swordfish was born, successor to the Sopwith Cuckoo, the Blackburn Dart, and the Blackburn Ripon. The Dart was a single-seater and had the great drawback that the pilot, as well as flying the machine, had also to work out the correct firing angle of his torpedo and operate the release mechanism. The Ripon, which followed, carried an observer as well as a pilot and, although its rate of climb was not quite so good as that of the Dart, it was both faster and had nearly twice the range.

The Swordfish, designed and built by the Fairey Aviation Company, was one of the most remarkable aircraft ever supplied to the Fleet Air Arm. It suffered to a certain extent from being a child of economy and was designed to serve a triple purpose. It was what was known as a " T.S.R." machine, the initial letters of torpedo, spotting, and reconnaissance. It was the " S.R." role which rather detracted from the " T " function, for its maximum speed of 184 miles an hour, while perfectly adequate for spotting and reconnaissance in which great speed might well prove a handicap, was woefully low for torpedo attack in which a plane has to run the gauntlet of massed close-range anti-aircraft fire.

Yet, in spite of this, the Swordfish put up so wonderful a performance during the early years of the 1939–45 war that its name will live for ever in the annals of the Fleet Air Arm. They were known throughout the Navy as " stringbags ", for they gave the impression of being tied together with pieces of string, and yet they were one of the most robust planes ever built. So much so that, on one occasion during the last war, two cylinders of the rotary engine of one of them were knocked off by an anti-aircraft shell and the Swordfish kept on flying ! They were very easy to fly and simple to land on a flight deck, making them almost the ideal naval aircraft for carrier-borne use, and it was only this lack of speed which, in the end, made them no longer a possible proposition. This was demonstrated forcibly in an action in the English Channel in early 1942 when, of six Swordfish attacking, all six were lost in particularly gallant circumstances. But until then they had had a most impressive record of success. It is a measure of their versatility that, in addition to being used as torpedo attack machines and for spotting and reconnaissance duties, they also at times performed the role of dive bombers with considerable success, carrying for this purpose a bomb-load of 1,800 pounds.

At the same time as the Swordfish replaced the Blackburn Ripon as a torpedo attack aircraft, the Fairey Flycatcher was replaced as a fighter by the Gloster Sea Gladiator, the sea version of the shore-based fighter of the same name. It was a biplane with a speed of some 250 miles an hour and, like the Swordfish, it was to write its name in letters of immortal glory in the story of the Fleet Air Arm.

In 1937 the Blackburn Skua was put into production as a fighter-cum-dive bomber, not entirely to supersede the Gladiator but to reinforce it. Time by now was running short and, with the new carriers ordered, it was necessary to build up a big reserve of aircraft. The Skua was not quite as fast as the Gladiator, but it was a monoplane and carried a heavier armament. Nor was it entirely a success, although during the war it had its moments of great achievement.

As the sands finally ran out in the early autumn of 1939, the Fleet Air Arm pinned its faith to the machines it had then, the ubiquitous Swordfish, the gallant Gladiator, the erratic Skua. Other, newer, machines were on the way, the Fairey Albacore to take the place of the Swordfish as a torpedo attack aircraft, the Fairey Fulmar to supersede the Gladiator and the Skua as a fighter. There were many others, of course, which made an appearance early in the war, for by that time almost anything that would fly was acceptable.

Mention must be made of the non-operational, or almost non-operational, Walrus, the amphibious machine carried by battleships and cruisers for reconnaissance, communication, spotting, and air-sea rescue duties. Slow and rather cumbersome in the air, they served a great variety of purposes and proved invaluable throughout the war. They were launched from a catapult and landed in the sea alongside their parent ship, being hoisted in by crane. A squadron of them served ashore in the Norway campaign, forced by circumstances to undertake the unfamiliar role of bombers, and they were not without their successes.

The catapult method of launching, fitted in battleships and cruisers and eventually to become an essential adjunct even of carriers, was first tested out at the Naval Aircraft Experimental Depot on the Isle of Grain during the First World War, but the experiments were not a success. A more ambitious series of experiments were carried out after that war at the Royal Aircraft Establishment at Farnborough, the first actual trial being made by a sheep. It was designed to test the amount of acceleration that a human body could absorb, but it was never determined whether a sheep was chosen because it was the nearest animal approach to a naval pilot that the scientists concerned could think of. Anyway, the sheep was strapped into the cockpit of the test aeroplane, sitting on its haunches in the pilot's seat with, it is said, a pair of goggles fitted over its eyes. It all looked most professional. The catapult was then released and the group of naval pilots watching the test—and at the same time watching the changing expression on the sheep's face as it shot away into space—doubled up with laughter. Some of them made themselves physically sick from laughing.

The sheep, however, suffered no ill effects from its involuntary experiment, nor did the naval pilots when they took over from this intrepid, if woolly, aviator. When the catapult was first fitted in ships, it consisted of a propulsive ram driven by high-pressure air. Although it worked quite satisfactorily, it proved rather too massive an installation to be fitted conveniently in a normal warship, and a much simpler form was evolved, worked by an ordinary explosive propellant, the size of the charge being regulated by the weight of the machine to be launched and the strength of the wind.

Occasionally, ships were given Swordfish to carry instead of the Walrus, and that ubiquitous machine could carry out the duties of a ship-borne aircraft just as well as the Walrus, with the exception of the air-sea rescue role. It was equally adaptable for launching from a catapult as for taking-off from a flight deck, and the two types of machine did yeoman service during the war in their ship-borne role.

The Struggle for Control

No SURVEY OF THE FLEET AIR ARM WOULD BE COMPLETE without some review of the political and administrative aspect that followed the amalgamation of the two flying services just before the end of the First World War. The original separation of its naval wing and its rebirth into the Royal Naval Air Service was not, as has so often been suggested, a selfish act of intransigeance on the part of the Admiralty. It came from an early realization that the sea role of air power was fundamentally different from the land role, involving a different application, different tasks, even different machines. In the traditional exercise of sea power, upon which the greatness and power of the nation had grown and been preserved, the new weapon in the air had a different part to play, but it could only play it effectively by complete integration into the naval scene so that it could act in full conformity with the main strategy of war at sea.

It was, therefore, no act of selfishness or greed that engineered the setting-up of a separate naval air service in the very early days of flying, for under the original conception of the Royal Flying Corps there lay a provision that the Admiralty was forced to find unacceptable. This was the proviso of a single joint-Service school of flying in which the training was the same for both naval and military pilots, with the declared policy of interchangeability of pilots of both Services. Whereas, to a limited extent, this was possible on the military side—in fact several complete naval squadrons were lent to the Army in France and fought with considerable success—it was quite the reverse on the naval side. A pilot pure and simple was not of very much use to the Navy. What was required was a trained naval officer or man who could fly, someone who already knew the difference between a battleship and a cruiser, who could estimate accurately courses and speeds, who knew from his training the capabilities and limitations of ships of different classes and different navies, who understood the intricacies of naval tactics and the effect of naval weapons.

Even at that early and embryonic stage of flying, the differences were clearly fundamental. Few, perhaps, could visualize the swiftness with which air warfare was to develop, or the immense power it would develop, but it was not that which was in question. It was the use to which it could be put in the naval field as an adjunct of sea power and a new element of naval strategy. Sea power, for all its immense and devastating strength, is a delicate instrument finely balanced, and in its exercise it calls for an expert touch, acquired only after years of training and experience. To try and graft a powerful new weapon on to so intricate a growth without expert knowledge and guidance was certain to end in confusion or chaos, and it was only the Admiralty that could supply that expert knowledge and guidance.

We have seen, in past chapters, something of how the new weapon was used in the war at sea in 1914 and 1918, and how the germ of fleet co-operation was born and developed. Under naval guidance, the appropriate types of aircraft were designed and tested, and were used in their proper strategical sphere ; for attack on targets beyond the range of naval guns, for fighter defence of the fleet, for distant reconnaissance beyond the range of human eyes, for taking over much of the essential patrol work of the Navy and freeing for alternative uses the ships that would otherwise have been employed in it, and, in the case of naval airships, for extended convoy escort duties. Thus was the new weapon harnessed to the exercise of sea power, extending its range and providing a new economy of force. There were, of course, many mistakes and in addition a good deal of antagonism from some of the "old school" senior officers, but taken as a whole the naval air service was intelligently used so far as the actual mechanical performance of the machines permitted.

To understand the destruction of this close and intimate association by the forced amalgamation of 1918 it is necessary to look more closely into the administrative side of flying during the war. Both the Navy and the Army, as we have seen, had their own flying services, separately administered by the Admiralty and War Office respectively. To co-ordinate the production of aircraft and allocation as between the two Services, a Joint Air

Committee was set up under Lord Derby on which members of both the Navy and the Army served. The committee was advisory only and, being bereft of all executive power, was unable to reconcile the two conflicting points of view. In his " Memorandum on the Organization of the Air Service ", prepared by Lieut.-General Sir David Henderson at the request of the Government and submitted in 1917, it is stated that :

> The Navy complained that there was really enough material available for both Services, which then [1915 and 1916] were very small, but that the methods of purchase by the Royal Flying Corps were slow and inefficient, and that therefore the Army were always trying to grab from the Navy material which the latter had been able to acquire. The Army, on the other hand, complained that the Navy purchased everything in sight, whether they required it or not, that their needs were not nearly so great as those of the Army, and that the material which they were purchasing was not required for proper naval purposes.

This inter-Service bickering did neither side any good and it was hardly surprising that the Henderson memorandum came out in favour of a unified air force.

> A department would have to be formed on the general lines of the Admiralty and War Office, with a full staff, and with full responsibility for war in the air. Undoubtedly some portion of our air forces must be considered as accessory to the Navy and to the Army, and such contingents would have to be allotted according to the importance of the sea and land operations in progress, but it does not seem necessary that such contingents should be composed of naval or military personnel ; any suggestion of that kind would only prolong the situation of divided responsibility. . . . The whole system of training, however, should be completely unified ; and it is only when pilots and mechanics begin to specialize, and then not in all cases, that it would be necessary to earmark them for service by sea or by land.

This recommendation, of course, lacked all appreciation of the distinctive role of naval aircraft and completely failed to grasp the enhanced value of sea power when allied to the air weapon. It was a somewhat pedestrian solution to an extremely complex problem, and at that time the answer lay not in the formation of a new body which would take entire control of all flying, irrespective of Service needs, but an air organization that, by tact and understanding, could strike the impartial balance as between the competing requirements.

The Joint Air Committee was succeeded by an Air Board under the chairmanship of Lord Curzon, but the new Board had little more success than the old Committee. Once again the chief protagonists were the naval and military representatives and the inter-Service squabbles persisted.

The Henderson Memorandum was submitted to the Government on 19th July, 1917, and four weeks later a committee, headed by the Prime Minister (Mr. Lloyd-George) and General Smuts, issued their report on Air Organization. It was strongly in favour of an Air Ministry to take over the whole of Service flying and, in some ways, an even more naïve document than that produced by General Henderson.

> . . . The day may not be far off when aerial operations with their devastation of enemy lands and destruction of industrial and populous centres on a vast scale may become the principal operations of war, to which the older forms of military and naval operations may become secondary and subordinate. . . . There remains the question of the new Air Service and the absorption of the Royal Naval Air Service and Royal Flying Corps into it. Should the Navy and the Army retain their own special Air Services in addition to the air forces which will be controlled by the Air Ministry? This will make the confusion hopeless and render the solution of the air problem impossible. The maintenance of three Air Services is out of the question, nor indeed does the War Office make any claim to a separate Air Service of its own. But, as regards air work, the Navy is exactly in the same position as the Army ; the intimacy between aerial scouting or observation and naval operations is not greater than long-range artillery work on land and aerial observation or spotting. If a separate Air Service is not necessary in the one case, neither is it necessary in the other. And the proper and, indeed, only possible arrangement is to establish one unified Air Service, which will absorb both the existing Services under arrangements which will fully safeguard the efficiency and secure the closest intimacy between the Army and the Navy and the portions of the Air Service allotted or seconded to them.

That this was the easiest way out of the difficulties caused by inter-Service disagreements none could deny, but that it was the right one is open to grave doubts. When the committee report was forwarded to Sir Douglas Haig for his opinions, he was emphatic in his condemnation of it.

> Apart from the question of advisability [he wrote], from the point of view of morality and public opinion, of seeking to end the war by "devastation of enemy lands and destruction of industrial and populous centres on a vast scale", I am unable to agree that there is practically no limit to such methods in this war or that—at anyrate in the near future—they are likely to "become the principal operations of war, to which the older forms of military and naval operations may become secondary and subordinate".

And later in his report he wrote:

> The Air Services with an army in the field are now as much a part of that army as are the infantry, artillery, or cavalry, and the co-ordination and combination of the efforts of all these services must be controlled directly by the Commanders of Armies, Corps, etc., under the supreme authority of the Commander-in-Chief. To expect that the relationship between a Commander and the Army generally, on the one hand, and "attached" units on the other, can ever be quite the same as if these units belonged to the Army, and looked to the other arms as their comrades and to the Army authorities as their true masters and the ultimate judges on whom their prospects depend, would be contrary to all experience. No system of liaison or of seconding military officers to serve for a period of years with the Air Service can ever establish the same relationship as springs from community of interests and the knowledge that we belong alike to one service.

It was, therefore, against the professional advice of the principal leaders in the field and at sea that the two main combatant Services lost their air components. It was not, of course, the whole story, for there undoubtedly existed a very serious quarrel between the Navy and the Army on the subject of supply and design. This naturally had a detrimental effect on the whole question of aerial development and supply, and there were too many interested people with too many ideas for any broad pattern of logical development to flow from the growing lessons of air fighting. It must be remembered that, in 1918, the whole problem of flight was still only emerging from the chrysalis stage and the inter-Service rivalry which hedged the industry with restrictive designs was, broadly speaking, a potent bar to rational development. Too much effort was being devoted to sidelines, not sufficient to the main stream.

For better or for worse, then, the Government decided compulsorily to amalgamate the two branches of warlike flying, sea and land, and to direct its growth under unified command. A White Paper was laid before the House of Commons in the autumn of 1917, was approved, and on 1st April, 1918, the amalgamation formally took place, sweeping into the Royal Air Force, as the new body was called, 103 naval airships, 2,949 naval aeroplanes, seaplanes, and flying boats, 126 naval shore air stations, and 67,000 naval officers and men.

For the next twenty years the story of naval flying is an unhappy one. The naval component of the Royal Air Force, not until 1924 to be called the Fleet Air Arm, suffered from apathy and neglect. It was not entirely the fault of the Air Ministry, for their main preoccupation was necessarily one in which a new foundation of war strategy had to be evolved, embodying a completely new technique of fighting. But it was undoubtedly a pity that there was not a broader vision at the head of the nation's air affairs, a vision that could appreciate not only the lessons of the war that had just been fought, but also those earlier ones which had established so firmly the immense force of sea power when properly wielded. The third dimension introduced by the invention of the aeroplane had in no way diminished the force of the lessons so hardly learned through three centuries of naval growth, and a wise reading of the application of sea power would have shown that the air had a vital contribution to make to it, if properly directed.

The first adverse result of the amalgamation was, it must regretfully be recorded, in the quality of the pilots and observers allocated by the new Air Ministry to service with the fleet. When appointed to flying duties at sea the Royal Air Force officer not only had to forego the pleasures of life on land, separation from wives and families, more comfortable living quarters, and so on, but also a loss of pay when compared with service ashore. There was little wonder in these conditions that, to the pilot in light blue, service at sea in aircraft carriers was unpopular and a drudgery to be passed through as quickly as possible. Their hearts were not in their jobs.

As the early peace years passed, the effects of Air Ministry control of naval flying caused a growing uneasiness at the Admiralty. Exercises at sea revealed a pathetic lack of skill, especially in spotting and reconnaissance, reaching its lowest pitch when a few fishing trawlers were reported during an exercise as a squadron of battleships. So inefficient a performance could hardly go unremarked and in 1921, as a result of very considerable pressure, the Admiralty managed to obtain approval for naval officers to be trained as observers. The first course of six officers began their training at Lee-on-Solent in April, 1921, and subsequent courses were formed for training at six-monthly intervals.

With that small success as a precedent, the Navy began its campaign for control of its own flying. The First Sea Lord, then Admiral Lord Beatty, persuaded the Government to set up a committee of inquiry in 1921 to study the question, but there was, as yet, insufficient evidence one way or the other to enable it to come to a joint decision. Another committee in 1923, under the chairmanship of Lord Salisbury, was equally non-commital over the major problem, but made some specific recommendations that helped, at any rate, to bring back a large measure of purely naval element in the matter of flying. It set out the desirability of all observers in aircraft at sea being naval officers not attached to the Royal Air Force and recommended that naval officers should be trained as pilots up to a maximum of 70 per cent of all carried at sea. These naval pilots were to be attached to the Royal Air Force and given equivalent R.A.F. rank in addition to their naval rank. At the same time the committee laid down procedure for discipline and administration for officers and men of either Service when serving with the other.

At the same time a minor reorganization was carried out for flying at sea. It had been found that the Royal Air Force squadronal organization was too cumbersome for use in carriers and, during 1923, units working with the fleet were reorganized into flights of six machines each to give a more flexible control in the air.

The compromise of the Salisbury Committee went part of the way towards meeting Admiralty fears on the future development of naval co-operation in the air. After his initial flying training carried out by the Royal Air Force, the naval pilot came to sea as a permanent naval pilot, no longer subject to the vagaries of " posting ", under which the former Royal Air

Force pilot in a carrier was liable to be appointed to a shore-based squadron just when he was really becoming useful at sea. One other administrative result of the reforms was to rename the carrier-borne branch as the Fleet Air Arm, a title which came into operation in April, 1924, and was to remain even after the Admiralty had reached a final victory in its struggle to obtain full control of naval flying. The full title, of course, was the Fleet Air Arm of the Royal Air Force.

There still remained one bone of contention between the Admiralty and the Air Ministry, even after the provisions of the Salisbury committee had come to full fruition. This was in the design and supply of aircraft, which remained a Royal Air Force commitment. With its faith pinned firmly to the land-based aircraft and the bomb as the true exponent of air power, the Air Ministry not unnaturally felt little inclination to spend very much time or trouble on specialized research into types of machine which ran counter to its own interests. The Fleet Air Arm, as a result, had to accept what the Royal Air Force provided, which generally consisted of sea adaptations of machines originally designed for operations from shore bases. There was little attempt to design aircraft purely for the sea role, nor indeed any real attempt to understand what the role of the air in relation to the sea was to be.

Here again such opinions as existed were based on entirely unknown factors. There had, for instance, occurred in 1923 a test carried out by the Royal Air Force and the Admiralty in which a radio-controlled target ship, the old battleship *Agamemnon*, was attacked by bombs from a height of 8,000 feet. Of eight bombs dropped, two were hits and the remaining six fell near enough to have caused considerable damage. From this simple example arose the cry that the battleship was an obsolete weapon, doomed to extinction by the bomb dropped from above. What was not taken into account was that in war, any ship of comparable size would not only have been escorted but would also have taken evasive action and have put up as heavy an anti-aircraft defence as possible. In addition she would probably also have had the protection of carrier-borne fighters. The *Agamemnon* test, as it was carried out, proved nothing. Yet it caused so violent a controversy that it held back normal development in the Fleet Air Arm for many years.

It was under these unfortunate drawbacks that the Fleet Air Arm struggled to reach some sort of efficiency during the inter-war years. The divided Admiralty-Air Ministry control prevented any clear-cut objective from being formulated and bedevilled all attempts to decide the proper role that air power should play in a true alliance with sea power, simply because the two controlling bodies were working to different sets of principles.

There came the time, inevitably, when at last the Admiralty won the battle for control of its own air force. The announcement was made in the House of Commons by the Prime Minister, Mr. Neville Chamberlain, in the summer of 1937, and under its terms the administrative control of the Fleet Air Arm passed to the Admiralty, in addition to the operational control which it already exercised. Land-based aircraft employed in co-operation with naval forces—later to be known as Coastal Command—remained with the Royal Air Force both administratively and operationally. It was envisaged in the parliamentary statement that the period of take-over would be two years, at the expiration of which all Fleet Air Arm personnel would be naval. At the same time, the new arrangement permitted the Admiralty to set up and operate shore bases for the Fleet Air Arm, and as a start naval stations were opened at Lee-on-Solent, Worthy Down, Donibristle, Evanton, Hatston, St. Merryn, and many other places.

The problem now was to find sufficient men not only to train as additional pilots and observers, but also to take over the " ground crew " duties of the R.A.F. personnel. It was solved by the formation of an Air Branch in the Navy and the acceptance of suitable men for a shortened term of service of seven years. The terms offered were sufficiently attractive to bring in many new men and also to persuade some of the older ones, who were facing retirement, to sign on for a new term of service. So successful, indeed, was the recruiting drive for the now entirely naval Fleet Air Arm, that by May, 1939, well within the two years allowed, the Admiralty was able to announce that the take-over from the Royal Air Force was complete. So far as pilots were concerned this was strictly accurate, but a few R.A.F. technical officers and many R.A.F. non-commissioned officers and men remained in the maintenance crews for some years more.

By May, 1939, too, there could no longer be any doubt that war was on the way. But the Fleet Air Arm was far from ready. The wasted years between the wars told their inevitable tale of obsolete aircraft and inadequate numbers. Good as were the Gladiators, Flycatchers, Swordfish, and Skuas, as fighting aircraft they were no match for the Messerschmitts, Focke-Wulfs, Heinkels, and Stukas with which Germany had largely equipped her air force, having neither the speed nor gunpower of the German machines. And, even by 1939, when the monoplane had almost completely replaced the biplane ashore, there were few who even considered feasible the landing of one of these high-performance single-wing machines upon the limited space of a carrier's flying deck. The power of the arrester gear had not yet been exploited to the full.

It was much the same story with carriers. In 1926 the only ships of this type in service were the *Furious*, *Courageous*, *Eagle*, *Hermes*, and *Argus*, and during the next ten years the *Glorious* was added to the list. All of these ships, of which only the *Hermes* was originally designed as a carrier, were of the First World War, or pre-First World War, vintage. In 1938 the new *Ark Royal* made her appearance, as has been described elsewhere, and in 1938 and 1939 the naval estimates included a provision for six more carriers, the *Illustrious*, *Indomitable*, *Indefatigable*, *Implacable*, *Formidable*, and *Victorious*. Although, under the spur of war, these six ships were built in record time, none was ready when the curtain rose on the war that most naval men had foreseen nearly two years earlier. This, too, was a legacy of those years of neglect and indecision, the wasted years of conflict between the diehards of two Services who had failed to appreciate the very special place that aircraft held in the exercise of sea power, still the most powerful weapon in the world.

Opening Shots in the New War

As in 1914–18, so in 1939 the german navy pinned its faith on the U-boat and the raider in its battle against the stranglehold of British sea power. Germany had failed in 1918 partly because so much of her naval resources had been devoted towards a vain attempt to match, ship for ship, the fleet of Britain. Even then the German U-boats had come near to success with their war against commerce. This fact could, in the German view, be taken as a blueprint to naval victory if, this time, it was waged with the maximum power from the very start. So Germany built the ships that she thought could win her the war at sea, medium- and long-range U-boats, heavy cruisers and battleships that could annihilate a whole convoy and its escorts, and long-range four-engined bombers that could dominate the seas within reach of their coastal bases.

There was one unknown quantity in their calculations, one risk as yet unresolved. That was the carrier, with her ability to take fighters and attack aircraft to sea and operate them far from any shore-based aerodrome. The U-boat, the raider, and the long-range bomber were all but powerless in the face of naval aircraft. The U-boat sighted from the air must dive and lose three-quarters of her mobility and her ability to reach an attacking position. The raider reported by aircraft must abandon her operational area, for she knows she will be hunted if she remains there. The long-range bomber is at the mercy of a fighter that is faster and infinitely more manœuvrable than herself.

The Germans, in 1939, banked heavily on a short war. If they could win in a year, or two years, the task they had set themselves would be completed before the new British carriers could be commissioned and before the unknown quantity could begin to exercise its influence on the war at sea. If also, during this period, Germany could reduce the carrier strength of Britain, so the time limit for victory could be prolonged. It was obvious to Germany that the crux of the naval war hinged on the carrier and its aircraft.

It needed little intelligence to realize that the first blows in the German naval effort were likely to be struck in the Western Approaches, those great focal points of sea-borne trade bound for Britain. The sinking of the *Athenia* on the first day of war bore out that contention, and it was, therefore, in that area that the first major efforts of U-boat hunting were made.

The fertile brain of Mr. Winston Churchill, then First Lord of the Admiralty, evolved a scheme in which the Fleet Air Arm could, perhaps, play an important part in this war against the U-boat. His idea was to use a carrier, with a hunting group of four destroyers, stationed near the great focal points as a means of keeping the area clear of the underwater threat to merchant shipping. The carrier's squadrons would patrol a wide area of sea, attack with bombs or depth-charges any U-boats sighted, and call up the waiting destroyers to carry on the hunt. But in the first trial of this idea, the result was unfortunate, for the U-boat struck first and H.M.S. *Courageous* was sent to the bottom, hit by two torpedoes from U.29. But it is a point of interest, that, later in the war, when the battle of the Atlantic was at its climax, the hunting group system based on the carrier played a decisive part in the final defeat of the U-boat. Even in 1939, the idea was excellent, but the general shortage at that date of carriers in the fleet made it impossible to risk them in operations of this sort, and after the loss of the *Courageous* the scheme lapsed until the advent of the smaller and more quickly built escort carrier made it a feasible operation of war.

In the meantime, however, the *Ark Royal* had been busy in the North Sea. On September 14th, three days before the loss of the *Courageous*, she had been similarly engaged in anti-submarine operations and had picked up a report from the S.S. *Fanad Head* that she had been torpedoed. Steaming down towards the position of the attack, she flew off three Skuas, and almost at once a torpedo was sighted running straight for her. It was, fortunately, sighted in time for her to evade it, and her escorting destroyers closed in to take over the hunt for the U-boat. Almost at once they picked her up on their Asdics. The first salvo of depth-charges blew the U-boat's engines off their beds and the second damaged her so much that she was forced to the surface. She was U.39. The whole of her crew was taken prisoner and the U-boat sunk by gunfire from the destroyers.

In the meantime the three Skuas, flying down towards the *Fanad Head*, sighted her, together with a U-boat shelling her. All three dived to the attack but the first two, diving too steeply, were unable to pull out and crashed into the sea alongside the U-boat, which happened to be U.30. The two crews of the Skuas were picked up by the submarine, which then dived again as the third Skua came in a second time to attack. Later still, six of the *Ark Royal*'s Swordfish made another attack on U.30, but although they claimed her as a victim, she was in fact only damaged and returned to Germany safely.

Twelve days later the *Ark Royal* was again in the news. She was part of a force sent out to cover the return of the submarine *Spearfish*, which had been badly damaged while on patrol off Horns Riff. As the *Ark Royal* was steaming along in company with the battleships *Rodney* and *Nelson*, her reconnaissance aircraft sighted three of the big German Dornier 18 flying boats which were shadowing the squadron. As soon as the signal reached the *Ark Royal*, she flew off nine Skuas. Two of the Dorniers were damaged and driven off, the third was shot down by Lieutenant B. E. McEwen and his air gunner, Petty Officer B. M. Seymour. It was the first enemy aircraft destroyed in the war by any Service. This was the famous occasion on which the *Ark Royal* was " sunk " by the German Press and the man responsible promoted and decorated with the Iron Cross. Shortly after the shooting down of the Dornier, a Heinkel came out from the clouds and dived steeply towards the carrier, releasing a 2,000-pound bomb. By using full helm, the *Ark Royal* just evaded the bomb, which burst about 30 yards away in the water. A few minutes later the Heinkel reappeared and sprayed the flight deck with machine-gun fire, but without causing any casualties. The only damage in the *Ark Royal* was a small amount of broken crockery, but the pilot of the Heinkel, Lance-Corporal Francke, was promoted to Lieutenant and given the Iron Cross for his action in " sinking " her.

Following this, the *Ark Royal* was detached from the Home Fleet and sent to the South Atlantic where, with H.M.S. *Renown*, she became " Force K ", based on Freetown, Sierra Leone. She was sent there to aid in the search for the pocket battleship

Admiral Graf Spee, which had been raiding in those waters. Although the *Ark Royal*'s aircraft never sighted the biggest prize, the *Graf Spee*, her Swordfish did intercept the German steamer *Uhenfels*, which was sent in to Freetown with a valuable cargo on board.

After a visit to Cape Town, occasioned by the sinking of the *Africa Shell* in the Mozambique Channel by the *Graf Spee*, the *Ark Royal* and *Renown* steamed at full speed for St. Helena, following the loss of the *Doric Star* off that lonely island to the *Graf Spee*'s shells. Then, dramatically, came the news that the *Graf Spee* herself had been brought to action on December 13th by Commodore Harwood's force of three cruisers and had sought refuge in the Uruguayan harbour of Montevideo. Force K crossed the Atlantic to Rio de Janeiro to take on fuel, with orders to proceed with the utmost despatch to the River Plate in case the *Graf Spee* should break out. The *Ark Royal* reached Rio at dawn on December 17th ; twelve hours later she had fuelled and was on her way, her Swordfish crews standing by to take off with torpedoes on the first report of the *Graf Spee* sailing. But it was not to be. Rather than face action again with British ships, the German battleship scuttled herself in the waters of the River Plate.

With the sinking of the *Admiral Graf Spee*, the waters of the South Atlantic were once again safe for British shipping and the *Ark Royal*'s task was over. During the search for the raider the carrier had steamed some 75,000 miles, while her aircraft had flown very nearly 5,000,000. She returned to Freetown to spend Christmas there, and later rejoined the Home Fleet for further operations round Great Britain.

In Europe, the war had not yet come to life. The two sides faced each other along the length of the Maginot Line, entirely static apart from an occasional patrol clash. But at sea the U-boats were getting into their stride, the great minelaying programmes of each side were starting to seal off wide tracts of ocean, the convoys were organized and running, and an occasional German warship crept round the north of Iceland and down the Denmark Straits to reach the Atlantic for a raiding cruise. There was plenty of work for the Fleet Air Arm to do, in flying searches for raiders, in anti-submarine patrols, in reconnaissance flights, and in providing fighter protection for the fleet when it went to sea. Most of the work was devoid of action, but none the less it was carried out with a thoroughness and skill that promised well for the trials that were so soon to come.

On April 7th, early in the morning, reports reached the Admiralty that the enemy was planning a new operation. The indications were that it was to be an attack on Denmark and Norway, but the reports were not taken seriously as at the time it seemed unlikely that the Germans would extend their front beyond that of their present commitments in Europe. Nevertheless a signal was sent to the Commander-in-Chief warning him of these reports, and that evening the Home Fleet sailed from Scapa Flow.

Just before eight o'clock the following morning, H.M.S. *Glowworm*, a destroyer, sighted what she took to be two enemy destroyers. She sent a sighting signal and engaged the nearer of them. An hour later she sent a further sighting signal, reporting another ship. There was silence for ten minutes, and then her wireless came up again with the start of a third signal. It faded away, and no more was heard. We know now that the third ship she sighted was the 10,000-ton cruiser *Hipper*, and that the *Glowworm* went down gloriously, ramming her great opponent and causing her severe damage. With her sinking, the curtain rose on the first great campaign of the war, the battle for Norway. It was to be the first chance of the new Fleet Air Arm to show its true mettle.

By the evening of April 8th the invasion was in full swing. German ships had penetrated to Oslo, Kristiansand, Stavanger, Bergen, Trondheim, and Narvik, and some of them were now within reach of aircraft of the Fleet Air Arm. At Bergen, for instance, lay the 6,000-ton German cruiser *Königsberg*, and the Commander-in-Chief ordered an attack by the aircraft of H.M.S. *Furious* on April 9th. On that morning, however, the fleet was heavily attacked by German bombers and, although the damage caused was slight, Admiral Sir Charles Forbes decided not to risk the *Furious*, who might well have been a tempting target with her aircraft away on a strike, but to leave the Bergen ships to the Skua aircraft based at Hatston, the Fleet Air Arm base in the Orkneys. Hatston, otherwise known as H.M.S. *Sparrowhawk*, was just within range, though it would mean that the Skuas would have to fly almost to the limit of their endurance.

Early in the morning of the 10th May they took off from the bleak Orkney airfield, two full squadrons of eight aircraft each of Nos. 800 and 803 Squadrons. Crossing the North Sea they flew up the Bergen fiord, winding through the high mountains that flanked it on either side. As they approached the harbour, the *Königsberg* was plainly visible, anchored out in Uud-fiord. The first squadron, led by Lieutenant W. P. Lucy, dived on to the target, releasing their 500-pound bombs. As they soared up and away the second squadron, commanded by Captain R. T. Partridge, R.M., repeated the manœuvre, the explosion of their bombs mingling with those already delivered. They, too, swept up over the mountains, to disappear on their way home to the Orkneys. As the observers looked back towards the target, all they could see was a high pillar of black smoke rising from the cruiser.

The *Königsberg*, still stationary at her anchors, had been hit by three bombs. A fourth, falling alongside, had burst just under water and had blown a large hole in the cruiser's side. For fifty minutes her crew struggled to save the ship, but their labour was of no avail. Slowly she filled, turned over, and sank in the deep waters of the fiord, the first major warship to be sunk by air attack.

This success heralded many further attacks, and although they did a good deal of damage, there was nothing quite so outstanding as the sinking of the *Königsberg*. On the 11th a squadron of Swordfish, armed with torpedoes, took off from the *Furious* with the intention of attacking two more cruisers reported to be at anchor at Bergen. They duly reached the target area, but the cruisers had already sailed, leaving only two small torpedo boats there. The Swordfish duly attacked, but the water was too shallow for torpedoes and no damage was done. But on the 19th the Hatston Skuas revisited Bergen, sinking the supply steamer *Bahrenfels* as she lay alongside the mole and setting one flying boat on fire at her moorings. Among other successes claimed by the Fleet Air Arm during this short campaign were two tankers set on fire, nine seaplanes sunk at their moorings, the oil fuel tanks at Bergen set ablaze, and considerable damage to port and harbour installations, warehouses, and aircraft hangars.

They met, of course, with considerable opposition, often fighting against tremendous odds. One flight of three Skuas, engaged in providing fighter cover to the Army ashore, shot down a Junkers 88, attacked three Heinkel 111s and destroyed one of them, and finally drove off another Junkers 88 and eight Heinkels, shooting down one and forcing the others to jettison their bombs, When last seen they were trying to make their escape out to sea, two of them with their engines ablaze. All three Skuas returned in safety.

Yet all that the Fleet Air Arm could do was on too small a scale seriously to affect the German campaign. The aircraft from the *Furious*, consisting in all of one Swordfish and one Gladiator squadron, flew almost incessantly in their attempts to provide fighter cover for the military landings at Namsos, Aandalsnes, and Narvik, protection for the Army as soon as it was ashore, and the bombing of enemy airfields and troop concentrations. Norway, of course, was out of range of the Royal Air Force fighters, and until they could be established on Norwegian fields, the whole of the work fell on the Fleet Air Arm squadrons. H.M.S. *Glorious*, who was recalled from the Mediterranean to assist, was used to ferry over some R.A.F. Gladiators, but no sooner were they ashore than the enemy attacked their airfield, which was a frozen lake, and made it untenable.

The *Ark Royal*, back from her South Atlantic operations, arrived off the Norwegian coast on April 24th, to reinforce the hard-pressed *Furious* with her four squadrons, two of Swordfish and two of Skua aircraft. They ranged the coast from Trondheim to Aandalsnes, harrying the German coastal traffic and bombing docks and railway sidings. It was still not enough to bring the German advance to a halt and, relentlessly, the superior enemy strength forced itself up the length of Norway, till only Narvik was left in Allied hands.

In the meantime the two battles of Narvik had been fought, the first on April 10th, the second three days later. With the first battle, in which Captain Warburton-Lee won the first Victoria Cross of the war for his gallantry in command of the 2nd Destroyer Flotilla, the Fleet Air Arm was not concerned, but in the second a Swordfish, fitted with floats and catapulted from H.M.S. *Warspite*, played a notable part. Piloted by Petty Officer F. C. Rice, and with Lieut.-Commander W. L. M. Brown as observer and Leading Airman M. G. Pacey as air-gunner, the Swordfish preceded the squadron up the long Ofot Fiord which leads to Narvik and Bjerkvik. In the words of the observer it was like "flying in a tunnel", for the low cloud only just cleared the mountains on either side of the fiord, and limited the height at which the Swordfish could fly.

Her work on that day was invaluable to the squadron of ships which came in to the attack. Seven enemy destroyers were known to be in the fiord, and they had a considerable tactical advantage in being able to position themselves for the best use of their torpedoes against the advancing British destroyers. Not only did the Swordfish report their positions back to the *Warspite*, but also controlled the battleship's heavy guns and reported the tracks of torpedoes fired by the enemy, thus enabling our own ships to take the necessary evading action. Finally, flying up the narrow Herjangs Fiord to Bjerkvik, the Swordfish sighted U.64 and sank her with bombs before returning to the *Warspite* to be hoisted in after her adventurous flight. In his despatch to the Admiralty on the battle, Vice-Admiral Whitworth wrote : " The enemy reports made by the *Warspite*'s aircraft were invaluable. I doubt if ever a ship-borne aircraft has been used to such good purpose as it was during this operation. In addition the aircraft bombed and sank an enemy submarine."

The campaign in Norway was the first real opportunity that the new Fleet Air Arm had of showing its paces in modern warfare. It had been given an almost impossible task, for its few machines, slow and obsolescent, had little chance against the more modern aircraft of the enemy. Though, perhaps, its successes had little effect on the whole on the German war plan for the campaign, one of the most encouraging features of the campaign was the skill with which the naval pilots handled their machines in the face of the enemy, often being able to outweigh the technical superiority of the German aircraft by their quickness of manoeuvre. The pilots and observers, it must be remembered, were all young men, and this was their first experience of war in the air. Well might the naval Commander-in-Chief, Admiral of the Fleet Lord Cork and Orrery, write in his despatch : " The Fleet Air Arm, however, did all that was possible—to the gallantry and activity displayed by that branch of the Service I desire to pay tribute."

But the difficulties of the Norwegian campaign, waged as it was with insufficient men, insufficient aircraft, insufficient bases, proved to be insuperable at that early stage of the war. The enemy, easily reinforced and enjoying the immense advantage of overwhelming air supremacy, could hardly fail to prevail. In the end a total evacuation was necessary, and the ships of the Royal Navy gathered off the Norwegian coast to bring the Army home. Among them was H.M.S. *Glorious*, and she assisted in the evacuation from Narvik by providing fighter cover for the withdrawal. Right at the end she was given a further task, that of taking off the two Royal Air Force squadrons which were operating from the airfield at Bardufoss. One squadron of Gladiators was successfully embarked, but it was feared that the remaining squadron of eight Hurricanes would have to be abandoned and destroyed. But the young pilots of the Royal Air Force showed that they had all the skill and the courage of their brothers in the Fleet Air Arm. They volunteered to fly their Hurricanes out from Bardufoss and to try to land them on the flying deck of the *Glorious*, a task never before attempted. Permission was given and all eight of them, fitted with makeshift arrester hooks, successfully made their landing on board. Not only was it, in itself, a most notable feat of airmanship and skill, but also one that was to have a profound effect on carrier technique in the immediate future, proving as it did that the carrier could operate the most modern type of fighter aircraft and paving the way for the adoption by the Navy of the Seafire, the naval version of the Spitfire, as a carrier-borne fighter.

But the gallantry of the Royal Air Force pilots was to have a sad ending. H.M.S. *Glorious*, screened by two destroyers, the *Acasta* and *Ardent*, was detached from the fleet with orders to return home. On her way she ran into the two German battlecruisers *Scharnhorst* and *Gneisenau*. Though she put up a gallant defence, and though her two escorting destroyers attempted to protect her with smoke-screens and were both sunk in doing so, she was no match for the enemy. Outranged and outgunned, she was hit repeatedly and sunk, with the loss of all her aircraft and a large number of her complement. It was a tragic ending.

The Epic of Taranto

WITH THE EVACUATION OF NORWAY, FOLLOWED SO rapidly by the withdrawal of the British Expeditionary Force from France, the war at sea entered a new phase. It was the chance for which Mussolini, the dictator of Italy, had been waiting, and he brought his country into the war on the side of the Axis powers. The uneasy peace which had existed in the Mediterranean since September, 1939, was shattered, and the Mediterranean Fleet faced a period of operations against a greatly superior enemy at sea, with its main base at Malta within easy bombing range from enemy airfields in Italy. Only in one respect was the Mediterranean Fleet superior, in the possession of one carrier, H.M.S. *Eagle*, shortly to be reinforced by the first of the new fleet carriers, H.M.S. *Illustrious*. Italy possessed no carriers.

The force of circumstances made it necessary for the main units of the Mediterranean Fleet to concentrate in the eastern end of that sea, based on Alexandria. At the same time another squadron, known as Force H, was formed and based at Gibraltar, at the western end of the Mediterranean. In this force was another carrier, H.M.S. *Ark Royal*, destined to play a considerable part in Mediterranean operations. Thus, broadly speaking, Great Britain held both ends of the Mediterranean in fairly considerable force, while Italy, with her fleet and her shore-based air force, dominated the central position.

The Mediterranean Fleet had not long to wait for its first action. Early in July it had been found necessary to pass two convoys, carrying stores for the fleet, from Malta to Alexandria, and Admiral Sir Andrew Cunningham sailed from the latter port to cover the merchant ships. The fleet moved up into the central Mediterranean, there to have its first brush with the enemy. It seems as though the Italian Fleet was similarly occupied, covering a convoy to Libya.

The enemy, consisting of two battleships, sixteen cruisers, and about thirty destroyers, was first reported by H.M.S. *Phoenix*, a submarine operating some distance south-east of Taranto. It was later picked up by reconnaissance aircraft operating from Malta and from then onwards shadowed more or less continuously until the Commander-in-Chief made contact on July 9th. With the fleet was H.M.S. *Eagle*, the antique carrier of the early 1920's. She had only seventeen Swordfish aboard, with largely inexperienced pilots, but she put up a most spirited performance and achieved one hit on the enemy.

The enemy fleet was sighted by one of H.M.S. *Eagle*'s Swordfish just before noon on the 9th, and a striking force of torpedo-carrying aircraft was flown off a few minutes later. It missed the main enemy fleet, which in the meantime had altered course to the southward, but attacked a cruiser without success. All the aircraft returned and landed on safely.

The first surface contact with the enemy was made during the afternoon of the 9th, but as it was at extreme gun range it remained indecisive. A second striking force was flown off from the *Eagle* during the afternoon, and this time one hit was obtained on a cruiser in the face of very severe anti-aircraft fire. Unfortunately it did not cause sufficient damage to slow her down sufficiently for the surface forces to engage, and the whole of the Italian Fleet was able to withdraw at high speed and under cover of smoke-screens to the shelter of its own harbours and its land-based air force. There was a slight recompense for the lack of success when, on the following evening, the *Eagle*'s Swordfish sank a small destroyer anchored off the Italian coast. But even then the main prize was missed. A reconnaissance during the day had shown three cruisers and eight destroyers in harbour at Augusta, but by the time the *Eagle*'s attacking force arrived, they had sailed, and only the small destroyer was left to fall a victim to their torpedoes.

The lack of success was probably due to two causes : the inexperience of the pilots and the speed of the enemy. Torpedo attack from the air on a swiftly moving target is a supremely difficult task, calling for a very high degree of skill and judgment. With the rapid war expansion of the Fleet Air Arm, it was only to be expected that, at this early stage, there would be many pilots who had not as yet had experience of the difficulties of such attacks.

During the two years previous to the war, however, in which the Fleet Air Arm had been completely under naval control, frequent exercises had been carried out to test the possibilities of making aircraft torpedo attacks on defended harbours and stationary ships. Time and again Malta had been the scene of these exercises, and the Grand Harbour had echoed to the roar of low-flying Swordfish. Many lessons had been learned from these exercises, the most important being that such an attack was almost certainly doomed to failure unless it could be carried out under cover of darkness. Even before the actual outbreak of war, as soon as it became apparent that Mussolini was going to hitch his wagon to the star of Hitler, plans for an attack on the Italian Fleet as it lay in its harbour at Taranto had been under consideration.

As soon, therefore, as Italy entered the war these plans were put into operation. An immediate sortie was out of the question, for much more training was necessary before it could hope to command success. With characteristic thoroughness the Fleet Air Arm pilots began intensive practice in night flying ; special reconnaissance machines capable of reaching and photographing Taranto were sent out to Malta ; and special long-range tanks ordered for the Swordfish who were to carry out the actual attack. The long-range tanks arrived in H.M.S. *Illustrious* in September, 1940, the Glenn Martin reconnaissance machines reached Malta in October, and by the middle of October the Fleet Air Arm pilots had reached the necessary degree of excellence in night flying to give promise of success. The stage was set for the operation.

It had been planned to make the attack on the night of October 21st, the 135th anniversary of Nelson's victory at Trafalgar, but a few days beforehand a fire broke out in the hangar of H.M.S. *Illustrious* which damaged a number of her aircraft. The night of October 30th was the next choice, but there was no moon and the attack would have called for the extensive dropping of flares of which the aircraft crews had had little experience. Finally November 11th, when the moon would be three-quarters full, was chosen, and the latest reconnaissance photographs taken the previous day showed five battleships at anchor, as well as several cruisers and destroyers. An evening patrol off the harbour flown by the Royal Air Force on the day itself reported that a sixth battleship had arrived.

H.M.S. *Illustrious* sailed with the fleet from Alexandria on November 6th. The *Eagle* was to have accompanied her, but two days earlier her petrol system was found to be defective, due to the service shaking she had had on many previous occasions when the Italians had tried to bomb her. Eight of her aircraft crews and five of her Swordfish were embarked in the *Illustrious*.

At 6.0 p.m. on the 11th the Commander-in-Chief, Admiral Sir Andrew Cunningham, detached the *Illustrious* and her screen of four cruisers and four destroyers, and they proceeded to the flying-off position, some 180 miles from Taranto. Two and a half hours later the first striking force of twelve Swordfish roared one by one down the flying deck of the carrier. In five minutes they were airborne. They took up their formation, some 8 miles ahead of the *Illustrious*, and at three minutes to nine flew off into the darkness, bound for Taranto and the Italian Fleet.

The second striking force consisted of only nine Swordfish, three having forced-landed in the sea during earlier flights. They were ranged on deck shortly after nine o'clock, and at half-past nine they followed the first striking force into the air. Only eight became airborne, however, one being damaged in a collision as it was taxi-ing forward. It was struck down into the hangar for repairs. While the pilot, Lieutenant E. W. Clifford, did his utmost to urge the maintenance and repair crews to make good the damage, the observer, Lieutenant G. R. M. Going, ran up to the bridge to ask the captain's permission for the Swordfish to take off as soon as the repairs were completed. Captain Denis Boyd, perhaps struck by the keenness of pilot and observer, gave his permission if the aircraft could be made ready in time. At five minutes to ten the Swordfish was on deck again ; at two minutes to ten it was airborne and setting a lonely course for the target 150 miles away.

By this time the first striking force, led by Lieutenant-Commander K. Williamson, pilot, and Lieutenant N. J. Scarlett, observer, was nearing Taranto. Of the twelve aircraft concerned, six carried torpedoes, four carried bombs, and two were armed with bombs and flares. As they neared their objective, they ran into thick cloud and the force was split up by the difficulty of keeping touch.

Just before eleven o'clock, the flare-dropping aircraft were detached. The leading machine laid a line of eight flares accurately along the eastern side of the harbour and then, accompanied by the other flare-dropper, made a dive-bombing attack on the oil storage depot. Although the two observers, looking back, could see no evidence of damage, the oil depot was, in fact, set on fire and blazed furiously throughout the remainder of the attack.

There followed the torpedo-dropping aircraft, led by Williamson and Scarlett. This machine failed to return, and was probably shot down on the way in, but the remainder successfully made their dive and fired their torpedoes at the battleships as they lay at anchor. Most of them had to pass through the balloon barrage both on their way in and also on their way back after attacking, and it was a tribute to their skill that all the pilots successfully evaded the mooring wires. As they came in, the air was filled with anti-aircraft fire from the battleships, cruisers, and batteries ashore. Nonetheless, all the twelve aircraft, with the single exception of the leader, returned safely to the *Illustrious* and landed on.

As they came to rest on the flying deck, the pilots and observers had many tales of success to report. Some had seen their torpedoes hit and explode on their targets, which had been the two big Littorio class battleships and one smaller Cavour class. The four bomb-dropping aircraft had penetrated into the inner harbour, the Mar Piccolo, and their targets there had been two cruisers laying at anchor, four destroyers secured alongside the dockyard jetty, and the seaplane station. Most of the pilots claimed hits.

Meanwhile the second striking force of seven Swordfish were attacking, one of the original eight being forced to return to the *Illustrious* with defects which developed in flight. The force was led by Lieut.-Commander J. W. Hale, pilot, and Lieutenant G. A. Carline, observer. Again the two flare-dropping aircraft were detached before the attack to illuminate the scene. As soon as their flares were alight, both machines made a second dive-bombing attack on the oil storage depot before returning. Of the five torpedo-carrying aircraft one failed to return, but the other four all made good attacks, the two Littorios again and a second Cavour-class battleship being the targets. As in the first attack, hits were claimed.

Finally, as the last Swordfish of the second striking force was leaving the scene of devastation, Clifford and Going arrived. They had, it will be remembered, been delayed by an accident during the take-off but had been given permission to proceed independently. Clifford came in over the land to the eastward of the harbour and, swinging to port, dived on the line of destroyers moored up in the Mar Piccolo. One stick of bombs was released over these ships, and a second over the two cruisers anchored off the dockyard. Turning to starboard, the Swordfish again crossed the land and sped out to sea towards the *Illustrious*, landing on some half an hour after the remainder. With her aircraft safely back on board, the *Illustrious* turned to the eastward and rejoined the Commander-in-Chief early in the morning of November 12th.

It remained to fly a reconnaissance over Taranto Harbour and to photograph the scene in order to assess the damage. Royal Air Force planes set out from Malta the following morning to carry out this task, and, when the photographs were developed, it was at last possible to discover the extent of the victory. The battleship *Cavour* had been hit, and the damage was so extensive that she later beached. The battleship *Duilio* (Cavour class) had been hit and had also been beached with her bows under water. The battleship *Italia* (Littorio class) had been extensively hit and was badly damaged. The cruiser *Trento* had been hit by a bomb, two destroyers (the *Libeccio* and *Pessango*) had been slightly damaged by bombs, two auxiliary vessels were sunk, the seaplane base badly damaged with one hangar completely destroyed, and the oil storage depot damaged by fire. The cost had been two Swordfish.

> Although the proper function of the Fleet Air Arm [wrote Captain Boyd after the attack] may perhaps be the operation of aircraft against an enemy in the open sea, it has been demonstrated before, and repeated in no uncertain fashion by this success, that the ability to strike unexpectedly is conferred by the Fleet Air Arm. It is often felt that this arm, which has had a long struggle with adverse opinions and its unspectacular aircraft, is underestimated in its power. It is hoped that this victory will be considered a suitable reward to those whose work and faith in the Fleet Air Arm has made it possible.

Before the Taranto battle, though, there had been the unhappy action in which the aircraft from H.M.S. *Ark Royal* had assisted in the immobilization of the French warships at Oran and Mers-el-Kebir. It had been hoped, on the fall of France, that it would have been possible to persuade the French Commander-in-Chief there, Admiral Gensoul, to agree to arrangements whereby the ships should not fall into the hands of the enemy, either by continuing the fight with Britain, or by internment in a British port, or by sending them to the French island of Martinique in the West Indies. Admiral Gensoul, however, at first refused to receive the British officer sent to talk to him, who happened to be Captain C. S. Holland, in command of the *Ark Royal*, and so the British proposals had to be signalled to the French admiral. After he had studied them he consented to receive Captain Holland, but finally all the British proposals were refused. There was nothing for it but to use force in preventing so powerful an addition to the German Navy.

Force H, in which the *Ark Royal* was serving, had arrived off Oran on July 3rd, 1940. It was on the 4th that the proposals were finally turned down by the French and at dusk the French battleship *Strasbourg*, screened by six destroyers, crept out of harbour, dodged Force H, and set off to the eastward at full speed. A flight of six Swordfish, carrying bombs, flew off in pursuit, but no hits were secured on the *Strasbourg*, though bombs fell close on either side of her. The bombers were followed by a squadron of Swordfish armed with torpedoes. They sighted the *Strasbourg* as she was steaming close to the African shore, and shadowed her until she should be silhouetted against the setting sun. They then came down to sea level to attack, but the pilots were still largely inexperienced in night torpedo attacks and dropped their torpedoes outside the destroyer screen instead of penetrating it first. As a result the French battleship got clean away, to be lost to sight in the fast-gathering darkness.

In the meantime, aided by spotting carried out by the *Ark Royal*'s aircraft, Force H had opened fire on the ships still lying at anchor in Oran harbour. Other Swordfish dropped mines in the harbour entrance. As a result of the bombardment, the old battleship *Bretagne* and two destroyers were sunk, while the modern battleship *Dunkerque* was slightly damaged and beached.

A reconnaissance carried out the following morning revealed that the *Dunkerque*, although ashore, had received only superficial damage and could easily be made operational again. It

(*Crown Copyright*)

In the act of taking off.   A Vickers Supermarine 529 leaving the flight deck.

A crash at sea.   A damaged Avenger bursts into flames on landing.

(*Imperial War Museum*)

(*Crown Copyright*)
A naval swept wing fighter, the DH 110, in flight.

A Vickers Supermarine Attacker in flight.
(*Vickers Armstrong Ltd*)

was decided to attack her with torpedoes, and early in the morning of the 6th two squadrons of Swordfish took off from the deck of the *Ark Royal*, divided into three flights. The first force, coming in low over the breakwater in line astern and directly in the path of the sun, achieved complete surprise, and four of their six torpedoes hit the target. The second and third flights met fierce opposition but all the aircraft returned safely, having made further hits on the *Dunkerque*. It was quite certain now that she would be out of the war for a very considerable time.

It was a most unhappy action, dictated purely by the necessity of preventing the ships of a fallen ally from being operated by our unscrupulous enemy. It was with sadness in their hearts that the pilots of the Swordfish loosed their torpedoes at these fine French ships, and there was no jubilation on board the *Ark Royal* when they returned to report their successes as there would have been had the ships been German or Italian.

As 1940 came to an end in the Mediterranean with the glory of the Taranto action, new carriers and new aircraft were arriving to reinforce Admiral Cunningham's fleet. H.M.S. *Indomitable*, a sister ship of the *Illustrious*, arrived ; and with her she brought ten of the new torpedo-carrying aircraft, known as Albacores, and thirteen of the new fighters, the Fairey Fulmars. They were very soon required to show their paces in action.

By March of 1941, the German invasion of Greece was under way and General Wavell's army in North Africa was called upon to supply a large force to help oppose the advancing enemy. That force, naturally, was carried by the Royal Navy, and its follow-up supplies also called for heavy naval escort against the threat of Italian submarine attack and German and Italian attacks from the air. There was the added danger, also, that the Italian fleet might make a rapid sortie from its bases on the western shore of the Adriatic in an attempt to intercept and annihilate a supply convoy on its way to Greece. Italy badly needed a naval victory and a successful attack on a British convoy would supply it.

A report on the evening of March 27th, 1941, gave an indication that the Italian Fleet was at sea with this object in view. An aircraft flying from Malta had sighted a group of Italian cruisers steering eastward, with the obvious intention of making a dash for one of the convoys to Greece. Our own cruisers, commanded by Vice-Admiral Pridham-Wippell, were already at sea south of Crete to cover the convoy, and Admiral Cunningham sailed with his battleships and with H.M.S. *Formidable* to reinforce them. It was well that he did so, for by the morning of the 28th the Italian cruisers, now with the modern battleship *Vittorio Veneto* to support them, were in the vicinity of Admiral Pridham-Wippell's cruisers.

An air search of four Albacores and one Swordfish was flown off from H.M.S. *Formidable* at dawn on the 28th, and almost at once enemy sighting reports began to come in. At first it was not clear from the reports as to how many of the enemy ships were at sea, but as the morning wore on it became apparent that three separate groups were engaged in the operation, one containing the *Vittorio Veneto* and the other two consisting of cruisers. From the picture given to the Commander-in-Chief from the various enemy reports it seemed as though the British cruisers under Admiral Pridham-Wippell were about to be caught between the fires of two of the enemy forces, the battleship to the northward and four cruisers to the westward. There was only one answer, to use the Fleet Air Arm in an attack on one of the two forces.

Accordingly the first striking force, consisting of six Albacores, led by Lieut.-Commander W. H. J. Saunt, and escorted by two Fulmars, was flown off. About an hour later it reached Admiral Pridham-Wippell's cruisers and sighted the *Vittorio Veneto*. Saunt decided to attack on her starboard bow and led his six aircraft into position. Just as they were peeling off for the attack they were threatened by two Junkers 88s, but the Fulmars were there to protect them. One of the Junkers was shot down into the sea, the other was driven off to leave the air clear for the Albacores.

As they came down to sea level to release their torpedoes, they met an intense anti-aircraft barrage put up by the battleship and her four attendant destroyers. In addition, the *Vittorio Veneto* was firing her 15-inch guns into the sea at minimum range to put up a splash barrage between herself and the low-flying Albacores. But the aircraft dodged the splashes and, closing in, released their torpedoes at a range of no more than 800 yards. The *Vittorio Veneto* took violent evasive action, making a wide turn to starboard, but it was of no avail. One of the Albacore's torpedoes hit her and she began to lose speed and turned for home, breaking off her engagement with the British cruisers. The first objective, which was the safety of Admiral Pridham-Wippell's force, had been achieved. The striking force returned to H.M.S. *Formidable* and landed on without loss.

Meanwhile, a sub-flight of three Swordfish from Maleme airfield in Crete had flown down to take a hand in the battle. They failed to find the battleship, but made contact with a group of three cruisers, attacking the *Bolzano*. They claimed a hit, but in fact the cruiser successfully evaded the torpedoes.

That ended the first part of the battle and the stage was now set for the second. The position at this juncture was that the *Vittorio Veneto* had turned away after her torpedo hit and was steering north-west towards her home base. The two cruiser squadrons were on similar courses, nearly 30 miles ahead of the battleship on either bow. The four British cruisers were withdrawing on the British battlefleet, which itself was some 60 miles astern of the *Vittorio Veneto*, and chasing at full speed.

It was obvious that, in such a position, Admiral Cunningham had no chance of catching the Italian Fleet unless he could again reduce the *Vittorio Veneto*'s speed. There was only one way of doing that, and that was through the medium of the Fleet Air Arm. If they could hit her again with torpedoes and cause enough damage to slow her down considerably, there was still a chance.

The Commander-in-Chief ordered a second striking force to be flown off from H.M.S. *Formidable*, and three Albacores, two Swordfish, and two Fulmars were ranged on deck. Led by Lieut.-Commander J. Dalyell-Stead, they flew off shortly before two o'clock and at twenty-five minutes past three they sighted the battleship to the south of Cape Matapan. Dalyell-Stead worked his aircraft up into the sun and from there dived down to sea level for the attack. The three Albacores went in first and, although the *Vittorio Veneto* took violent evasive action, one torpedo hit her. The Albacores were followed by the Swordfish. By the time they attacked, the Italian battleship had steadied down on to her course again. They selected a perfect dropping position for their torpedoes and both scored hits. One aircraft, the leading Albacore piloted by Dalyell-Stead, failed to return, but the remaining six all landed on without mishap, though they had all attacked through a fearsome anti-aircraft and splash barrage.

So far as the enemy was concerned, the *Vittorio Veneto* was now reduced to a speed of only 13 knots. She called in the two cruiser squadrons to protect her and, with them in close attendance, continued her homeward journey. But now there was a chance of her being caught, a chance which would become a certainty if she could be hit again.

The Commander-in-Chief decided to send out a third force, to consist of every available machine on board the *Formidable*. Six Albacores and two Swordfish were armed with torpedoes and, led once more by Lieut.-Commander Saunt, they flew off into the dusk of a Mediterranean evening.

Two of the shore-based Swordfish on Crete were already shadowing the enemy and they guided the striking force on to the target. Just as the sun was setting the attack went in, to be met with a tremendous barrage from every ship in company. In his official report of the battle Vice-Admiral Pridham-Wippell, who at that time was in sight of the enemy and witnessed the Fleet Air Arm attack, wrote :

> The enemy's retaliation to the dusk torpedo attack by our own aircraft could be distinctly seen from my squadron some 12 miles away. The sky was filled with streams of tracer ammunition of various colours, and they must have been very gallant men who went through it to get their torpedoes home.

The barrage, in fact, was so intense that the force was unable to attack as a squadron but had to break up and go in independently. As a result, to the danger of the anti-aircraft fire was added the danger of collision in the air with other attacking aircraft. But that was a risk that had to be accepted, for a squadron attack with all aircraft coming in from the same direction would have given the enemy an opportunity to concentrate his anti-aircraft fire. The attack then would have been suicidal.

The battleship herself was not hit during this third strike, but the last Swordfish to go in landed her torpedo against the side of the 10,000-ton cruiser *Pola*, and brought her to a complete stop. The Italian admiral ordered two other 10,000-ton cruisers, the *Zara* and *Fiume*, to stand by the *Pola*, and it was these three cruisers which Admiral Cunningham caught later that night and sank in his night action. As for the *Vittorio Veneto*, she managed to make her escape and by daylight the following morning was already under her shore-based air cover.

The battle of Matapan is an interesting one from the Fleet Air Arm point of view, for it shows the development and exercise of a tactical move in which the air and surface forces are admirably designed to collaborate. The same move, but with more positive results, will be seen again when the description of the hunting of the German battleship *Bismarck* is given. In this battle can be seen to advantage the added flexibility which the naval aircraft gives to the surface ship, for in the conditions in which the opposing fleets found themselves, there could have been no action without the intervention of the air arm. The Italians, already too far ahead of the British battle fleet for surface action as soon as the relative positions were established, could have maintained that safe distance without difficulty.

It was the first air attack that gave hope of some positive result, for when the *Vittorio Veneto* was hit, her speed was reduced, though only fractionally. But even this was enough to justify a prolongation of the chase, for what had been done once could be done again. The second strike, carried out in the afternoon, did all that the Commander-in-Chief hoped, for three hits at least were scored and the enemy battleship was down to 13 knots. For a second time the air arm had achieved its object, and to most observers at that time it seemed obvious that the *Vittorio Veneto* was doomed. Once again the striking power of the air had been demonstrated in its relation to surface force, making possible the continuation of the battle. Even as it was, and without any further air attack, there was a good chance of Admiral Cunningham and his battleships reaching the damaged Italian ship, though this chance would become a certainty had the third strike been as successful as the second. Perhaps it was a pity that the third strike hit and stopped a cruiser, rather than the battleship, for the summary execution of her and her consorts when the battlefleet reached them inevitably delayed the Commander-in-Chief and gave the *Vittorio Veneto* an added lead. None-the-less, the destruction of three powerful cruisers was a most welcome result and made possible only by the torpedo hit from the Swordfish. Without that, the cruisers would have escaped just as did the remainder of the fleet.

The battle of Matapan demonstrated in emphatic terms the tactical value of the air weapon in the hands of a Commander-in-Chief at sea and made plain its essential place in a modern fleet in wartime. For it was not only by the strike aircraft that Admiral Cunningham was so faithfully served. The reconnaissance aircraft played their part well in building up the picture for him on which he could base his tactical plans. It is true that, in the initial reconnaissance, quite a number of wrong reports were received, due in the main to lack of adequate training of the observers, but it was nevertheless to these aircraft reports that the Commander-in-Chief owed his early knowledge of the three separate enemy groups. Where the initial reports were chiefly inaccurate was in the composition of the three squadrons.

There was one more aspect of the air weapon that the battle of Matapan made clear, and that was that the strike aircraft would have been of little value had they not been piloted by men of rare personal courage. It is not unduly difficult to locate an enemy squadron at sea from the air when it is known to be in a certain sector. It is not difficult to manœuvre the aircraft into a favourable attacking position. But it does take a rare courage to come in through a heavy barrage such as a big ship can throw up and to release the torpedo at a range of something like 800 yards or less. To ensure a good attack, the aircraft must come in low and on a steady course. As she does that, she offers a much easier target to the close-range guns than if she came in "jinking". When the captain of the *Pola* was rescued, he said that he had never seen such courage as that displayed by the crew of the aircraft which attacked him, which had flown in at point-blank range in the face of withering fire.

Comparisons are notoriously odious, but an attack made by two Italian S.M. 79s on the *Formidable* while she was flying off her second striking force bears out the point made above. These two aircraft came in low on a good approach course, but the fire of the *Formidable*'s anti-aircraft guns, and the close-range weapons of her two attendant destroyers forced the Italians to drop their torpedoes at a range of 2,000 yards. The *Formidable* had no difficulty in avoiding them, as she had time at that range to alter course and comb the tracks. To be sure of a hit, an attacking aircraft must fly through the barrage and only drop her torpedo when it is too late for the target to avoid it by altering course.

In the meantime, in the western Mediterranean, the *Ark Royal* was having her share of action. Her first main operations after the affair at Oran were the bombing of Cagliari, on the southern coast of Sardinia. The airfield there was attacked on three occasions and mines laid in the entrance to the harbour. These attacks were diversionary, in order to distract attention from the passage of convoys to Malta, and they not only succeeded in their object but also caused a good deal of damage to aircraft and hangars at Elmas aerodrome, just outside Cagliari, as well as destroying one wing of the military headquarters there. The cost of three raids on the port was one Swordfish, of which the crew was taken prisoner.

It was to be expected, however, that sooner or later the enemy would attempt to intercept one of the convoys to Malta, and Admiral Somerville, in command of Force H based on Gibraltar, had this possibility always in mind. It came as little surprise, therefore, when enemy forces were reported to be at sea on November 27th, 1940, while an east-bound convoy was taking stores to Malta and Alexandria. A Swordfish from H.M.S. *Ark Royal* was sent out on reconnaissance duties and soon made contact with the enemy south-west of Cape Spartivento, the southern tip of Sardinia. As later off Matapan, the enemy was sighted in three separate groups, two of them composed of cruisers, the third of two battleships and a flotilla of destroyers.

Admiral Somerville, with Force H admirably disposed between the enemy and the convoy, increased to full speed in the hope of catching the enemy. As yet, the Italians seemed to have no knowledge of Force H, for they were steaming on a westerly course and closing Admiral Somerville. But at noon, with the advanced cruisers in sight of each other, the enemy became aware for the first time of the presence of a British squadron and, turning 180°, set a course for Cagliari.

Here was the same problem as was later to appear at Matapan, how to slow the enemy down and enable the battle fleet to make contact. The answer, of course, was the same and H.M.S. *Ark Royal* was ordered to fly off a striking force of Swordfish. Led by Lieut.-Commander Mervyn Johnstone, eleven torpedo aircraft took off and set a course for the enemy fleet. It was a typical Mediterranean day, with the sun shining in a cloudless sky, giving no chance of an unobserved approach.

Nevertheless, so inefficient were the Italian look-outs, that the approach was unobserved right up to the last moment. The Swordfish attacked out of the sun, and it was not until the leading aircraft was committed to her run in that the Italian battleships opened fire.

When they did so, however, the barrage was intense, and augmented by the fire of their seven screening destroyers.

As the Swordfish, peeling off individually and diving to sea level, released their torpedoes, a column of smoke and water was seen to rise above the leading battleship, which was the *Vittorio Veneto*. It looked to be a hit and was claimed as such, but in fact the ship was not hit at all. The *Vittorio Veneto* thus had no difficulty in maintaining her long lead over Admiral Somerville's force. A second striking force from the *Ark Royal* was equally unsuccessful, and, in fact, attacked one of the cruiser squadrons instead of the *Vittorio Veneto*.

This action off Cape Spartivento, so similar in every respect to the battle of Matapan, which followed some five months later, came too early in the war to show the Fleet Air Arm at its best. Those years of frustration between the two wars were telling their tale, coupled with the very rapid expansion of pilots and observers which the war had brought in its train. There was all the personal gallantry that was required in both these actions, but in the first, that of Cape Spartivento, there was a certain absence of skill that was attributable to lack of training opportunities, a state of affairs that still existed, though to a lesser degree, at Matapan.

Just as the Fleet Air Arm activities at Matapan, judging purely by results, were a great improvement on those at Cape Spartivento, so those a couple of months later in the wastes of the Atlantic were an improvement, again on results, to those at Matapan. This was in the chase and destruction of the German battleship *Bismarck*, where once again the similarity of the action points to a definite and increasing function of naval air work, the damaging of an enemy ship to enable our own to make contact. As yet the great naval battles of the air, as fought by the Americans, lay in the future; in 1941 the Fleet Air Arm was still the servant of the battle fleet, opening the range of operations but still, in the last resort, relying on the concentrated fire of naval guns to bring about the *coup de grâce*.

The "Bismarck" Operation

We had fairly good warning that the Germans were proposing to send the new battleship *Bismarck* and the new cruiser *Prinz Eugen* into the Atlantic as a task force for commerce raiding. In spite of all the precautions the Germans could take to keep the break-out of these two ships secret, they were sighted on the morning of May 20th by the Swedish warship *Gotland* in the Kattegat as they were steering northwards. The news was soon public, and a special Royal Air Force photographic reconnaissance was sent out in search of them.

The two ships were photographed in Korlsfiord, near Bergen, on May 21st, and that night there was a bombing raid on the fiord, carried out by the Royal Air Force. It was in vain, for the fiord was empty and the two birds had flown. Even as the bombs dropped, they were 100 miles away to the northward.

An attempt at reconnaissance on May 22nd was abortive, for thick cloud was down to 200 feet and there were patches of fog along the Norwegian coast. Admiral Sir John Tovey, Commander-in-Chief Home Fleet, was waiting anxiously for news at Scapa Flow, for on the movements of the enemy ships depended his dispositions of the Home Fleet.

It was in these conditions of anxiety, and of the imperative need for the Commander-in-Chief to be informed, that the Fleet Air Arm first came into the picture. With the failure of the daytime reconnaissances, desperate measures were required. Captain H. St. J. Fancourt, who was commanding the Royal Naval Air Station at Hatston in the Orkney Islands, decided to send out an aircraft to try to break through the fog barrier that lay off the Norwegian coast and bring back the essential information. He selected as pilot Lieutenant N. E. Goddard, R.N.V.R., and with him sent one of the Navy's most experienced observers, Commander G. A. Rotherham.

The aircraft set off on the evening of May 22nd. The low

cloud and fog forced it to fly only a few feet above the surface of the sea, but it succeeded not only in reaching the Norwegian coast but also in penetrating Korlsfiord, where the two ships had been photographed on the previous day. As we know, they found it empty. Not content with this information, the aircraft next flew up the fiord to search Bergen harbour itself, in case the two ships might have moved up there after the bombing of the previous night. In the face of heavy anti-aircraft fire they flew round the harbour. Neither the *Bismarck* nor the *Prinz Eugen* were there. Satisfied at last, they flew out to sea and signalled to base that the two ships had sailed. The information reached the Commander-in-Chief at eight o'clock that night, and two hours later the Home Fleet was at sea.

From that moment until she was finally sunk on the morning of May 27th, five days later, the chase of the *Bismarck* was followed anxiously by millions of eyes, for the news that she was out was known all over the world from May 24th onwards. The long-drawn-out drama of the action gave an opportunity for all arms of the Service to contribute their quota towards the final result.

With the Home Fleet sailed the carrier *Victorious*. She was only newly out of the builder's yard and had had as yet few opportunities of working up to full operational efficiency. Before the *Bismarck* came out she had been loaded up with crated Hurricanes for Malta ; these were unloaded, and a squadron of Swordfish, and two sub-flights of Fulmars, the only aircraft available at such short notice, were embarked. The Swordfish squadron, No. 825, was under the command of Lieut.-Commander Eugene Esmonde, later to lead a gallant and forlorn sortie against tremendous odds and to lose his life as the result.

The *Bismarck* was first sighted by H.M.S. *Suffolk* in the Denmark Strait on the evening of May 23rd, and was shadowed by radar and visual contact by herself and H.M.S. *Norfolk* throughout the night. When the " enemy in sight " signal was received by the Commander-in-Chief he was able to make new dispositions and to steam westward to try to make contact with the *Bismarck* and the *Prinz Eugen* when they emerged from the Denmark Strait. He already had two ships, H.M.S. *Hood* and H.M.S. *Prince of Wales*, up to the southward of Iceland,

and these were in a good position already to intercept. Also he had the *Victorious*, with her tiny force of Swordfish and Fulmars, and with these he planned, as Admirals Somerville and Cunningham had planned in their battles, to slow the *Bismarck* down with torpedo hits.

All through the night the enemy was shadowed, the two cruisers *Norfolk* and *Suffolk* hanging on to her by their radar throughout the hours of darkness. By daylight on the 24th they were able to direct the *Hood* and the *Prince of Wales* to the *Bismarck*'s position, and there occurred that brief, sharp battle in which the *Hood* was lost and the *Prince of Wales* damaged. But before the *Hood* went down she had hit the *Bismarck* with one salvo. The *Prince of Wales* had hit her with three salvoes. Although the damage was superficial, one 15-inch shell had passed through two oil fuel tanks and the *Bismarck* had lost not only the oil fuel in those two tanks but also all that stored in tanks forward of the hit, for that oil could not now be pumped through the damaged section. It amounted to 1,000 tons and was to have a considerable effect on the battle.

With the abrupt ending of the action between the *Hood* and *Prince of Wales* and the *Bismarck* and *Prinz Eugen*, the Commander-in-Chief realized at once that he would be unable to intercept the enemy ships if they continued to the southward. He fell back on to the Fleet Air Arm and that Swordfish squadron in the *Victorious* to solve his problems. It was for them to attack and to slow her down. He detached the *Victorious* with orders to steer the best course to reach a position within 100 miles of the *Bismarck* and then to fly off her Swordfish. It was a tactical risk, for if the attack failed and the *Bismarck* shook off her shadowers during the night, then he would need the *Victorious* and her aircraft to search on the following day. If he detached her now she would be too far away on the morrow. But it was a risk that had to be taken, for the most essential thing now was to try to reduce the *Bismarck*'s speed. At three o'clock in the afternoon of the 25th the *Victorious* parted company with the fleet, her Swordfish already ranged on the after flight deck in readiness for their attack.

As the *Victorious* steamed away to reach a favourable position for flying off, the weather began to deteriorate. It had been threatening to do so for some time, but now the threat became a reality as a cold front made its way across the Atlantic. Heavy cloud hung low in the sky and fierce rain squalls considerably limited the visibility. A short, confused sea made conditions on board uncomfortable.

As we know the *Victorious* was but newly commissioned and her crew had had little time to get used to her. Her aircraft were new to her, too, and the pilots, especially of the Fulmars, had not had as full facilities for training as could have been desired. But in command of the Swordfish squadron was Lieut.-Commander Esmonde, an experienced, indomitable, and tenacious leader who knew the value of an attack at close range and was always prepared to take his aircraft through the fiercest barrage to reach a proper firing position.

By ten o'clock that night the *Victorious* was some 120 miles from the *Bismarck*. One by one the Swordfish took the air, formed up, and set off in search of their target. An hour later three Fulmars were flown off for shadowing duties, followed two hours later by two more. In those far northern latitudes, the summer sun did not set until after midnight, and the light was good enough for visual sighting.

By excellent navigation, No. 825 (Swordfish) Squadron found the *Bismarck* at half-past eleven, sighted her through the cloud, and turned away to the south to obtain a good attacking position from ahead. There they ran into thick cloud and lost touch with the ship. After a short search they made contact with H.M.S. *Prince of Wales* and H.M.S. *Norfolk*, and were directed by them back on to the target. As they were still flying in cloud, they used their ship detection sets to give them warning of the target below. A few minutes later their sets indicated a ship and they broke cloud cover to find, below them, not the *Bismarck* but a United States coastguard cutter. Six miles away the *Bismarck* herself was visible but, as the aircraft sighted her, so did she sight the aircraft, to open a heavy and accurate anti-aircraft fire. So accurate was it, indeed, that Esmonde's aircraft was hit at a range of 4 miles.

Nevertheless he continued to lead his flight of three Swordfish in to the attack, in full view of the enemy and under continuous and very heavy fire. At exactly midnight he fired his torpedoes from abeam of the *Bismarck* to port. The second flight, led by Lieutenant P. D. Gick, made an unsatisfactory approach, broke

off the attack, reformed, and came in again to fire on the
Bismarck's port bow.   Lieutenant H. C. M. Pollard, leading the
third flight came in on the starboard bow to fire after circling
the ship.   One of his three aircraft became detached in the thick
cloud and failed to locate the target.   As the attacking aircraft
swept up over the ship after releasing their torpedoes, they
sprayed the bridge and control positions with machine-gun fire
at almost point-blank range.

The return of the squadron was something of a nightmare.
The *Victorious* had been steaming towards the *Bismarck* in order
to shorten the passage of the homecoming aircraft, but shortly
before they were due to land on the homing beacon on board
the carrier broke down.   The Swordfish, just as they were about
to sight her, ran into a rain squall which blotted out all visibility
and they flew past without seeing her.   They were finally found
by direction-finding procedure and given a course to steer, the
Victorious making her position apparent by burning a small
searchlight and sweeping it round the horizon like a lighthouse.
This was a dangerous procedure in waters close to an enemy
ship and possibly patrolled by U-boats, and it was a great relief
when the striking force landed on just before two o'clock.
They were then almost at the end of their endurance and down
to the last few gallons of petrol.   Two of the Fulmars failed to
return, but the crew of one was later picked up by a merchant
ship after an uncomfortable period of floating in the northern
Atlantic.

One hit on the *Bismarck* had been scored, but it was not
sufficient to reduce her speed.   But it did have one fortunate
result.   The shock of the explosion shifted the collision mats
used to cover the holes made by the *Hood*'s and *Prince of Wales*'s
shells and also the shores holding up the bulkhead of the damaged
boiler-room.   The compartment was flooded and the *Bismarck*
thereby lost the use of another 1,000 tons of oil.

Some four hours after the attack by the *Victorious*'s aircraft,
contact was lost with the *Bismarck*.   She turned momentarily to
the westward, shook off the shadowing *Suffolk*, turned back on
a south-easterly course and got clean away.   The *Prinz Eugen*
had already parted company and was steaming down to the
southward towards a waiting tanker where she could replenish
with oil fuel.   She had, in fact, already passed out of the picture

and no one was bothering about her in view of the bigger game represented by the *Bismarck*.

The Commander-in-Chief was thus confronted with two main possibilities. The enemy could, and most probably would, try to make some port where she could repair her damage. That meant either breaking back into the North Sea to try to reach the coast of Norway, or steering south-east towards the Bay of Biscay ports, probably Brest. The other alternative was for her to steer westward, where it was thought that replenishment tankers were waiting for her, refuel, and disappear into the Atlantic where she could threaten the vital convoy routes from Canada and America. Since the latter possibility was by far the more dangerous to the whole war effort, Admiral Tovey acted on that assumption and concentrated his search in that direction. The *Victorious*, whose captain had been planning a search to the south-east, which would almost certainly have discovered the missing ship, was ordered instead to search to the north-west. The Swordfish and the Fulmars spent the morning flying over an empty sea.

Yet, in the absence of precise information, Admiral Tovey was strategically correct in his decision. It was the right thing to guard against the more dangerous of the two alternatives. As we now know, Admiral Lutjens in the *Bismarck* had already decided to make for Brest and was steering directly for the port. Every minute, therefore, took him further away from the danger of action.

Admiral Lutjens, however, was unable to keep his mouth shut. He felt he had to tell Hitler about his action with the *Hood*, and shortly after nine o'clock on the morning of the 25th he made a long wireless message to tell of his triumph. It was a fatal move, for every direction-finding station in the Empire was keeping watch on his transmitting frequency and within a matter of minutes wireless bearings were pouring into the Admiralty plotting-room. It was not a particularly good " fix ", for the angle of cut was a narrow one, but it was enough to show that the *Bismarck* was well to the south-eastward of her former position and was therefore making for Brest.

These wireless bearings were immediately signalled out to the Commander-in-Chief, but a plotting error in H.M.S. *King George V* made it appear that the *Bismarck* was some 80 miles north of her real position. To the Commander-in-Chief, it looked as though she were breaking back towards the North Sea, hoping to escape through the Faeroes-Iceland gap to the shelter of a Norwegian fiord. He therefore himself altered course to the north-east.

Fortunately his signal, ordering the new dispositions to be taken up on this assumption, was read by the Admiralty. Aware of what had happened in the flagship, the Admiralty now sent out the actual position obtained from the direction-finding bearings and followed it up with a further signal stating that their appreciation of the situation was that the *Bismarck* was making for Brest. On its receipt the Commander-in-Chief altered course to south-east, and the chase was on.

In the meantime, Force H, based on Gibraltar, had been ordered up to join in the action. This had been a far-sighted action on the part of the First Sea Lord, Admiral Sir Dudley Pound, who had long before visualized the possibility of such a move on the part of the *Bismarck* and had ordered Force H to sail even before the action with the *Hood*. Admiral Somerville was flying his flag in H.M.S. *Renown* and with him was H.M.S. *Ark Royal*, now commanded by Captain L. E. H. Maund. She had two squadrons of Swordfish on board, piloted by men who by now had had considerable experience of aerial warfare at sea in the Mediterranean. In the ensuing operations they were to play a vital part.

For the remainder of the 25th, the *Bismarck* steamed alone in an empty sea, unfound, unshadowed, and completely lost to the searching ships. Astern of her, and now far behind, came the Home Fleet, steering a parallel course. Down to the southward was Force H, at full speed in a steadily mounting sea, endeavouring to cut her off from her base. And from far away to the south-westward, having intercepted the many signals and hoping that she might still arrive in time, came the battleship *Ramillies*, which had been escorting a convoy to Sierra Leone.

By nightfall of the 25th, with the *Bismarck* still unfound, hopes were beginning to falter. The oil fuel situation in the fleet was beginning to cause concern, and there was little more than enough for two more days' steaming. And the *Bismarck* herself had learned wisdom, for her wireless was silent and there were no more exuberant signals to Hitler.

At daybreak on the 26th, there was still no news. But if the Admiralty appreciation were correct and she was, in fact, making for Brest, she must now be approaching an area that could be covered by air search, both from England with long-range aircraft, and from the *Ark Royal*'s Swordfish. Early in the morning the aircraft were sent out, Catalina flying boats of Coastal Command from the Cornish base of St. Eval, Swordfish from the *Ark Royal*. The Swordfish searched three sectors, one based on the *Bismarck*'s maximum speed from her last known position, one based on medium speed, and the third based on low speed.

It was the Catalina of Coastal Command that won the race, sighting the *Bismarck* through a break in the clouds. That she was still a ticklish customer was evident in the fact that she opened fire on the Catalina at maximum range and drove her off by the accuracy of her anti-aircraft gunnery. But fourteen minutes after the Catalina had lost touch first one, and then a second, Swordfish found the enemy ship and stuck to her through thick and thin. Shortly afterwards they were joined by a second Catalina from Coastal Command, and between them they kept the Commander-in-Chief and Admiral Somerville fully informed of the *Bismarck*'s movements.

But though the *Bismarck* was found, she was too far ahead now to be caught. H.M.S. *King George V* was 130 miles behind her, and H.M.S. *Renown* was no match for the *Bismarck*'s guns, for she was an old ship and comparatively lightly armoured. In the words of the Commander-in-Chief: "It was evident that she [*Bismarck*] had too great a lead for H.M.S. *King George V* to come up with her unless her speed could be further reduced or she could be deflected from her course; our only hope lay in torpedo attack by the aircraft of H.M.S. *Ark Royal*."

Early in the afternoon Admiral Somerville detached H.M.S. *Sheffield* to close and shadow the enemy, now some 40 miles to the south-west. At about the same time an attacking force of fifteen Swordfish was ranged on the flight deck of H.M.S. *Ark Royal*, armed with torpedoes, and ready to fly off as soon as a favourable position was reached.

To the pilots and crews waiting for the order to take off, the flight deck of the *Ark Royal* appeared a frightening place. The sea by now was so rough that the stern of the carrier was rising

(*Crown Copyright*)

The Sea Venom, the naval version of a famous R.A.F. fighter.

A squadron of anti-submarine Whirlwind helicopters in flight.

(*Crown Copyright*)

A Fairey Gannet anti-submarine aircraft seen in a carrier's lift.
(*Crown Copyright*)

A Fairey Gannet coming in to land on.
Crown Copyright)

and falling as much as 56 feet in the huge seas. The deck itself was swept by the waves and covered with sea water to a depth of an inch or more, while a fierce wind made it almost impossible to retain the Swordfish on deck.

Just before three o'clock the fifteen Swordfish took off. One had to return because of engine trouble, but the remaining fourteen continued on their way. Almost at once they ran into thick cloud and had to rely on their ship detection sets to make contact.

As the squadron of Swordfish approached the target area, the ship detector apparatus registered a ship. Coming down through the clouds the aircraft sighted her and formed up to attack, using cloud cover as much as possible. As soon as they had worked into a favourable position they dived in line astern through the clouds, flattened out almost at sea level, and released their torpedoes. Only the last three forbore to fire, for as they were coming in they recognized the target. It was H.M.S. *Sheffield*, detailed by Admiral Somerville to shadow the *Bismarck*.

By magnificent ship handling and increasing to full speed, the *Sheffield* managed to avoid the eleven torpedoes fired at her. As one of the Swordfish lifted and flew over her after firing, the observer seized the Aldis signalling lamp and flashed a message. " Sorry for the kippers," it read.

The first striking force flew back and landed on. Their mission had been unsuccessful and the *Bismarck*, still able to steam at over 20 knots in the heavy sea, continued unchecked on her course towards the safety of Brest.

On board the *Ark Royal* there was bustle to prepare a second striking force of fifteen Swordfish. With so many aircraft committed to shadowing duties, there were not enough Swordfish on board to make up the number and so some of those returning from the first strike were hurriedly refuelled and rearmed. Three of the first striking force crashed on landing, for the gale had increased and the *Ark Royal* was pitching even worse than before.

The fifteen aircraft of the second force were ready shortly before seven o'clock in the evening. They were led by Lieut.-Commander T. P. Coode, with Lieutenant E. S. Carver as his observer. Leader of the second wave was Lieut.-Commander J. A. Stewart-Moore. The pilots had been ordered this time to make contact with H.M.S. *Sheffield* before attacking, the

K

Sheffield then directing them on to the *Bismarck*. All aircrews, too, were told of the vital necessity of obtaining hits on the *Bismarck*, for this was the last chance. No more striking forces could be flown off that night.

At seven o'clock the *Ark Royal* turned into the wind and reduced speed, for the force of the gale was already producing a wind speed of over 40 knots on the flight deck. The Deck Control officer had to have a rope passed round his waist to enable him to stand upright, and the ratings at the chocks, holding the wings of the Swordfish, had to bend double to prevent themselves from being blown overboard. Added to the noise of the wind and the heavy slap of the sea was the roar of the Swordfish engines as they revved up for the take-off.

Waiting his opportunity, the Commander Flying, on the bridge above, watched the movements of the ship. As the bow rose he dropped his green flag and the leading machine sped down the flight deck to rise and disappeared into the gloom. One by one the others followed until all fifteen were safely airborne and circling the ship. Taking up formation, they set a course for H.M.S. *Sheffield*, carrying with them the hopes and good wishes of the whole fleet. On them alone now rested the fate of the whole operation.

In the meantime H.M.S. *Sheffield* had made contact with the *Bismarck* and was carrying out shadowing procedure, keeping just out of range of her 15-inch guns. When the Swordfish reached the *Sheffield*, she was able to direct them on to the target. The weather seemed ideal for a synchronized attack, with fairly thick cloud down to 2,000 feet. The squadron would be invisible to the *Bismarck* as they formed up above the cloud. They could then dive down in formation with only the minimum of time out in the open.

But the weather over the *Bismarck* was very different from that over the *Sheffield*. The German ship was advancing under a cold front, with thick cloud down to 700 feet and icing conditions above 5,000 feet. Shortly before nine o'clock, the Swordfish caught a glimpse of the *Bismarck* through a break in the clouds, but before they could take up an attacking position they became split up into small groups in the thick banks of cloud. So, in twos, threes, and fours, the Swordfish dived through the cloud on to the *Bismarck*, flattening out and flying in under a tremendous anti-aircraft barrage put up by all the close-range weapons of the German ship. So great was the volume of fire that in one Swordfish, when she landed on again, were counted no fewer than 175 holes. Another Swordfish, piloted by Sub-Lieutenant A. W. Duncan Beale, lost touch with his flight, flew back to the *Sheffield* to obtain the range and bearing of the enemy, and returned again to press home a lone attack and to hit the enemy amidships with his torpedo.

By half-past nine the attack was over and the aircraft on their way back to the *Ark Royal*. In appalling weather, and with the flight deck rising and falling some 60 feet, all were safely landed on. The pilots, air gunners, and observers were immediately interrogated in order to assess the probable damage and to signal the result to the Commander-in-Chief.

There were two certain hits, one amidships on the port side, the other aft. Two of the aircraft had had to jettison their torpedoes, and the *Bismarck* had succeeded in avoiding the other eleven. But those two hits were just what the Commander-in-Chief wanted. The hit aft had damaged the rudders and the *Bismarck* could no longer steer. She turned two complete circles, reduced to eight knots, and came up into the wind, to head approximately north.

From that moment she was doomed, though there was still a lot of fight left in her. On one occasion H.M.S. *Sheffield* approached within range, and the *Bismarck* fired six 15-inch salvoes at a range of 9 miles. So accurate still was her shooting that some damage was caused, one man was killed and ten wounded, of whom two died later. The *Bismarck* was determined to sell her life dearly.

Until half-past two that night, the *Ark Royal*'s Swordfish, fitted with special long-range tanks, continued to shadow and to report alterations of course and speed. Their task, if less spectacular than that of the torpedo attackers, was no less vital in the information they provided. "Particular credit", wrote Admiral Tovey in his despatch, "is due to the crews of these aircraft whose part, though unspectacular and often forgotten, is as important and frequently as dangerous as that of the aircraft which attack with torpedoes." On one occasion one of the Swordfish momentarily lost touch, and flew around looking for the *Sheffield* to obtained a new bearing and distance. Sighting her, or what the observer thought was her, the pilot flew down for information. On the signalling lamp the observer flashed a question—" Where is the ruddy *Bismarck* ? " The answer was immediate—in the form of a burst of anti-aircraft fire from the *Bismarck* herself.

As the last shadower left the enemy in the gathering darkness, the watch was taken up by the 4th Destroyer Flotilla, which had been detached from convoy duties and arrived in the nick of time. All through that wild night they kept in touch, darting in when the opportunity offered to attack with their torpedoes. And in the morning they were still there to hand the *Bismarck* over to the big guns of H.M.S. *King George V* and H.M.S. *Rodney*, who reached the scene of battle as the dawn broke on May 27th.

Aboard the *Bismarck* herself we have a picture of the scene as painted in the words of survivors. After the torpedo attack the Iron Cross was offered to anyone who would enter the flooded steering compartment and free the rudders. One diver did go down and managed to get one of the rudders amidships. But the other defied all his efforts, and the ship remained unmanageable.

The men on board knew that it was the end. They knew that, at dawn, the Swordfish would come back. What they did not know yet was that an even more terrible fate was approaching from the west in the avenging guns of the *King George V* and the *Rodney*. The crew was told over the ship's broadcast system that dozens of U-boats and squadrons of aircraft were coming to their assistance, but none believed the words. There was an exchange of heroics between Hitler and Admiral Lutjens, but it brought no comfort to the desperate men on board.

At dawn the Swordfish from the *Ark Royal* again appeared in the sky, armed with more torpedoes. But already they were too late, for from the westward, shrouded in the tempestuous weather, came the long grey shapes of H.M.S. *King George V* and H.M.S. *Rodney* to settle the account opened 72 hours earlier with the sinking of the *Hood*. H.M.S. *Norfolk* and H.M.S. *Dorsetshire* were there, too, to flank mark for the battleships, as well as the destroyers that had hung on so gamely throughout the night.

It was the final act of the drama. One by one the *Bismarck*'s turrets were put out of action until she lay no more than a hulk at the mercy of the battleships' guns. In the end the torpedoes of H.M.S. *Dorsetshire* put her out of her misery. She turned turtle, floated for a moment or two, and then slid below the waves, her ensign still flying.

In this action the Fleet Air Arm first demonstrated its full value as a striking force at sea. The course of the action, in many ways, followed closely the pattern of Matapan, but with a far more decisive result. The *Ark Royal* had been at sea for eighteen months and her air crews were well trained and experienced, a factor that led directly to the crippling attack of the 26th. At Matapan, the Swordfish crews had not had the experience of many months at war and, though their attack had been pressed home with great gallantry, it had not met with all the success that Admiral Cunningham had hoped for. In the case of the *Bismarck*, Admiral Tovey was admirably served by his Fleet Air Arm squadrons, both those of the *Victorious*, which had first slowed the *Bismarck* down, and those of the *Ark Royal*, which had stopped her. Without their contribution at a vital moment the *Bismarck* might well have reached the security of Brest before being brought to action.

With the morning flight of Swordfish landed on, the *Ark Royal*, with H.M.S. *Renown*, returned to Gibraltar. As she steamed into harbour on May 29th every man of the garrison turned out to give her a tremendous welcome. All who could do so crowded into boats to greet her, and she proceeded through the harbour to her berth to the cheers of countless thousands. It was a spontaneous, thrilling welcome, a tribute to those men of the Swordfish who had played so signal a part in the destruction of the pride of the German Navy.

War against the U-Boats

IT WAS, HOWEVER, NOT ONLY IN FLEET ACTIONS OR IN attacks on enemy harbours that the Fleet Air Arm was solely engaged. As important a duty, though one much less spectacular, was the long battle of the Atlantic, fought unceasingly throughout the war against the U-boat menace. In a later chapter will be told something of the story of the convoys to Malta and North Russia, operations that later developed into major fleet actions. This chapter deals with that continuing struggle in the Atlantic and with the final defeat of the U-boat, in which aircraft played so large a part.

It is a story shared with Coastal Command of the Royal Air Force, which for most of the war came under the operational control of the Admiralty. For a long time it was Coastal Command that bore the burden alone, until the provision of large numbers of escort carriers and additional naval aircraft enabled the Fleet Air Arm to take a fuller share.

So much in the war depended upon keeping open the sea lanes of the Atlantic that every arm of the Service had to be called in to their defence. Increasingly large forces had to be allocated to the Atlantic battle and until at least the end of 1942, increasingly large losses accepted. For this was the one vital seaway in which the loss of control would eventually have meant the loss of the whole war.

The Atlantic battle started quietly, for Germany in September, 1939, had no more than fifty-seven operational U-boats, of which not more than one-third could be at sea at any one moment. But during these early weeks the German shipyards were busy and by the spring of 1940 new boats were appearing in increasing numbers. The real battle was on.

An initial broad line of strategy soon became apparent. Every submarine's speed and range of visibility is severely limited when it is submerged. So it followed that if the U-boats could be kept under water, convoys would have a greater chance of getting clear by their superiority in speed when attacked or sighted. The easiest way of enforcing this was by air patrol over the convoy, for the wide area which aircraft could search would force U-boats in the vicinity to submerge to prevent discovery. This was to be one of the primary tasks of Coastal Command, although during the early days of the war they had neither the number of aircraft, nor machines of sufficient endurance for the task. So it was but a scattered effort, fortunately coinciding with a period of very limited U-boat activity. Both sides were building up their forces for the struggle that was to come.

The fall of France in June, 1940, was the signal for the battle to start in real earnest. To the U-boat command under Admiral Doenitz fell the inestimable advantage of new bases on the Norwegian and Biscay coasts, bringing the U-boats some thousand or more miles nearer their hunting-grounds. To their help, too, came new air bases in France and the big four-engined Focke-Wulfs, which could search the eastern Atlantic for convoys and home the U-boats to their prey by wireless. The combination of aircraft and submarine was formidable indeed.

But it was not entirely a " one-way " deal. In January of 1940 radar had been fitted in a few aircraft of Coastal Command, and though it was still in an elementary stage of development, it could yet locate a surfaced U-boat at a range of about 10 miles. And in that same month of January a Coastal Command Sunderland of No. 228 Squadron had detected a U-boat west of Ushant and, with the aid of surface forces called to its area, had destroyed it. The writing was on the wall, though very faint to see as yet.

The early combined operations of Coastal Command and surface forces had two quick effects. They drove the U-boats westward, where the chances of air observation were more remote, and they forced the U-boats to concentrate on attack at night rather than by day. By the autumn of 1940 the pattern was becoming clearer, with U-boats operating mostly beyond the range of Coastal Command aircraft and concentrating their attacks during the dark hours when their detection became even more difficult. The hard-pressed escort vessels, relying in the main on Asdic search, were quite unable to compete with the growing threat, for attacks were made with the U-boat surfaced and the Asdic was useless in those circumstances.

The big Focke-Wulf aircraft, too, were playing an increasing part in the attack on Allied shipping. Ranging far out into the Atlantic, not only did they act as the eyes of the U-boats but themselves could attack and sink merchantmen. There was but one answer to that threat, and it was contained in a directive issued by the Prime Minister early in 1941. It contained the following clauses :

1. We must take the offensive against the U-boats and the Focke-Wulf wherever we can and whenever we can. The U-boat at sea must be hunted, and the U-boat in the building yard or in dock must be bombed. The Focke-Wulf, and other bombers employed against our shipping, must be attacked in the air and in their nests.
2. Extreme priority will be given to fitting out ships to catapult, or otherwise launch, fighter aircraft against bombers attacking our shipping. Proposals should be made within a week.
3. All the measures approved and now in train for the concentration for the main strength of the Coastal Command upon the north-western approaches, and their assistance on the east coast by Fighter and Bomber Commands, will be pressed forward. . . .

It was with the second requirement of the directive that the Fleet Air Arm was most directly concerned. The Royal Air Force's Hurricane fighter was speedily adapted to naval use and in May the first merchant ship fitted with a catapult and carrying a single Hurricane sailed in convoy. The Hurricane, of course, could not land on again once it had been catapulted, and the procedure was for the pilot to jettison his aircraft after an attack and himself to descend by parachute near enough to one of the escorts to be picked up out of the water. This method was first tried out by pilots of the Fleet Air Arm, and when it was found to be practicable, it was turned over to Fighter Command to operate. These catapult ships were known as Camships (catapult aircraft merchant ship), and more than one marauding Focke-Wulf was shot down at sea by these gallant pilots.

The Camship gave place to the Macship (Merchant aircraft carrier ship), which was a great step forward and was to lead to the rapid development of the small escort carrier. The Macship was an ordinary merchant vessel with a flat superstructure built over her to act as a flying deck. They carried six Martlets, new ship-borne fighters of American construction, permanently parked on deck, for they had no hangars and no lifts. These Macships proceeded in convoy and their Martlets were flown off, not only as a fighter defence against attack and shadowing by Focke-Wulfs, but also as anti-submarine patrols above the convoy.

The first of the Macships was the *Empire Audacity*, formerly the German ship *Hanover*, which had been captured while trying to run the blockade. She was a ship of 5,600 tons and after her conversion in July, 1941, she had a flight deck of just over 400 feet in length and some 60 feet in width. She was a Diesel-engine ship and had a maximum speed of 14 knots.

Her first trip was with a convoy bound for Gibraltar, and within a matter of three days her aircraft were in action. One of them drove off a U-boat, two days later a second shot down a shadowing Focke-Wulf. For the remainder of the voyage the *Empire Audacity* flew anti-submarine patrols over the convoy and kept the U-boats at bay by forcing them to submerge well out of range.

This limited success of the *Empire Audacity* proved that the idea was likely to be a profitable one. The Admiralty took her over as a ship of war and renamed her H.M.S. *Audacity*. On her return journey her convoy came through unscathed.

The third convoy, again to Gibraltar, reached its destination without loss, though three Focke-Wulfs were shot down for the loss of one Martlet. On the return trip the convoy was beset with U-boats, no fewer than seventeen being sighted during the course of the first few days. As they were sighted, the Martlets called the escorting destroyers and corvettes to the scene, and three of the seventeen were sunk. Two Focke-Wulfs out of four that attempted to shadow were shot down on the seventh day out from Gibraltar.

That night, December 21st, the *Audacity* was hit by a torpedo from a U-boat. She began to settle in the water, but remained afloat with her after gun-platform awash. For twenty minutes she remained stationary and preparations were made to take her in tow. Just as it looked as though she might be saved, a second torpedo hit her forward. For a few minutes she remained afloat and then, her forepart filling with sea water, she plunged under as her stern rose vertically in the air. Her Martlets broke adrift and shot down the short flight deck, smashing her boats.

As she went under she carried with her many of her pilots and observers, men who could ill be spared.

In her short career, H.M.S. *Audacity* had provided the final answer to the U-boat menace, though as yet it was a long way in the future. It was not the Macship in herself that could beat the U-boat, for she could not operate a sufficient number of aircraft to maintain permanent air patrols, and the lack of hangar space was a drawback in that it exposed the aircraft to damage in heavy seas. But she showed the way, and the answer was something larger, complete with hangar and a small workshop. This was the escort carrier, a miniature aircraft carrier built on a merchant ship hull, but with most of the amenities of their larger sisters.

This answer, however, lay in the future, for the escort carrier had first to be provided. In the meantime, the battle of the Atlantic swayed to and fro, with each side for a time gaining the advantage. For some months toward the end of 1941 and the beginning of 1942 the U-boats found their main success in the areas of mid-Atlantic, beyond the range of Coastal Command aircraft, and it was during this period that the pendulum swung far in the direction of the German Reich. But the gradual acquisition by Coastal Command of the very long-range Liberators, the rapid development of airborne and ship-borne radar, and the provision of special improved depth-charges filled with Torpex for use from aircraft, began to send the pendulum back again on its swing to the west.

For a long time it hovered, uncertain of its final swing, as the battle increased in ferocity. The new U-boats were being delivered fast now, and in early 1943 Germany could keep over 100 of them at sea. But with the greater numbers operating there came as a counter-measure the greater expansion of the escort groups, the greater skill in attack of the Coastal Command machines, and the first of the new escort carriers to help cover that bare gap in mid-Atlantic which was still beyond the range of Coastal Command. The Fleet Air Arm was now able to take an increasingly vital part in the battle, though it was still Coastal Command that was bearing the lion's share. The other Royal Air Force commands, Fighter and Bomber, also did much valuable work, the former in taking over the escort of the coastal convoys, the latter providing some of their long-range machines for use with Coastal Command and also carrying out many raids on the U-boat bases. Although these bombing raids rarely did any damage to the U-boats themselves—they were too securely sheltered in massive concrete pens—they did at least harry the U-boat crews and allow them little rest while in harbour.

By the summer of 1943 the U-boats were beginning to falter under the ceaseless attack. The " wolf-pack " attacks of 1941 and 1942 no longer paid such immense dividends and the packs themselves were beginning to break up. With the mid-Atlantic gap becoming smaller and smaller every day as more and more escort carriers arrived on the scene, convoys could begin to count on continuous air cover from departure to arrival.

It was at this juncture that the Allies moved from defence to attack. While the convoys still, of course, had their escort groups to shepherd them across, support groups and hunting groups could work independently of convoys and search out the U-boats in the empty wastes of the ocean. It was in this work that the escort carrier really came into her own, for her aircraft could cover wide areas and could call on the attendant frigates, corvettes, and sloops to deal with any U-boat they sighted, or attacked. And it was in this work, too, that the Swordfish, already being ousted for fleet work by the faster and more heavily armed Barracudas, once again came into their own.

For work with an escort carrier, the Swordfish was ideal. The comparative smallness of the flight deck held no fears for them in flying off and landing on, and their extreme manœuvrability and the way they could be flung about in the sky made them formidable opponents to a U-boat on the surface or in the act of diving. Doomed to extinction as the newer torpedo-carrying aircraft came along, the escort carrier gave the Swordfish a reprieve and a new lease of valuable and productive life.

So, in the end, the pendulum made a final swing westward and the long and vital battle was won. Neither the air nor the escort vessel won it alone, but the two combined forged a weapon powerful enough to eliminate the under-water threat. Similarly, neither the Fleet Air Arm nor Coastal Command could claim the exclusive mastery in the air ; once again it was the combination of the two that closed the gap and forced the U-boat under.

If the battle of the Atlantic was long and bitter, if it entailed heavy and grievous losses, it yet taught one tremendous and enduring lesson, that of a close and friendly co-operation with the Royal Air Force in maritime affairs. In the various naval command areas, in which convoy or other combined operations might take place, were set up combined headquarters in which the naval and air officers sat and worked side by side. In this way all movements were known both to the naval and air elements and all arrangements for patrols, strikes, searches, fighter cover, and so on, were worked out in full agreement. Such close co-operation led not only to personal friendships and a smooth and efficient plan, but also proved a most useful medium for understanding and appreciating the varying problems and methods of either Service. All the little animosities engendered during the period of divided control before the war were automatically dissolved, and in its place grew a genuine admiration for the way each Service tackled its problems. And it was this admiration and understanding which led to so signal a success in the great battle.

The Gallant Sortie

IT IS NECESSARY NOW TO MOVE BACK AGAIN TO 1941 and to follow the fortune of Lieut.-Commander E. Esmonde's squadron of Swordfish. We have already seen how it flew off from H.M.S. *Victorious* on the night of May 24th to carry out the first of the air attacks on the *Bismarck* and to score one torpedo hit. A few weeks later the squadron was transferred to H.M.S. *Ark Royal* in Force H, and in her it carried out many raids on enemy bases and installations.

On November 13th the *Ark Royal* was torpedoed by a German U-boat 30 miles from Gibraltar. One man was killed by the explosion and all the remainder were taken off. Although the Swordfish were lost when the ship sank fourteen hours later, the pilots, observers, and telegraphist-airgunners were saved.

Esmonde returned to England to reform the squadron. It had to be reduced to six aircraft as some of the pilots had been appointed elsewhere. With these six Swordfish Esmonde began to work up his squadron to full operational efficiency at Lee-on-Solent. It was earmarked for service in one of the new escort carriers just beginning to come over from America.

Late in January, 1942, the squadron had been ordered to move north for final training and working-up, and the move was expected to take place early in February. A few days later it was cancelled, the squadron being required to stand by for a very different operation. On February 4th Esmonde went up to Buckingham Palace to be decorated by the King with the D.S.O. which had been awarded to him for his part in the attack on the *Bismarck*. On his return he found new orders awaiting him and, in execution of them, took off from Lee-on-Solent with his squadron and flew to a Royal Air Force station in Kent. There was a blizzard blowing during the flight and snow lay on the ground as the Swordfish landed. All through the morning of the 6th the maintenance crews were kept busy digging the six aircraft out of snow and keeping the runway clear. The engines were run periodically to keep them warmed up, and the squadron was placed at five minutes' notice to take off.

At this time there lay in Brest harbour the two German battle-cruisers *Scharnhorst* and *Gneisenau*, and the 10,000-ton cruiser *Prinz Eugen*. All these had taken shelter there after raiding operations in the Atlantic, and had lain there for many months. But within the last week there had been indications that the three ships were preparing for sea and a break-out was expected in the next "no moon" period, sometime in mid-February.

It was appreciated in the Admiralty that the ships would take the Channel route rather than the much longer voyage round the north of Scotland. Although they might have to face opposition as they passed through the narrow Straits of Dover, they could, by hugging the coast of France, count on strong and continuous fighter cover for the whole of their passage, an advantage well worth the risk of discovery and action. They could count, too, on surface escort by destroyers, E-boats, and R-boats, and that, too, was worth the risk. In the Admiralty's opinion, the Channel route was almost a certainty.

The necessary precautions were taken to obtain early information of any move. A submarine was sent to patrol an area off Brest and to report the sailing of the three ships. Three daily and three nightly air patrols were flown across the probable course of the three ships by Coastal Command, using aircraft fitted with ASV, as air-borne radar was called in those days. It was hoped, by these means, to enable plenty of time to be gained for an attack from the air to be mounted while they were in the Channel. A flotilla of six destroyers, used for escort duties on the east coast, was also earmarked for an attack on the ships further east, though that, of course, depended on whether the flotilla was in the neighbourhood at the crucial moment. It was not possible to take them away from their normal escort duties until definite information was forthcoming.

Although the Admiralty had been correct in their appreciation that the enemy would use the Channel route, they were wrong in their estimate of the timing. It had been thought that the enemy would leave Brest in daylight in order to pass through the Channel narrows during the dark hours. For this reason

Esmonde had been told to expect a night attack and the Royal Air Force had arranged to send out fighters as flare droppers to illuminate the target. But the enemy had different plans. The three ships left Brest in the dark hours of February 11th and by daylight of the 12th were well on their way up Channel.

The submarine on patrol off Brest missed them in the darkness. The most westerly of the patrolling aircraft which should have picked up the three ships off Brest, met a Junkers 88 on the way to its patrol line, and its ASV, when switched on, was unserviceable. The second aircraft fared no better. In the official inquiry after the event, its ASV was stated to be suffering from a fault of an " obscure and unusual nature which is still under investigation ". The third aircraft missed the ships altogether. It was, in fact, the Germans themselves who revealed that the break-out was taking place when they began to jam our south coast radar stations. As a result a new reconnaissance was flown and the three ships sighted, although first reported as a convoy. By this time they were approaching the Dover Straits.

Thus it was that the news of the break-out of the three ships was not received until it was too late to deliver a properly co-ordinated attack. The long-range batteries installed in the cliffs above Dover opened fire, but the visibility over the Channel was so poor that accurate spotting was impossible. Destroyers and motor-torpedo boats made an attack, but their torpedoes were successfully avoided. All now depended on the six Swordfish of Edmonde's squadron.

As the news was telephoned to the airfield shortly after twelve o'clock the pilots, observers, and air-gunner-telegraphists ran out to their machines, putting on their flying kit as they went. As they ran, Esmonde gave his instructions. " Fly at 50 feet, close line astern, individual attacks, and find your own way home. We shall have fighter protection."

By 12.30 p.m. the six Swordfish were in the air, circling over the airfield. As they formed up into line astern a squadron of ten Spitfires came up as fighter cover, and Esmonde led the force out over the Channel. After twenty minutes' flying, the enemy was sighted, steaming in line ahead, led by the *Prinz Eugen*, with the *Scharnhorst* and *Gneisenau* following in her track. Escorting them were German destroyers, E-boats, and minesweepers.

Above them flew their fighter force, composed of Messer-schmitt 109s and Focke-Wulf 190s, the biggest fighter screen ever seen over a naval force. It was to be an attack against tremendous odds.

Esmonde never faltered, leading his sub-flight in in line astern through a hail of anti-aircraft fire. Inevitably his Swordfish was hit. It staggered for a moment in the air, but he straightened it out and levelled off just above the sea to deliver his attack. Out of the clouds above him dived about fifteen Messerschmitt and Focke-Wulf fighters. As they sped downwards they were attacked by the Spitfires but the fighter escort was too small to compete with them all and enough of them got through to attack the much slower Swordfish. Esmonde was now com-mitted to his firing course and his only chance of a hit with his torpedo was to maintain a steady course and refrain from taking evasive action. Although he must have known that he was facing certain death he flew on direct for his target. He was hit again and again, but still he held on. At last the concentrated fire of the German fighters ripped the top of his main plane completely off and his Swordfish, now out of control, dived straight down into the sea.

Following Esmonde in the second Swordfish was Sub-Lieu-tenant B. W. Rose. His machine was attacked from ahead and astern simultaneously. His rear gunner, Leading Airman A. L. Johnson was killed and Rose himself was hit by splinters from a cannon shell which exploded against the bulkhead behind his seat. His observer, Sub-Lieutenant E. Lee, stood up in the after cockpit and directed him in order to evade the enemy attacks by shouting "port" or "starboard" as the German fighters came in.

Rose's Swordfish was being continually hit and the engine was beginning to falter under the heavy fire of the fighters. With Esmonde's plane crashed into the sea, Rose was now leading the flight and he decided that the attack must be now or never. Ignoring the fighters on his tail he steadied the machine on to its proper firing course and held straight on towards the enemy ships. He aimed at the *Prinz Eugen* and closed to a range of 1,200 yards, when he dropped his torpedo. He kept on a steady course long enough to see that it was running correctly, and then swept up and away, his machine now heavily damaged.

We shall return to his Swordfish after describing the attacks by the remainder of the squadron.

Following Rose was Sub-Lieutenant C. M. Kingsmill. His Swordfish was early damaged, a direct hit from one of the ships' anti-aircraft guns landing on the engine and shooting away the two top cylinders. Miraculously, the engine continued to function, although it and the upper port wing caught fire. Two Focke-Wulf 190s dived on to the blazing Swordfish, but the rear gunner, Leading Airman D. A. Bunce, shot one of them down into the sea.

The whole of the Swordfish's crew were now wounded, but Kingsmill was determined to bring her in and complete his attack. Taking as his target the *Scharnhorst*, the second ship in the line, he managed to get within range and drop his torpedo. Like Rose before him he was able to see it running properly before breaking away and heading for home.

Nothing is known of the exploits of the second sub-flight of Swordfish, piloted respectively by Lieutenant J. C. Thompson, Sub-Lieutenant C. R. Wood, and Sub-Lieutenant P. Bligh. When last seen they were flying over the destroyer screen and closing in for their attack against a defence that was as fierce as ever. All three of them were shot down and there were no survivors to bring back the story of their attack.

Meanwhile, both Rose and Kingsmill were having their adventures. Rose, after his attack, soared away over the port wing of the destroyer screen in order to make as much height as possible. His Swordfish was hard hit and he knew that he would never be able to bring her back to the English coast. As he reached a height of 1,200 feet his observer, Lee, told him that the starboard petrol tank was punctured and that the petrol was pouring out of it over the machine. It was, perhaps, a stroke of good fortune that at that moment his engine cut out, otherwise the Swordfish might have been set ablaze. Down below him, some 5 or 6 miles away, he saw a group of motor-torpedo boats, and he glided towards them. He landed in the sea about 4 miles short.

The aircraft dinghy, kept in the top of the main plane, was automatically blown up when the aircraft ditched and was washed into the sea, upside down. Rose, though severely wounded in the arm, managed to recover it and get it right side up. Lee held it steady as Rose climbed down from the sinking Swordfish and got aboard, then he tried to remove Johnson from the after cockpit. Johnson was dead, however, and Lee was unable to lift him out. For several minutes he wrestled with the difficulties of freeing Johnson, unwilling to leave him without burial, but in the end he was forced to abandon the attempt. He then joined Rose in the dinghy and cast it off from the Swordfish.

The sea, already rough, was becoming rougher and within a few minutes the dinghy was full of water. The two men used their flying helmets to bale it out, but they only just managed to keep the dinghy afloat with such inefficient balers. Next they recovered the waterproof bag which contained the emergency gear. They took out the tins of aluminium dust, which when scattered on the water forms a silver pool and is visible for a considerable distance, and flung the dust out. But they threw it to windward and it blew back on them, covering them with a silver sheen so that they looked like a couple of highly polished tin soldiers.

With the empty tins, however, they were able to resume baling and at last managed to get the dinghy nearly dry, so that it was floating high enough in the water for immediate safety. They then took out the marine distress signals and fired them. They were seen by a couple of motor-torpedo boats, which closed.

For a few moments, as the two boats were approaching, Rose and Lee were a bit apprehensive as they might well be German E-boats, which had a very similar silhouette to our own craft. But they were hailed by English voices, and in another minute or two they were both hauled on board to safety. They had been in the dinghy for an hour and a half and Rose, seriously wounded, was in poor shape when he was picked up. Both of them were numb with cold.

We left the other Swordfish, piloted by Kingsmill, on fire after having delivered its torpedo attack. Sighting a flotilla of motor-torpedo boats, Kingsmill tried to land near them, but they turned out to be enemy E-boats and greeted him with a burst of anti-aircraft fire. Although he was wounded and handling the plane was an effort, he kept on flying and evaded the gunfire. But his engine, with two cylinders shot away, was faltering badly, and the fire was getting serious. Finally, the engine packed up completely and Kingsmill made a pancake landing on the sea. British motor-torpedo boats were near at hand and the three men were soon rescued.

So, out of eighteen men who set off soon after noon on this day, only five remained alive two hours later. Of the six Swordfish, all were lost. Writing in his official report of the action, the Flag Officer Commanding at Dover, Vice-Admiral Ramsay, said : " In my opinion, the gallant sortie of these six Swordfish constitutes one of the finest exhibitions of self-sacrifice and devotion to duty that the war has yet witnessed."

Lieut.-Commander Esmonde, who led the squadron in, was posthumously awarded the Victoria Cross, the first member of the Fleet Air Arm to win this award during the war. The four surviving officers each received the D.S.O., and Leading Airman Bunce, who was the telegraphist-air-gunner in Kingsmill's Swordfish, the Conspicuous Gallantry Medal. All the remainder were posthumously mentioned in despatches.

This action in the Channel on February 12th had wide repercussions. The public was angry and many questions were asked in the Press and in Parliament as to the supply of aircraft to the fleet. As a result the Admiralty was given some priority in the design and constitution of war machines, and a marine version of the Spitfire fighter was developed for use in carriers. This was certainly a step in the right direction, but it came too late, for by now the Government was committed to the big bomber policy of the Royal Air Force and the priority given to the Admiralty meant, in actual fact, very little since the manufacturing capacity did not exist to undertake this extra commitment.

The answer, as it turned out, was only just around the corner. If Britain could not produce the aircraft, America could, and within a few months the United States was in the war. Naval aircraft came across the Atlantic from America in ever-increasing numbers, and the new carriers joining the fleet were largely armed with Barracudas, Wildcats, Hellcats, Martlets, and many other machines of American origin.

Work of the Shore Bases

It was, however, not only on the sea and from carriers that the Fleet Air Arm served during the war. At its outbreak, in 1939, the Admiralty already had a few shore stations, placed at strategic positions, and as the war developed these grew in number. The fleet anchorage at Scapa Flow, for instance, was protected by shore-based squadrons at Hatston, armed with Skuas, Rocs, and Gladiators, and they had a number of engagements with enemy bombers, and not entirely without success considering the general antiquity of the fighters concerned.

During the Battle of Britain, too, pilots of the Fleet Air Arm were able to play a part, though a small one in comparison with that of the Royal Air Force. Soon after the evacuation from Dunkirk the Admiralty offered to the Air Ministry the loan of any pilots under training who might volunteer. The offer did not include executive officers as these, already trained as naval officers, were too urgently needed for work with the fleet, but some forty pilots under instruction at the fighter school in H.M.S. *Raven*, one of the naval air stations ashore, all volunteered for temporary service with the Royal Air Force. They left H.M.S. *Raven* and were distributed to operational training units in order to learn to fly Spitfires and Hurricanes. They finished their course in July, 1940, and were then posted to operational squadrons for the defence of Britain. They were there for the opening shots of the battle of Britain and remained with the Royal Air Force until it was over. Throughout they wore naval uniform and received naval rates of pay, but in all other respects were administratively and operationally under the control of the Royal Air Force.

For the rest, there was never any lack of action or work for the shore-based squadrons. In modern warfare, the strategic disposition of fleets depends very largely on intelligence of the enemy's movements, which in itself depends very largely on reconnaissance. To be really effective, reconnaissance needs to be an almost daily task, especially in such a place as the Norwegian coast, which was used extensively by enemy shipping. By a careful daily watch on the movements of shipping, information was built up from which intelligent forecasts of movements could be made and which enabled the fleet to carry out several successful sweeps along that rugged coastline.

Much of the work of the shore-based squadrons was routine, the flying of patrols across wide areas of sea to maintain the economic blockade of Germany, the endless reconnaissance flights across the North Sea to search out the Norwegian fiords for enemy shipping. Occasionally these daily tasks might be enlivened with a strike against shipping, or the bombing of German naval units at sea or in harbour, but for the most part it was dull, monotonous work. Nevertheless, it is this sort of work that forms the background of sea power, and history has many examples to show of how this sort of routine work wins wars. So it was in this case, and even if much of the daily duty of those squadrons was automatic and uninspiring, without it the war would have been a longer and more costly affair.

A great deal of this work was done under the operational control of Coastal Command, controlled through the area combined head-quarters, in which naval and Royal Air Force officers sat side by side. Some of it was done under the control of Bomber Command, especially such tasks as minelaying, while at one period forty naval bomber pilots were lent to the Royal Air Force, flying Whitleys and Wellingtons with R.A.F. crews in the big bomber attacks on Germany.

Side by side with these operational squadrons were those of the second-line, which were used for a variety of purposes. Their main task, of course, was in training, in producing the ever-increasing numbers of pilots, observers, and air-gunners required to maintain the rapidly growing strength of the Fleet Air Arm at sea. Target-towing, spotting for practice firing by ships, exercises to test anti-aircraft gunners on board, all these were duties every bit as essential to the successful outcome of the war as the actual air attacks on the enemy. The communication squadrons, too, did invaluable service, even if of a more humble type than that of the operational machines. One of the communication squadrons, based on Donibristle, was composed entirely of pilots and engineers of the Jersey Airways Company, who offered themselves as a going concern to the Admiralty when the Channel Islands were overrun by Germany in the summer of 1940.

Malta was another outpost where Fleet Air Arm machines operated from land. At the beginning of the war there was a large training squadron of twenty-four <u>Swordfish</u> based in the south of France designed to produce pilots and aircrew for Mediterranean operations. Led by Lieut.-Commander G. C. Dickens, it carried out the first raid on Italy after Mussolini had entered the war on the side of Germany, bombing Genoa on June 14th, 1940. Being a training squadron, it had no bombs of its own, and the Swordfish were fitted out with French bombs borrowed for the occasion. Since the bombs were of a size that could not be carried normally by the Swordfish, they were fused before take-off and secured to the machines by spunyarn.

With the fall of France and the signing of the armistice with Germany, the squadron was ordered to leave its station at Hyères. It flew to Bône, in Algeria, and then split up, the training half returning to Britain via Casablanca and Gibraltar, the operational half flying to Malta, via Medjez-el-Bab. There, under the leadership of Lieut.-Commander F. D. Howie, they were soon in the thick of the Mediterranean battle.

They began their operations with raids on the Italian mainland, one of their more successful attacks being on the oil tanks at Augusta, where considerable damage was done to the installation. Another successful raid was on the airfield at Catania. This, however, was to use the aircraft for a purpose to which they were not really suited and one, moreover, which had little influence on the naval war in that area. It was a waste of machines designed for attacks with torpedoes to use them in a bombing role ashore. Before long, however, with the build-up, first of Italian, and later of German troops in Tripolitania and Libya, the really worth-while targets appeared to test their mettle.

It was the one source of weakness of the Axis campaign in North Africa that all military stores had to be carried by sea. On the face of it, with a big Italian fleet available for escort duties and the only British base in the central Mediterranean, Malta, rendered unavailable for use by the British Fleet by attack from the air, it might have seemed a not too difficult task. But any hopes the Axis powers may have had of an easy passage for supplies were soon dispelled by the work of the Fleet Air Arm squadrons in Malta and by the submarines which operated from there. This was warfare for which the Swordfish, and later the Albacores which came out to reinforce them, were ideally suited, and it was warfare, moreover, which could demonstrate the classical use of sea-power by denying to the enemy his essential supplies. It was to be a long battle, but in the end it was to draw the net tight round Rommel's armies in North Africa and force them, inevitably and remorselessly, into defeat.

The general pattern for these attacks on the enemy's seaborne supplies was to sight and shadow by day, and to attack by night. It was never easy work, for in addition to the defences of the convoy itself there was often an enemy fighter patrol in the vicinity of Malta at dawn waiting for the return of the striking force. There were, too, the incessant daylight raids on the island, with the risk of damage to the Swordfish by bomb or splinter. In an attempt to disrupt these convoy attacks, the Germans frequently kept a handful of bombers over the island all night, dropping one or two bombs on the airfields at short intervals to try to prevent the Swordfish from taking off. The Swordfish pilots, however, were not to be discouraged when there was a chance of air attack, although, as one of the pilots wrote when describing this night bombing : " This practice made it very uncomfortable while taxi-ing to the take-off position, and sometimes entailed taking-off without knowing whether bomb splinters or shrapnel had penetrated any vital part of the air-craft."

There were so many attacks on enemy convoys that a description of them all would be tedious. An account of one of them must suffice as a pattern of them all.

The convoy in question was sighted by a Royal Air Force reconnaissance machine during the afternoon of 23rd February, 1942. It consisted of four liners carrying troops, escorted by one Italian battleship, four cruisers, and fifteen destroyers, and was proceeding southwards from Sicily, bound for Tripoli. When it was sighted it was ploughing into a rough sea, for there was one of those Mediterranean storms, known as *gregales*, blowing. Conditions aloft, with heavy rainstorms and a fierce north-easterly gale, were just as bad as they were below.

With the report of the convoy the Fleet Air Arm pilots prepared for battle. Shortly after 8.0 p.m., in the gathering darkness of the winter night, a mixed force of Albacores and Swordfish took off from Malta. They were led by Lieut.-Commander F. H. E. Hopkins in an Albacore, the remainder of the striking force consisting of seven Swordfish and one more Albacore.

The Swordfish, battling against the gale, were unable to reach the convoy as their supply of petrol was not sufficient to enable them to make enough headway against the fierce wind. All seven had to turn back to Malta. But the two Albacores kept on and at last, after a long search, they made contact. By that time, however, they too were reaching the limit of their endurance and there was insufficient petrol remaining in their tanks to make an attack. Hopkins therefore decided to return to Malta, collect another striking force, and attempt an attack later. As he now knew the position of the convoy the aircraft need not waste time in searching and should be able to get there, make an attack, and return without anxiety over petrol.

As he and his companion flew back the storm got worse. The two Albacores just made it, their tanks almost empty as they landed. Hopkins quickly organized a second striking force of six machines and at 2.45 a.m. on the 24th he took off again. Two of the six aircraft lost contact in the darkness and the blizzard and had to return, but the other four kept together and in due course found the convoy. Forming line astern, they swept down on the Italian ships and scored two hits with their torpedoes on the 24,000-ton liner *Victoria*. All four machines landed back on the aerodrome at Malta at 9.15 a.m., having flown for an hour above their permitted endurance. Hopkins himself had been in the air for a total of 11 hours 50 minutes, and that in conditions which would normally have been considered unfit for flying. He had already won a D.S.C. for a former operation ; for this attack he was given an immediate award of the D.S.O.

During this attack a squadron of Albacores, based in Libya at an airfield near Benghazi, had been detailed to make a second attack on the convoy. Only five machines, led by Lieut.-Commander J. W. S. Corbett, were available, and they met the same difficult conditions of weather as the aircraft from Malta. They had no difficulty in finding the convoy, so well had its movements been reported, and as they made contact the Albacores separated, each to attack a different target. Corbett was last seen attacking the battleship, his machine being shot down on the run in. Lieutenant H. M. Ellis, though attacked by two Junkers 88s, fired his torpedo at the *Victoria*, already hard hit by the Malta machines, and saw it explode against the ship's side. The *Victoria* sank later as a result of the two attacks. Another of the Albacores hit one of the escorting destroyers.

So the battle of the Sicilian straits was waged, with cruisers, destroyers, and submarines to supplement the activities in the air. Here, indeed, was the true expression of sea power, the denial to the enemy of his vital sources of supply, but a sea power made more flexible and more powerful by the tactical possibilities of the Fleet Air Arm. The co-ordination achieved was superb, and the combination not only extended the range of attack by nearly 250 miles but also brought a far wider area of visibility, through air reconnaissance over an immense area. The Malta squadrons, by themselves, sent to the bottom nearly half a million tons of enemy shipping during the course of the North African campaign, vital shipping on which the Axis relied to carry on the battle. They had a hand in the destruction of nearly as much again through their co-operation with the surface forces engaged, sighting and reporting convoys and leading the cruisers and destroyers to their targets.

Farther east, shore-based squadrons of the Fleet Air Arm were in operation in the Aegean Sea and even in the Western Desert, although in that theatre of war they were taking over a shore role in support of the Army.

The aircraft operating in the Aegean were based on the airfield at Maleme, in Crete. The first squadron came from H.M.S. *Illustrious*, whose flight deck had been seriously damaged in a dive-bombing attack on February 10th, 1941. Unable to operate her aircraft, they were divided between Malta and Crete and became temporarily shore-based while the *Illustrious* was taken in hand for large repairs.

The squadron at Maleme consisted of Swordfish, under the command of Lieut.-Commander J. de F. Jago, and it was later reinforced by a squadron of fighters, consisting of Fulmars and Buffaloes, led by Lieut.-Commander A. Black. During the Italian attack on Greece, the Swordfish squadron moved to

Eleusis, near Athens, and from there carried out a number of attacks on the Italian convoy routes from Brindisi to Durazzo and Valona. For five weeks they dominated this area of sea, sinking many ships and laying minefields, until finally they were forced back to Maleme by the German advance through Jugoslavia into Greece.

The story of the Fleet Air Arm's defence of Crete is a tale of heroism against tremendous odds. The two squadrons, one of torpedo-carrying Swordfish, the other of mixed Fulmar, Gladiator, and Buffalo fighters, were faced with a task that was impossible from the outset. They were clearly unable to provide fighter cover for the fleet, which was, for the purpose of these operations, divided into five separate forces each operating in different parts of the sea surrounding Crete. To them, therefore, fell the task of attempting to defend Crete itself from the attacks made on the island from the air. It was hoped that the naval forces, even operating without air cover, would be able to beat off any attack from seaward.

Maleme airfield was the first area to be attacked, raids beginning to come in during the first week in May. After a few days it was obvious that the Swordfish were going to be of little value in this type of warfare. Already they were receiving losses, from attacks in the air, from bombs on the runways, from damage received through frequent forced landings. They were finally withdrawn to Alexandria, while three more of the antique Gladiators were flown in from there to Maleme as a reinforcement for the hard-pressed naval fighters still left in Crete.

The Gladiators were, unhappily, soon eliminated. Three of them ran into a force of twenty-five Junkers 88s and, though the pilots fought like tigers, all of them were shot down into the sea. The remainder, together with the last of the Fulmars, were finally destroyed on the ground during a bombing raid after an almost ceaseless battle against tremendous odds in the air. The Buffaloes, one by one, had already disappeared in combat, until all that remained were three Hurricanes, taken over from the Royal Air Force and flown by naval pilots. These three, on May 6th, engaged a mixed force of fifteen Messerschmitts and thirty Junkers. Two of them were shot down, two of the enemy were destroyed, and the third Hurricane survived to land at Maleme. It was piloted by Lieutenant A. R. Ramsay, and was the only machine left on the island when the enemy launched his invasion from the air.

Maleme airfield, still under naval command, was one of the first targets of the Germans as they came in from the air on May 20th. One of the naval officers who was present has described the scene.

> Shortly before dawn on 20th May all the troops stood-to. The sun rose, and everyone was dispersed to wash and breakfast. Then, while the troops were scattered and in different stages of undress, the air raid warning sounded and they took cover in the nearest shelters. Almost immediately wave after wave of enemy fighters and bombers streaked round the airfield, shooting up the camp and paying particular attention to the defence positions all round. The actual landing ground was left alone.
>
> For two hours they continued to circle round at heights from 100 to 150 feet, gunning and bombing, creating dust, smoke, and noise which was frightening in its intensity. Overhead were swarms of troop-carrying aircraft from whose interiors hundreds of parachutists were dropping. Some had already landed, and the air was full of reinforcements as an endless stream of aircraft came and went.

It was the end, so far as the Fleet Air Arm was concerned, though the remainder of the story is as full of courage and endurance as the beginning. It is, however, a story of ground fighting, of a long and courageous defence of the airfield, and of a final skilful withdrawal through the mountains to the evacuation beaches of Sphakia, in the south of the island. Led by their officers, the Fleet Air Arm personnel put up an almost incredibly gallant show in the hand-to-hand fighting, and played a worthy part alongside the Army in the tragic battle that followed the invasion.

Finally must be told the story of three Swordfish, operating temporarily from a Royal Air Force airfield at Sidi Barrani. The aircraft came from H.M.S. *Eagle*, lying at the time in Alexandria Harbour, and had been borrowed temporarily by the Air Officer Commanding, Western Desert, for the purpose of dealing with enemy shipping off the coast of Africa.

The Swordfish flew first to Ma'aten Bagush, and from there carried out many coastal patrols, though without finding any target worthy of attack. But a few days later information came through to the operations room that the evening patrol of

Blenheims had reported a submarine depot ship lying in Bomba Bay, just opposite El Gazala, with an Italian U-boat approaching from seaward. The three Swordfish were, therefore, flown to Sidi Barrani, to await the result of the dawn patrol. If the ship were still there, it would prove a very worth-while target.

The early morning reconnaissance brought news that the ship was still at anchor, and at 10.30 a.m., on August 22nd, 1940, the Swordfish took off, with Captain Oliver Patch, Royal Marines, leading them. The other two were piloted by Lieutenant J. W. G. Wellham and Lieutenant H. A. F. Cheesman. Patch led his flight some 50 miles out to sea in order to prevent observation by Italian fighters or shore stations and then turned westward, flying parallel to the coast. As they came opposite Bomba Bay they turned to port and approached the coastline.

The navigation was in the hands of Patch's observer, Midshipman C. J. Woodley, and it was so accurate that, as the Swordfish closed the land, the depot ship was sighted dead ahead. There were other vessels alongside her, but at that distance it was impossible to distinguish what they were. More important, however, was an Italian U-boat, steaming slowly on the surface some 4 miles off shore and obviously making for the depot ship. So sure were the crew of safety in these Italian-dominated waters, that they had brought up their laundry and hung it on the jumping wire to dry in the morning sunshine.

Telling the other two Swordfish to make for the depot ship, Patch decided to deal with the U-boat himself. He swung away to starboard to open the range and then, coming down almost to sea level, made straight for the U-boat, which opened fire with its close-range weapons. He dropped his torpedo at a range of 300 yards and a few seconds later the U-boat disappeared in a tremendous explosion.

The two remaining Swordfish swept on into the bay, to discover that the two vessels alongside the depot ship were a destroyer and another U-boat. With the plan of attack mapped out between them, the two pilots separated, Wellham to attack from the east and Cheesman from the west. With Wellham as his observer was Petty Officer A. H. Marsh, and they let go their torpedo on the starboard beam of the depot ship. As Cheesman was attacking from the west his observer, Sub-Lieutenant F. Stovin-Bradford, noticed that the water was too shallow for the torpedo to run. In order to prevent wasting it in the sand, Cheesman flew his Swordfish to within 350 yards of the three ships before dropping it. It ran straight and hit the U-boat, which was lying on the outside. At almost the same instant Wellham's torpedo hit the depot ship. The simultaneous explosions did severe damage to the U-boat and set fire to the depot ship. For a few minutes she blazed fiercely and then blew up as the fire reached her magazines. By that time the destroyer was also on fire and, a few seconds later, she too disappeared under a vast cloud of smoke and steam.

The attack [wrote the Commander-in-Chief in his official report], which achieved the phenomenal result of the destruction of four enemy ships with three torpedoes, was brilliantly conceived and most gallantly executed. The dash, initiative, and co-operation displayed by the sub-flight concerned are typical of the spirit which animates the Fleet Air Arm squadrons of H.M.S. *Eagle* under the inspiring leadership of her Commanding Officer.

Although a subsequent reconnaissance, on which Sir Andrew Cunningham based his report, indicated that the four ships had been sunk, only one in fact had been completely destroyed, the Italian submarine *Iride*. But the other three ships had been so severely damaged that it was many months before they were back in service.

The Convoy Battles

COMMAND OF THE SEA, WHICH HAS ALWAYS BEEN, AND always will be, a prerequisite of final victory, involves widespread duties. Not only does it mean the denial of the sea lanes to enemy warships and merchant vessels, but also the safe carriage of troops, supplies, guns, ammunition, aircraft, fuel, and all the great host of requirements issued to sustain our own forces in the field. Until the flying machine emerged as a potent force of war, the task was a relatively easy one, for the battle was in two dimensions only on the surface of the sea. But when the aircraft reached maturity, command of the sea entailed command of the air above it as well, for ships are as vulnerable to attack from the air as they are to attack from the sea. So it was that one of the greatest burdens which fell upon the Fleet Air Arm was that of gaining a temporary command of the air above the actual operations of sea power.

From mid-1940 until the end of 1942, two of the greater tasks of the Navy were the sustenance of the island of Malta and the supply of weapons of war to our eastern ally, Russia. To both of them the only passage in the early days was by sea, though later in the war an alternative land route to Russia was opened through Persia. But even with that additional road, the needs of Russia's immense armies were still so tremendous that the sea route round the North Cape of Norway had to be maintained in addition and used to its fullest capacity.

The epic story of the defence of Malta has been told many times, but the Navy's share is, perhaps, not so well known. Beset by overwhelming air strength but an hour's flying distance away, every article of defence needed by the gallant garrison had to be brought by sea. An underwater supply service by submarine was run to the beleaguered island, but this could carry only a fraction of the total supplies needed. The vast bulk of the remainder had to be borne across the surface of the

Mediterranean, running the gauntlet of every form of enemy action designed to stop it. The convoys to Malta developed into great naval operations of war, supported by fleets and protected in the air by many squadrons of Fleet Air Arm fighters.

It would be beyond the scope of this book to try to tell the story of all these operations, though each in itself is a fine saga of gallantry and determination. Broadly speaking, the overall pattern was the same. The ships of the convoy, tankers, ammunition carriers, cargo vessels, and usually one of the older carriers loaded with Royal Air Force fighters and their pilots destined for Malta, would gather at a British port, sailing secretly out into the Atlantic, and then southward, wide of the Bay of Biscay and the coast of Spain. The passage of the Straits of Gibraltar would be made at night in order to avoid if possible the chance of being sighted by enemy agents and reported to the German and Italian high commands. So the convoy, with its close escort of cruisers and destroyers, would enter the Mediterranean, on its last and most dangerous leg of the journey.

In the meantime, the fleets in the Mediterranean would be taking up their stations as a more distant cover for the vital convoy. From Gibraltar would sail Force H, later to become known as Force F, strengthened for the purpose with additional modern carriers. They would provide cover to the northward, placing themselves between the convoy and the enemy's naval and air bases. The overall plan might well contain diversionary raids on enemy bases in order to preoccupy his forces and detract attention from the passage of the convoy. Additional distant cover was normally provided by the Mediterranean Fleet from Alexandria, standing by to the eastward to engage should the main Italian Fleet come out, while from Malta would sail the local forces to sweep a passage through the minefields which the enemy invariably laid outside the Grand Harbour.

It was this general pattern that covered the passage of a convoy during the summer of 1942, which was given the code-word "Pedestal". Operation "Pedestal", indeed, provided the opportunity of carrying out three subsidiary operations all connected with the main task : an aircraft carrier co-operation exercise before entering the Mediterranean, a reinforcement of the Malta air defence by Spitfires carried in the *Furious* and flown off at sea, and the return from Malta to Gibraltar of a small convoy of empty ships.

The main convoy sailed from the Clyde on the night of August 2nd, and consisted of fourteen ships, of which one was a tanker. They and their immediate escort passed through the Straits of Gibraltar on the night of August 9th, and by daylight of the 10th were out of sight of the Spanish coast. Yet, in spite of the darkness, the passage of the convoy had been seen and reported, and ahead the enemy forces were gathering.

While the main convoy was steaming down from the Clyde, the heavy ships which were to cover them were also gathering. On July 31st, Rear-Admiral A. L. St. G. Lyster (Rear-Admiral Aircraft Carriers, Home Fleet) sailed from Scapa flying his flag in H.M.S. *Victorious* with the older carrier *Argus* in company. They steamed down to rendezvous with the *Eagle*, from Gibraltar, and the *Indomitable*, from Freetown, both of whom were to be added to the covering force inside the Mediterranean. On meeting they carried out their co-operation exercises, so that when they, too, less H.M.S. *Argus*, passed into the Mediterranean they were fully prepared with a plan of action worked out for dealing with the enemy raiders when they should appear.

With the carrier force were two battleships, the *Nelson* and *Rodney*, six cruisers, thirty-two destroyers, and four corvettes. Such was the importance of the supplies to Malta that this tremendous force had to be gathered to fight the convoy through. Much was to depend on the fighter squadrons embarked in the carriers.

This particular convoy was probably the most fiercely contested of any that sailed to the help of Malta. It is a particular maxim of sea power that where the prize is great, great risks may be taken. In this case the prize was the continued retention of Malta, with its great strategic threat to the supply lines to the Axis forces in North Africa. Although this particular operation cost the loss of many ships, both naval and merchant, the proportion of the convoy that got through with its supplies more than offset the cost.

Embarked on board the three carriers were some seventy fighters, with further replacements on board the *Argus*, which remained behind at Gibraltar. The fighters carried were Sea Hurricanes, Fulmars, and Martlets. In the *Furious* were Spitfires,

(*Crown Copyright*)

A Wyvern naval interceptor during her take-off run down the flight deck.

A view from the air of a modern light fleet carrier.

(*Crown Copyright*)

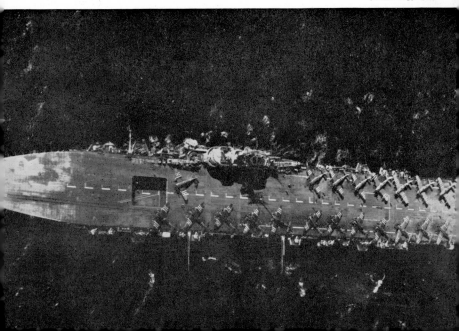

(*Crown Copyright*)

With flaps down and arrester hook trailing.   An Attacker coming in to land on.

A Vickers Supermarine 510 (Swift) during deck-landing trials in H.M.S. *Illustrious*
The 510 is virtually a swept-wing version of the Attacker.   The two tubes under th
wings are for rocket-assisted take-off.

(*Crown Copyright*)

but these were Royal Air Force machines, destined for Malta, and not part of the air defence of the fleet.

The first day was a quiet one, for the waters near Gibraltar were too far removed from the enemy's sea and air bases for any threat to develop. The only danger to be expected was from U-boats, which of course could operate anywhere. Anti-submarine patrols were flown ahead of the escorting forces and the convoy, while the close escort of destroyers swept the waters with their Asdics.

August 11th, the second day out into the Mediterranean, saw the first blows struck. The close air patrol sighted an Italian Savoia reconnaissance machine during the morning and fighters from the *Indomitable* drove it off, but it had seen enough to report back by wireless the position and course of the convoy. As the morning drew out, other shadowing machines made their appearance. Their presence made it clear that the convoy was not to go through without a fight.

That afternoon, a tremendous explosion shook the *Eagle*. A few moments later she lay beneath a great cloud of smoke as a fire raged on board. A torpedo from a U-boat had hit her and, within ten minutes, she rolled over and sank, taking with her many of her aircraft. Those that were already in the air landed on the *Victorious* and the *Indomitable*. Almost the entire complement of the *Eagle* was saved, 67 officers and 862 ratings being taken off.

Later that afternoon the *Victorious* also was nearly hit, a torpedo passing close ahead of her bow. Intensive air patrols and the anti-submarine measures of the destroyers kept most of the U-boats submerged and so unable to approach close enough to attack, though six of them were sighted during the afternoon.

During the evening one of the objects of the convoy operations was achieved. The distance to Malta was by then within the range of the Spitfires carried in the *Furious* and they were flown off to make their own way to Malta in order to reinforce the fighter defence of the Island. As soon as they were clear, the *Furious* was detached to return to Gibraltar, her part of the operation being concluded.

That evening saw the first of the large-scale air attacks on the convoy, between thirty and forty German Junkers carrying out a high-level attack. They were met by a squadron of Hurricanes from the *Indomitable* which was carrying out a combat air patrol, and by a squadron of Fulmars flown off from the *Victorious* on the first report of the enemy. Some of the bombers got through, to be met by the anti-aircraft fire of the carriers and their escort, and two at least were shot down. So accurate was the fire that the Junkers were unable to make accurate bombing runs and no ships were hit, although H.M.S. *Victorious* was shaken by two near misses. The merchant ships in convoy came through unscathed, the carriers and the close escort taking the brunt of the attack.

On the 12th the convoy began to move into really dangerous waters. Italian airfields in Sicily and Sardinia were now within fighter range, and the enemy bombing planes could count on a fighter escort, to make the task of defence even greater. In range, too, were light craft of the Italian Navy, motor-torpedo boats and motor-gunboats, and were they to reach the merchant ships they could do immense damage. It was up to the air cover of the convoy to keep a close watch and to report their presence in time for the destroyer screen to intercept.

Throughout that day the enemy sent over wave after wave of attackers, high- and low-level bombers, Cant torpedo-carriers, and Italian Reggiane fighters. Hour after hour the air was filled with the roar of aircraft engines as Fleet Air Arm fighters, Hurricanes, Fulmars, and Martlets, broke up the formations and harried the attackers, shooting many of them down into the sea.

The day's fighting cost the enemy over forty aircraft destroyed for the loss of eight Fleet Air Arm fighters. And in only one instance did an enemy formation get through, a group of some twenty dive-bombers which took the *Indomitable* as their target. Although they failed to hit her, a very near miss buckled her forward lift and made her unable to operate her aircraft. Those of her squadrons in the air at the time had to land on the *Victorious*.

With the coming of night the attacks ceased, and the convoy was able to continue its passage unmolested from the air. It was approaching Malta now, and by daylight would be within range of the R.A.F. Beaufighters from the island. As the dawn of August 13th broke, contact was made with the British shore-based fighters and the Fleet Arm Arm turned over to the Royal Air Force the duties of providing air cover. It was unsafe to take the carriers farther to the east. Their task was over now. They handed the convoy over to the Beaufighters and altered course to the westward, leaving the battle behind them.

In his despatch on the operation Vice-Admiral Syfret, commanding Force F, paid a glowing tribute to the magnificent work carried out by the Fleet Air Arm. "Flying at great heights," he wrote, "constantly chasing the faster Junkers 88s, warning the fleet of approaching formations, breaking up the latter, and in the latter stages doing their work in the face of superior enemy fighter forces—they were grand!"

Such an action as that of August 12th called for an all-out effort, not only from the pilots of the fighters involved, but also from the flight-deck parties and the maintenance ratings in the hangars. It was estimated that the flight-deck party in the *Victorious*, in addition to their normal work of placing the chocks, folding wings, releasing arrester hooks, and so on, ran over 20 miles up and down the flight deck, ranging aircraft and striking them down. In the hangars below the maintenance crews worked ceaselessly in the glare of electric lights at the height of a Mediterranean summer, and in an atmosphere of petrol and oil fumes. Without that work, carried on without a break throughout the day, the fighters could never have got up into the air.

Yet, with all this great escort and the grim fighting that accompanied the passage to Malta, the convoy did not get through unscathed. Of the fourteen ships that passed through the Straits of Gibraltar, but five reached Malta, and most of those bore scars of the long action. The price was high, but the need was vital, and the supplies carried by those five ships were enough to keep Malta going for a time. Of the three operational carriers involved, the *Eagle* had been sunk and the *Indomitable* damaged, though she made her own way safely back to Gibraltar.

The passage of this convoy is an example of what can happen when the command of the air in the theatre of operations is disputed. Valiantly as the carrier-borne, and later the shore-based, fighters strove to drive off the enemy, enough of them got through to cause heavy losses, not only to the merchant ships but also to many of the escorts as well. Without the Fleet Air Arm fighters, no ships at all could have got through, and the small percentage that did succeed is probably in close relation to the degree in which the fighters managed to win a temporary command in the air, a command that was never more than spasmodic. Later in the war, as more and more strength at sea was brought to bear on the German and Italian forces, and as shore fighter stations were established along the north coast of Africa, a permanent command of the air along the Mediterranean routes was achieved, and the convoys to Malta could run through unscathed.

A similar problem was that of ensuring supplies to Russia. There the enemy had bases in northern Norway from which they could operate aircraft, U-boats, and surface forces. In this area, too, it was a question of winning the command of the air before the convoys could pass in safety. In many respects, the general pattern was similar to that in the Mediterranean, though the situation in the northern waters was complicated by the resolute action of the German U-boats, which were far more potent a menace than were the Italian U-boats in the Mediterranean. One other point of difference was that, while a fleet carrier was normally included in the covering force of heavy ships, an additional escort carrier accompanied the later convoys as part of the close escort. One reason for this was that the covering force could not remain with the convoy once it had passed the longitude of Bear Island, almost directly north of Tromsö, without running a disproportionate risk. A second reason was that it had to operate in waters a long way south of the convoy route, so as to be within air striking range of the German capital ships should they leave their Norwegian bases.

Let us, once again, take the case of one of these convoys and see the part played in its passage by the Fleet Air Arm. The convoy was known as P.Q.18. It sailed from Loch Ewe on September 2nd, 1942, and arrived off Iceland on the 7th. On the following day it was joined by its ocean escort for the passage to Russia, which included the escort carrier *Avenger*, carrying twelve Sea Hurricanes and three Swordfish.

Cloudy weather prevented the enemy from making his usual small-scale air attacks while the convoy was still well to the westward, a fact which prevented the fighter pilots in the *Avenger* from getting in a little practice against slight opposition. As it turned out, this was to prove a considerable drawback, for when the first attack developed from the air on September 12th, the Hurricanes expended their energy on the shadowers and allowed the attacking torpedo bombers to slip through. Some forty or fifty Heinkel IIIs, each carrying two torpedoes and flying very low, got among the merchant ships and sank eight of them. Only one Heinkel was shot down.

On the next day it was a very different story. The commanding officer of the *Avenger* decided to change his tactics and only kept two Hurricanes in the air on patrol, each returning at short intervals to refuel so that, when the enemy came, those in the air should still have enough petrol to engage in combat. The main force of fighters was kept on board the carrier, ready to fly off only when the big-scale attacks came in. The two in the air were enough to deal with shadowers and to discourage the smaller attacking forces.

Two heavy attacks came in on the 13th, one of twenty-two and the other of twenty-five Heinkels. In addition, there were two high-level bombing attacks. In each case the fighters got among the formations as they came in, breaking them up and preventing them from making calculated attacks. As a result only one ship was sunk. On the 14th, seventy bombers made a prolonged attack on the convoy and again the Hurricanes got among them. No ship in the convoy was sunk, though the attack lasted for over three hours.

During these two days, over forty German aircraft were shot down, some by the fighters, some by the close-range weapons of the escort. Four Hurricanes were lost, though three of the pilots were safely recovered.

It was this convoy which proved the turning-point in the North Russian operations. The one that had preceded it, P.Q.17, had been cut to pieces and had suffered immensely heavy losses. The inclusion of an escort carrier in the close screen had, after the first day, proved a satisfactory answer to the German torpedo aircraft, and the fighters carried by her had been sufficient to attain a reasonably decisive state of command of the air above the immediate convoy route. The U-boat packs, which had made contact with the convoy on September 10th and had shadowed it throughout, were unable to score anything but a very mediocre success. They sank but three ships, and at a cost to themselves of three of their number.

They were satisfactorily kept down during daylight hours by the anti-submarine patrols flown by the three Swordfish carried in the *Avenger*. Several U-boats were attacked with depth charges, and in one case at least the Swordfish led an escorting destroyer on to a U-boat, which was attacked and sunk by her. This was U.88, sunk by H.M.S. *Onslow*, after the Swordfish had made the sighting and brought the *Onslow* to the spot.

The passage of these convoys called on occasions for operations which, although connected with their safety, did not involve the close cover given to the ships described in the operation above. Such an operation was that carried out during April, 1944, when another convoy to Russia was running. Included in this convoy was the battleship *Royal Sovereign*, which was being lent to Russia in place of one of the Italian battleships which fell to her share after the surrender of the Italian Fleet. It was known that the German battleship *Tirpitz*, lying in Kaafiord, right up in the northern tip of Norway, had succeeded in repairing the damage she had sustained in the attack by British midget submarines in September, 1943, and was once again operational. In order to safeguard the *Royal Sovereign*, it was proposed to make the *Tirpitz* immovable once again, if only for the few days during which the *Royal Sovereign* would be off northern Norway during the passage of the convoy.

Kaafiord was well beyond the range of shore-based bombers, and it was only from the air that the *Tirpitz* could be reached. So it fell to the Fleet Air Arm to mount the attack which, it was hoped, would immobilize the great battleship for a time. It was too much to hope that she could be sunk by the relatively small bombs carried by carrier-borne bombers.

So, as the time for the convoy drew near, the carriers gathered for the strike. There were six of them in all, the *Victorious*, *Furious*, *Emperor*, *Fencer*, *Pursuer*, and *Searcher*, under the command of Admiral Sir Michael Denny, and they carried forty-two Barracuda bombers and eighty Corsair fighters.

Kaafiord was not an easy place to attack from the air ; indeed it had been selected by the Germans as an ideal anchorage for the *Tirpitz* largely because the high, steep sides of the fiord made it quite impossible for a torpedo-carrying plane to fly low enough for an attack. But in another way Kaafiord was rather less of an asset. The high mountains surrounding it would cut off the noise of an approaching plane and so assist an attacker in reaching the area unheard. It gave a chance of achieving a surprise attack.

The carriers reached their flying-off position before dawn on April 3rd, and the planes were in the air while it was still dark, although to the south, above the Norwegian mountains, the sky was lightening. The weather was calm and settled, giving the promise of a fine, sunny day later. Forty-two Barracudas were flown off in two groups of twenty-one each, and the whole force of eighty fighters took the air to give them cover. A continuous patrol was also flown above the carrier force to guard against attacks from U-boats or from the air.

Inside Kaafiord the *Tirpitz* was getting ready to run steaming trials in Altenfiord. The gate in the anti-submarine net defences was being opened to let her pass through. It was the first time she had been able to move under her own power since she had been damaged by the midgets and on board there was a feeling of pleasure, almost of excitement, that she was at last a whole ship again. The long winter days of immobility were over.

Everything in Kaafiord was quiet. The sun was shining out of a cloudless blue sky, there was no more than a light breeze to raise a tiny ripple on the water. The war seemed a very long way away on that lovely spring morning.

Quite suddenly, over the top of the high hills, an aircraft flew. The silence of the fiord was shattered as it screamed down in a dive. Others followed it, coming in at top speed from different directions, yet all converging on the unhappy ship. To the roar of their engines was added the shattering explosions of their bombs and the fire of the ship's anti-aircraft guns as the crews leapt to action stations. But the guns were manned too late and the damage had been done before anyone on board had realized what was happening. One minute later the Barracudas had gone and the noise died away, only for it to leap up again into an ear-splitting roar as the second striking force of twenty-one aircraft came in. The pilots found the fiord full of smoke and had to drop their bombs blind. That attack, too, was over within a minute and Kaafiord returned to its accustomed quiet, as the Barracudas and their escorting fighters winged their way back to the carriers.

The *Tirpitz* was not to carry out her steaming trials that day,

or for many a day to come.   She had received fifteen direct hits,
apart from additional damage from several near misses.   The
bombs had been 500- and 1,000-pounders and although none
had penetrated the armoured lower deck, they had done great
execution between decks, and had started a fire amidships.
Some of the bulkheads were shattered, steam pipes had been cut
or fractured, a large area of the upper deck had been ripped
open.   Some 300 of the ship's complement had been killed, and
many others wounded.

The success of this raid, and the ease with which the *Tirpitz*
had once more been immobilized, were responsible for further
strikes against her.   On July 17th the Fleet Air Arm was
back again off northern Norway with the carriers *Formidable*,
Indefatigable, and *Furious*.   They flew off forty-five Barracudas,
escorted by fifty Corsairs, but after her experience on April 3rd
the *Tirpitz* was taking no more risks.   A system of look-outs
had been established on the hilltops and a radar station erected
to give warning of the approach of aircraft.   When the Barracudas arrived on July 17th, they found Kaafiord full of artificial
smoke and the *Tirpitz* invisible beneath it.   Although they aimed
at the point from which the anti-aircraft fire was emerging, they
made no hits and the ship only received superficial damage from
splinters and near misses.

One month later the carriers tried again.   The same three, the
Formidable, *Indefatigable*, and *Furious*, were once more employed,
this time with the escort carriers *Nabob* and *Trumpeter*.   It was
decided that, in an effort to defeat the smoke, the *Tirpitz* was
to be attacked continuously in the hope that before the end, the
smoke pots would be exhausted and the anti-aircraft crews tired
out.

The attacks began on August 22nd.   On the following day
the Barracudas were surprised when they ran into a barrage some
15 miles from the fiord.   It was the *Tirpitz* firing her main
armament which was being controlled from an observation
point on a mountain top.   So on the 24th the striking force
took a wide sweep on the way in and delivered their attack
from the south.   And this time they hit the ship again, a 1,000-
pound bomb bouncing off the bridge, penetrating the upper
deck, and coming to rest on the lower armoured deck behind
the main switchboard.   But the bomb failed to explode and

was rendered harmless by the quick action of two petty officers who dismantled it.

The attack on August 25th was once again frustrated by the smoke-screen, and after the aircraft had landed on, the carriers left the scene of action. That morning the *Nabob* had been hit by a torpedo from a U-boat and it was certain that other U-boats would be called in if the carriers remained off the coast.

Convoys to Russia continued throughout the war, but with the Fleet Air Arm providing continuous air cover from escort carriers their losses were slight. The initial success of the *Avenger* in the close escort had provided the answer to attack by German aircraft, and the heavy ships were no threat after the *Scharnhorst* had been sunk and the *Tirpitz* damaged. There remained the danger of the U-boats, but these could very largely be kept quiet by a combination of the escorting destroyers and carrier-borne aircraft. Indeed, it turned out to be the Fleet Air Arm contributions to the escort that proved to be the key to success, for the aircraft carried could combine the dual role of fighter and anti-submarine patrol. Sea Hurricanes, Corsairs, and Seafires, the naval version of the Spitfire, provided the fighter element, while Swordfish, Albacores, and Barracudas, combining with the anti-submarine surface escort, were enough to keep the U-boats at bay. As in the case of the Mediterranean convoys, it was demonstrated that command of the sea was not enough, and that it had to be combined with command of the air above before the supplies could pass in reasonable security.

It has been shown in an earlier chapter how it was the part played by the air that proved to be the deciding factor in the war against U-boats in the Atlantic. This was the same lesson, but given a more urgent twist since the convoys in question were subject to massed attack from the air as well as from under the waves. But in each case the result showed that naval aviation, as an addition to the flexibility and striking force of sea power, had a tremendous influence even on the less spectacular duties of the naval war.

Close Support of the Army

IT SAYS MUCH FOR THE VERSATILITY OF NAVAL AIRCRAFT that they proved themselves fitted for duties in almost every condition of warfare. We have already seen them in action with the fleet, timing their blows in a fast moving operation fought at 30 knots. We have seen them in night attack against a heavily defended naval port, striking home with supreme accuracy in the darkness and through a heavy curtain of anti-aircraft fire. We have seen them engaged in anti-submarine warfare, patrolling over a 7-knot convoy, keeping the U-boats under, and attacking them when they presented themselves as targets. The fighters of the fleet have been seen in operation against bombers and torpedo aircraft at sea, against reconnaissance machines, and fighting with the Royal Air Force in the Battle of Britain and in the desert campaign in North Africa. Let us now look at them in yet other roles, in support of combined operations with the Army, or acting alone in raids on enemy installations.

Isolated attacks on enemy-held coastal points have long been recognized as a sound strategic operation in a continental war. The elder Pitt was a master of such moves during the Seven Years War, and though the raids he planned and executed had no military value of any permanence, they served to spread the defence and to tie up enemy forces. So it was in the Second World War, when once again raids on the enemy coast served the same purpose. Sometimes they were amphibious, or Commando raids, when the Navy carried the Army to the scene of operations, supported them ashore by gunfire or carrier-borne fighter cover, and then re-embarked them for the return home. Sometimes they were purely air strikes, launched from carriers some 80 or 100 miles to seaward of the point of attack. Sometimes the military value was considerable, resulting in the destruction of vital factories, of stocks of oil fuel, or of important installations, sometimes it was the political value that counted the most, the reason for the attack being the need to hearten the resistance movement in countries overrun by the enemy. But whatever the motive, it was to the Fleet Air Arm that the forces engaged looked for their air support, since most of the objectives were out of range of fighter bases ashore in Britain, and only the carrier could bring air cover to the required destination and operate it when the time came.

There were many of these raids up and down the coasts of enemy-held Europe, some of them large, many of them small. They served their purpose well on the whole, keeping the enemy on the jump and encouraging the men and women ashore in their defiance of the occupation troops. Some of them were made only at the expense of considerable loss in aircraft and aircrews for very little material gain. Such a raid was that carried out by squadrons from H.M.S. *Victorious* and H.M.S. *Furious* on Kirkenes and Petsamo, up on North Cape, at the end of July, 1941. The primary objective here was to keep vigorous the morale of our allies in that area, the secondary objective being to attack any German shipping that might be found in the two harbours and to damage oil tanks and other harbour installations.

Each carrier flew off three squadrons, two each of Albacores, one of Fulmars, and one of Hurricanes. As the aircraft were taking off, the forces were unfortunately sighted by a German reconnaissance machine and the aircrews knew, as they flew in towards the shore, that they were going to meet fierce opposition. The essential element of surprise had been lost, the visibility was excellent, and enemy fighter stations were within easy reach of the two targets. Yet the political advantages of the raids were held to justify the risks that were inevitably run.

It says a great deal for the pilots and aircrews that, in the face of that knowledge, they all pressed home their attacks to the very minimum range. It was, perhaps, an additional hardship that when they did reach the target area, there should be practically no shipping worth attacking in either port. In the event, three aircraft were lost from H.M.S. *Furious* and thirteen from H.M.S. *Victorious*, a heavy price to pay for so little tangible result. But in its way it was a little epic of gallantry and one that can be remembered as an example of the high morale and superb discipline that animated the Fleet Air Arm. In his despatch to the Admiralty on this attack the Commander-in-Chief, Sir

John Tovey, wrote : " The gallantry of the aircraft crews, who knew before leaving that their chance of surprise had gone and that they were certain to face heavy odds, is beyond praise. . . . I trust that the encouragement to the morale of our Allies was proportionately great."

Effective as many of these isolated raids were, it was usually when working in co-operation with troops ashore that the more material gains were made. During 1941 there were many subsidiary campaigns being waged in various corners of the world, and in these the Fleet Air Arm frequently provided the air cover and support that was needed for the men ashore. Typical campaigns of this nature were those fought for the reconquest of British, and the conquest of Italian, Somaliland, the pro-German outbreak in Iraq, and the campaign against Vichy France in Syria. While each one presented a different set of problems for the naval aircraft taking part, they all fell within a broad pattern which, when developed into a closer understanding and co-operation with the army, was to pave the way to more ambitious adventures.

It was the campaign for the conquest of Italian East Africa that paid the highest naval dividend, for the Italian forces in that part of the world included several naval units based at the port of Massawa. Aircraft from H.M.S. *Hermes* assisted the troops ashore in their advance against Kismayu by flying strikes against Italian strong points and by bombing the fortification of the town as the army approached. Aircraft from H.M.S. *Formidable* did the same in the case of Mogadishu and Massawa, taking in the process a heavy toll of Italian shipping in Massawa, which included serious damage to three destroyers and one submarine. But it was H.M.S. *Eagle*'s machines which were able to claim the largest share of the damage caused to Italian naval units. Although the carrier was lying in Alexandria harbour, seventeen of her Swordfish were detached and flew down to Port Sudan to assist in the East African campaign. Led by Commander C. L. Keighley-Peach, the Swordfish patrolled the waters north of Massawa and were rewarded, on the morning of April 3rd, by the discovery of five Italian destroyers attempting to escape from their base. Only eight machines were on patrol at the time, the remainder being at Port Sudan, bombed up and in a state of instant readiness.

Two Swordfish made the first sighting. In his report of the action Keighley-Peach describes how his attention was drawn to the ships by seeing his accompanying machine diving down towards the sea. " On following him down through the clouds, I saw a lovely fat Italian destroyer right beneath me and a second later another just zigging away ahead of her," he wrote. He attacked but his bombs missed just astern. Leaving the other Swordfish to shadow the ships, he flew back to Port Sudan and brought back the remainder of his squadron. As each Swordfish dropped its bombs it returned to Port Sudan for a second load and came back at top speed to continue the attack. A Swordfish piloted by Midshipman E. Sergeant scored six hits on the *Nazario Sauro* with a stick of six bombs, and she sank in half a minute. Another, with Sub-Lieutenant S. H. Suthers as pilot, scored two hits amidships on the *Daniele Manin*, causing her to abandon ship and, later, to sink. Two more destroyers, the *Pantera* and *Tigre*, were driven ashore, where they were finally destroyed by gunfire from H.M.S. *Kingston*. The fifth, the *Cesare Battisti*, turned back to Massawa and succeeded in reaching the harbour, only to scuttle herself to avoid capture when the town finally surrendered to British troops.

It was these comparatively small local operations, in which the Fleet Air Arm showed that it was fully capable of carrying out close support of troops ashore, that led to the first of the major operations calling for a yet higher degree of co-operation between ship-borne squadrons and assaulting troops ashore. This was the capture of Madagascar from the French, the operations beginning on May 5th, 1942. The naval force was under the command of Rear-Admiral E. N. Sypret, flying his flag in the battleship *Ramillies*. He also had in his squadron two of the large fleet carriers, H.M.S. *Illustrious* (Captain A. G. Talbot) and H.M.S. *Indomitable* (Captain T. H. Troubridge). The two carriers and their aircraft were commanded by Rear-Admiral Denis Boyd, Flag Officer Commanding Carriers, Eastern Fleet.

The operations against Madagascar were made necessary by the threat to Allied shipping using the Mozambique Channel by Japanese submarines, and the detailed planning of the assault involved a very closely timed schedule of air support for the troops as they were landed on the assault beaches. It was the first time that the Fleet Air Arm had attempted such close support of troops, the plans calling for air patrols and attacks only a few hundred yards ahead of the men ashore. As it turned out, this close co-operation was perfectly achieved and the carrier-borne aircraft successfully carried out every task for which the army called. Great accuracy was necessary in order to prevent accidents and to protect the civilian population, but there were no untoward incidents and the whole initial operation, which resulted in the quick capture of the town and harbour of Diego Suarez, went like clockwork.

At dawn on the day of the landing, May 5th, a squadron of Albacores from H.M.S. *Indomitable* flew off to bomb the aerodrome. Runways on the airfield were pitted with bomb craters and the hangar was set on fire. Martlets from the same ship attacked the shore batteries and shot up French fighters as they attempted to take off. At the same time Swordfish from the *Illustrious* attacked the anchorage. They torpedoed the armed merchant cruiser *Bougainville* and sank the submarine *Bevezières* with depth charges. In a second attack the sloop *D'Entrecasteaux* was hit with bombs and driven ashore, to be finally destroyed in a follow-up bombing attack by three more Swordfish.

In the meantime the troops were going ashore in assault landing craft, covered by Martlets from the *Illustrious*. The aircraft patrolled the beaches as the men landed, attacking machine-gun posts, carrying out tactical reconnaissance for the landing parties, and keeping a watch for French fighters and bombers. A few of these made a brief appearance but all were quickly shot down before they could do any damage.

For three days the operations continued, Diego Suarez capitulating on May 8th. Throughout this period the aircraft from the two carriers maintained complete air superiority over the area, giving the assaulting troops every assistance in their power. Many of them ranged far afield to deal with enemy strong points and emplacements and one Swordfish, piloted by Sub-Lieutenant F. H. Alexander and operating off Antsirane, sank the submarine *Le Heros* with depth charges.

The capture of Diego Suarez was but the prelude to the occupation of the whole island, an operation which took another six months to complete. As it was obviously impracticable to tie up two carriers for so long a time, some of the Fleet Air Arm squadrons were based ashore on the island, where they co-operated with squadrons of the South African Air Force. Throughout the campaign they maintained the essential air superiority required by the various forces converging on the capital, Tananarive, and proved particularly valuable for long-range reconnaissance and for attack on the final French positions. It was a new role for the Fleet Air Arm, but one which demonstrated to the full its flexibility and versatility.

The experience of close support gained in Madagascar made possible the same role for the bigger operations of the landings in North Africa and the bridgehead battle of Salerno. At both these places, as in Madagascar, the scenes of the landings were beyond the range of Royal Air Force fighters, tied as they were to airfields ashore. It is true that a few Spitfires from Gibraltar were able to reach the westernmost beaches of the North African landings, but even those were almost at extreme flying range and the beaches farther to the east were far beyond their reach. As a result, almost the whole of the close support for the operation was provided by carrier-borne aircraft until the capture of airfields ashore made possible the bringing up of Spitfires and Hurricanes of the R.A.F. to take over.

In some aspects the North African landings differed from those carried out six months earlier in Madagascar. One of the most essential requirements was the capture of airfields intact and with as little damage as possible to them. Another was the unknown quantity of the opposition. In some areas it was expected that the French would allow the troops to come ashore unopposed, in others it was not known what would happen, especially as the invasion was an Anglo-American one and good relations existed between the United States and Vichy France. Nevertheless, even in the face of expected non-resistance in some places, no risks could be run and the Fleet Air Arm was required to organize as heavy a supporting programme as possible.

A large force of carriers was set aside for these crucial landings, and as the troops left the landing ships on the morning of November 8th, bombers and fighters of the fleet flew off to provide cover, carry out tactical reconnaissance, and smother the opposition by attacks from the air. At the same time Albacores from Force H, covering the two assault forces, were required to fly anti-submarine patrols to discourage torpedo attack on the fleet and the transports.

While these air operations were going on, a force of Martlet
fighters was sent to carry out an air patrol over Blida aerodrome
to prevent French fighters from taking off. Blida was some
30 miles from Algiers and a valuable prize if it could be captured
intact for the Royal Air Force. Only two fighters were seen
at Blida, and they were discouraged from moving by a few bursts
of machine-gun fire.

The first flight of Martlets over Blida was relieved by a second,
led by Lieutenant B. H. C. Nation, and it was to him that the
honour of capturing the field must go. After flying round for
a few minutes he noticed a group of French officers waving their
handkerchiefs and reported back to his carrier by wireless that
he thought the officers might be prepared to surrender the airfield.
He was given permission to land and, with the three other
Martlets giving him such support as they could by flying low
above him, he took his machine down and landed near the
hangars. As he climbed out of his Martlet the French officers
escorted him to the commandant of the air station, who greeted
him in friendly fashion. The commandant then tore a sheet
off his writing pad and wrote on it : "La base de Blida est
disponible pour l'atterissage des armées alliés"—"The base
at Blida is available for the landing of the Allied armies." He
handed this document to Nation, who retained it and remained
in conversation with the Frenchman on the ground until Commando troops arrived to take it over.

The big civil airfield of Algiers, Maison Blanche, was also
captured on the day of the landings, again without opposition.
But in this case it was the army who made the capture, being
protected in their task by Fleet Air Arm fighter cover above.

Opposition in the harbour of Algiers was fairly stiff, the
destroyers entering the port being held up by gunfire from the
naval forts that guarded the entrance, as well as from elements
of the French army ashore. They signalled to the carriers for
assistance and two flights of six Albacores each took off. They
bombed the forts on the Jetée du Nord and silenced the guns,
and then went on to carry out the same tasks on Fort du Perré,
which was holding up the Commandos. From there they flew
to Fort Matifou, where they were equally successful.

While these eastern landings were going on successfully round
Algiers, the western landings were making good progress at Oran,

(*Crown Copyright*)

H.M.S. *Eagle*, the Navy's largest carrier, meets a heavy sea in the Denmark Straits.

Deck scene in a modern carrier.   Attackers on the flight deck of H.M.S. *Eagle*.

(*Crown Copyright*)

(Crown Copyright)

A bow view of H.M.S. *Glory* lying at anchor.

H.M.S. *Eagle*, a modern large fleet carrier, at anchor.

(Crown Copyright

though there the military airfield of La Senia gave far more trouble than did that at Blida, near Algiers. Here the French defenders were far more aggressive and the attacking squadron of Albacores, led in by Lieutenant J. G. A. Mcl. Nares, was met by fighters and both heavy and light anti-aircraft fire. It was unfortunately necessary to bomb the hangars in order to prevent further fighters from taking off, and forty-seven aircraft were destroyed on the ground. After that the resistance was only spasmodic and the airfield fell to an American armoured column advancing from the coast. Nares lost his life during the attack when his Albacore was set on fire by a Dewoitine fighter. Although he could have escaped by parachute he remained in his machine and led the rest of his squadron on to the objective. He made his attack with his Albacore in flames, though he must have known that he was facing certain death.

With the vital airfields in Allied hands, the Royal Air Force was able to send in fighter squadrons to take over the close support duties with the advancing troops. The main task of the Fleet Air Arm had been completed and nothing remained but the normal duties at sea of fighter patrols above the congested shipping areas and routine anti-submarine patrols for the fleet and for the build-up convoys.

This North African landing was known as Operation " Torch ", and it was part of the overall plan that led to the final expulsion of German and Italian forces from the whole of North Africa. The course of the Mediterranean war after that was a steady advance towards the heart of the enemy resistance. We have already seen in an earlier chapter how Fleet Air Arm squadrons based in Malta and Tripoli took a savage toll of the supplies required by Rommel during the North African campaign, hastening his inevitable end, and it is a matter of history now how, after having driven the enemy from Africa, the assault was carried to Sicily and, later, Italy. The lessons learned during Operation " Torch " helped the Fleet Air Arm to repeat the assistance given to the Army in an even greater amphibious assault in this theatre of war nearly a year later. This was the landing in the Gulf of Salerno, known as Operation " Avalanche " and carried out in September, 1943.

There was some similarity between the two operations. The Salerno beaches were just within range of land-based squadrons in Sicily, but the distance was such that fighters operating from airfields there would be unable to remain in the fighting area for long. And as in North Africa, it was difficult to estimate the degree of resistance that would be met, for news of the Italian armistice was made public on the eve of the landings. It was obviously going to be a race between the assaulting forces getting ashore and the Germans taking over the shore-defences from their erstwhile allies. As it turned out, the race was won by the Germans and Salerno was defended by them with a ferocity and tenacity that called for every ounce of determination from the assaulting forces, but that was not discovered until the landing craft were actually on their way in.

Operation " Avalanche " was on so much larger and fiercer a scale than operation " Torch ", that the naval air support had to be organized as a two-stage affair. For work ashore with the Army an escort carrier group, consisting of the *Hunter*, *Stalker*, *Battler*, and *Attacker*, was provided under the command of Rear-Admiral Sir Philip Vian, and all the aircraft operated by these small carriers were at call for tasks required by the assaulting troops. A second force of fleet carriers, H.M. Ships *Illustrious* and *Formidable*, part of Force H, had the task of maintaining the air defence of the escort carriers while their own machines were operating over the beach-head. By this means the smaller carriers could concentrate on their one essential task, which was the support of the men ashore, without having to worry about their own safety.

The battle of Salerno was, as is well known, one of the stiffest that the Fifth Army had to fight. The prize was the port of Naples, essential to future operations in Italy as the only port on the west coast that could handle supplies in sufficient bulk to maintain the armies in the field. It was certain that, with so great a prize, the enemy would fight back hard, but in the original planning it had been hoped that he would have been taken unawares by the landing and that swift progress could be made to seize a large bridgehead before the defence could be fully mobilized. This hope had led to the expectation that Monte Corvino airfield would be captured on the day of the landing and that it would be possible to operate shore-based fighters from it on the following day. The initial task for the Fleet Air Arm was envisaged as air support for two days only, with Royal Air Force squadrons moving up from Sicily to take over.

As it turned out, Monte Corvino was not captured on the first day, and even when it was taken later it was under constant artillery fire from the neighbouring hills, and unable to be used by aircraft. Instead of two days, for which the carriers had been ammunitioned and stored, the escort carriers had to operate for four, a heavy strain both on aircrews and the ship handling-parties. And even then an airstrip had to be constructed ashore and two squadrons of naval planes landed for further support ashore while the carriers themselves returned to Palermo for replenishment.

Just as Operation "Torch" paved the way for "Avalanche", so did "Avalanche" for "Dragoon", the landings on the southern coast of France in August, 1944. Here again the beaches were beyond the range of shore-based fighters, making it necessary to use the Fleet Air Arm for fighter cover and support. But whereas Salerno was bitterly defended, the fighting on the southern coast of France was relatively light. All the first-line German troops had been moved north to deal with the Allied landings in Normandy, leaving low-grade divisions to hold the Mediterranean shore. Nevertheless, it was six days before the work of the naval aircraft was completed, and though their operations called for little air fighting, the ceaseless patrols were only carried through at the cost of a tremendous physical effort on the part of the ships' companies. That the casualties ashore in this operation were so light was due largely to the efficient support given by the naval squadrons flying from their carriers.

In all, five carriers took part in the British sector of the landings, with two other British carriers included in the American task force covering the U.S. landings. The carriers engaged in supporting the British landings were the *Emperor*, *Khedive*, *Searcher*, *Attacker*, and *Pursuer*, under the command of Rear-Admiral Thomas Troubridge. In the six days in which they were operating their aircraft flew nearly 1,000 sorties. Included in their work was the destruction of 20 tanks, 64 railway trucks, and 5 bridges, while 18 roads and 14 railways were cut, and 190 motor vehicles were damaged. In addition 7 small ships were sunk, including one motor-torpedo boat.

The progress of the war had brought many new tasks to the

Fleet Air Arm, tasks which had, perhaps, not been fully envisaged in the early days when naval aviation was still in the making. But the development of the carrier, and her ability to operate her aircraft under all conditions, had made possible the planning of long-range amphibious operations far beyond the range of the shore-based machine, a factor that gave the Allied powers a tremendous flexibility in their conduct of the war. It was a flexibility that kept the enemy always guessing about the next point of attack and so made possible the priceless element of surprise. Without the carrier and her aircraft, the task of the Army would have been wellnigh impossible in such operations as have been described above, and the course of the war would inevitably have been painfully pedestrian, each move forward having to await the establishment of airfields ashore to cover the advance. Amphibious operations such as those just described could only have been made at a tremendous cost in casualties, were it not for the floating aerodromes provided by the Fleet Air Arm, a cost that might well have proved disastrous.

War in the Pacific

As the war approached its end in Europe, the eyes of the Navy turned naturally, and more urgently, to the Pacific. Since the fall of Singapore in February, 1942, it had been possible only to keep a token force in those waters, since the main British naval effort had to be concentrated in the European theatre and in holding the flank of the Japanese attack in the Indian Ocean. One of the fleet carriers, H.M.S. *Victorious*, had for a time operated with the American Fleet in the Pacific, but it was not until the tide had fully turned in the Atlantic and the Mediterranean that it became possible to build up a self-contained British fleet in those waters.

Yet, during these years, the war against Japan had in no wise been neglected. Although the Pacific Ocean was, throughout, very largely an American commitment, the holding of the Japanese in the Indian Ocean fell to the Royal Navy. There a small fleet, operating under great handicaps and from distant bases, successfully prevented the penetration of a Japanese naval force into those vital waters. There, too, the Navy lost one of its older carriers when the *Hermes* was sunk by Japanese aircraft during April, 1942, while she was operating off Ceylon.

The Pacific Ocean presented something of a new problem to the Navy, when, in 1944, the time came to build up an effective fleet in those waters. The years of naval warfare since the Japanese attack on Pearl Harbour in December, 1941, had produced something of an enigma in the spectacle of purely naval actions fought at ranges of up to 250 miles, the weapons being aerial torpedoes and bombs, while the main targets were the carriers of either side. It was a facile solution of the problem to see in this new type of naval warfare the pattern of future battles at sea, relegating the battleship to the lowly status of an anti-aircraft gun platform for the defence of the vital carrier, and it required a good deal of penetrative thought to reduce the problem to its proper perspective.

Generally speaking, the vastness of the Pacific makes it a theatre of war where the aircraft must become the predominating weapon of a fleet. It is also an area of the globe where the weather presents more continuous opportunities for flying under good conditions than any other. It is, in addition, an ocean in which the actual scene of naval operations may be some thousands of miles from a fleet's main, or even subsidiary, base. All these conditions operate in favour of the carrier and her aircraft, so that the admiral in command comes to rely on the air strike as his main weapon. Certainly the experience gained by the Americans in their battles at sea led them to pin their faith to their carrier-borne aircraft in the naval war against the Japanese, the battleships rarely finding the chance of employment in their classic role.

Initial British experience in the conflict against Japan tended to support that view. The *Prince of Wales* and *Repulse* were both victims of enemy air attack off Malaya ; the *Hermes*, together with the 10,000-ton cruisers *Cornwall* and *Dorsetshire*, had fallen to the same medium of attack in the Indian Ocean. But what might at first sight have been attributed to the striking power of naval aircraft was, in fact, the result of lack of air cover, the penalty of attempting to operate in distant waters without making provision for the necessary command of the air above the sea which the ships required for their adequate protection. It was not difficult to appreciate this, and by the time the British Fleet had been built up in the Pacific it was a balanced force, with battleships and cruisers to support the carriers. Obviously, in view of the nature of the operations to be carried out, the carriers were the preponderating element, since the " island-hopping " method of advance towards the Japanese main islands called, in the main, for great air strength to neutralize the Japanese garrisons.

The British carriers operating in the Far East were at first attached to the East Indies Fleet, based mainly on Trincomalee, in Ceylon, where their main task was to harry the flank of the Japanese occupied islands stretching down towards Australia. Here there was an obvious crack in the Japanese armour, for it was largely on the oil and petroleum spirit obtained from the Borneo and Indonesian fields that the enemy's ships steamed and his aircraft flew. A strike at those refineries was not a difficult operation for a carrier-borne force and it was one which could most easily be mounted from the Indian Ocean.

The two main refineries, which produced at least half the oil required by the Japanese Navy and three-quarters of the aviation spirit needed by the Air Force, were those of Pangkalan Brandan and Palembang, both in Sumatra. The targets selected for attack were those at Palembang, where the two chief installations were at Pladjoe, the largest and most important refinery in the Far East, and at Songei Gerong.

The attack, which took place in two sorties in January, 1945, was carefully rehearsed and admirably planned. A preliminary taste of such operations was provided by two small-scale operations against oil installations in northern Sumatra during the previous month, and in exercises off Ceylon early in January the forming-up of a large contingent of aircraft from carriers had been practised. As the proposed strike entailed a force of forty-eight bombers and sixty fighters, together with a fighter sweep of a further twenty-four machines, all of them flying off from four carriers, the proper co-ordination in the air after take-off was a matter of considerable organization.

The main force, consisting of the battleship *King George V*, the carriers *Indomitable*, *Indefatigable*, *Illustrious*, and *Victorious*, together with its attendant cruisers and destroyers, sailed from Ceylon on January 16th. It was under the command of Rear-Admiral Sir Philip Vian, Flag Officer Commanding Aircraft Carriers, who was flying his flag in the *Indomitable*.

The first two attempts to mount the attacks were cancelled because of bad weather and unfavourable forecasts, but on the night of January 23rd–24th the fleet reached the flying-off position with every hope of a reasonable flying day. The visibility was good and the cloud was high. So, shortly after six o'clock that morning, the first range of aircraft took the air, the second range, which consisted of the fighter sweep and a squadron of Fireflies of the main striking force, flying off shortly afterwards. The whole force consisted of forty-eight Avengers, escorted by thirty-two Corsairs, sixteen Hellcats, and twelve Fireflies, who had an additional role of making rocket attacks on the refinery. The main force was bound for Pladjoe refinery, with a fighter sweep of twenty-four Corsairs to attack the Japanese airfields of Lembak, Palembang, and Talangbetoetoe, and a small subsidiary strike of four Avengers and four Hellcats to deal with the airfield at Mawa. The main striking force was under the control, for the approach and withdrawal, of Major R. C. Hay, Royal Marines, the squadron commanders being responsible for the actual attack of their individual units.

The first blow was struck by the fighter sweep, which reached the Lembak airfield undiscovered. They were able to put it out of action unmolested, but by the time they reached the other two fields, the warning had been given and they met a good deal of opposition from anti-aircraft fire. Nevertheless, on the three airfields visited by them, they put out of action thirty-four aircraft on the ground and damaged many others. Their success added much to the actual bombing strike by efficiently crippling the Japanese fighter defence, and so giving the Avengers and Fireflies a much clearer run-in to the target.

While the twenty-four Corsairs on the fighter sweep were doing their work, the bombers were crossing the coast and forming up for their attacks. A few enemy fighters which had been in the air during the attacks on the airfields attempted to intercept, but they were successfully driven off by the escorting Corsairs. The next " hurdle " to be overcome was a balloon barrage on the edge of the refinery, with balloons flying at various heights between 4,000 and 6,000 feet. Both Avengers and Fireflies ignored it, diving down through it in order to press home their attacks.

There was intense heavy and light anti-aircraft fire over the refinery, but fortunately it was inaccurate and did little to stop the bombers and the Fireflies. With their bombs and rockets they devastated the main buildings of the refinery, and photographs taken during the raid showed very extensive damage.

Five days later the same carriers carried out a similar strike on the Songei Gerong refinery. Once again forty-eight Avengers, with an escort of Corsairs, Hellcats, and Fireflies, dived through the balloon barrage to make sure of hitting their targets. The bombing was excellent and all the main targets were hit and largely destroyed. The photographs which were taken during the raid showed that the power house and distillery areas were a sea of fire.

Shortly after the striking force had landed on, the fleet was attacked by Japanese aircraft. At the time an air patrol was being flown by Seafires from the carriers and seven of them, forming the low patrol, were vectored out on to the approaching raid. Although the formation was broken up by the Seafires, the individual machines continued independently, diving down on the ships in a manner that made it appear that they were manned by suicide crews. The defending Seafires had orders to break off the engagement as soon as the enemy came within range of the Bofors anti-aircraft guns of the ships, but on this occasion, with a total disregard of their own safety, they followed the Japanese machines right in. They shot down all but one of the raiders, the last one falling to the guns of the ships.

This was the first large-scale action carried out by the Fleet Air Arm against the Japanese, and its success was most encouraging. The two refineries had been a major factor in the ability of Japan to continue the war in the islands, and their destruction was to play a large part in the future operations in the Pacific, partly by immobilizing enemy ships, partly by grounding enemy aircraft, through the resultant shortages of oil and aviation spirit. Even in May, four months after the attack, the Songei Gerong refinery was still completely out of action, while that at Pladjoe was producing less than half its normal output.

As important as the destruction of the two refineries was the victory in the air gained over the Japanese by the Fleet Air Arm. The whole operation had cost the Navy forty-one machines, including those which had ditched or had been lost in deck crashes ; only sixteen had fallen to enemy action. The Japanese losses were thirty certainties and seven probables shot down in the air, and thirty-eight destroyed on the ground. The figures proved that the machines now flying in the Fleet Air Arm were more than a match for the Japanese.

After these operations the carriers and their escorts returned, not to Ceylon but to Fremantle, in Western Australia, in preparation for further operations in the Pacific proper. From here, after embarking necessary stores and topping up with oil fuel, the ships sailed to Sydney to play their part in the war against the eastern enemy.

The Pacific presented many new problems to the Navy, problems that took a great deal of work and planning to circumvent. The chief requirement was for a method of keeping the fleet at sea for periods long enough to enable it to carry out sustained operations in very distant waters. For this purpose a Fleet Train had been formed and sent out to the East, a massive assembly of ships that formed almost a floating dockyard, able to accompany the fleet to sea. It could supply everything required by the ships, from spare aircraft to a packet of pins, from oil fuel and aviation spirit to bombs and ammunition, from fresh water and food to spare clothing and machinery. Included, too, were repair ships, with trained personnel to make good damage received in action. With its aid the British Pacific Fleet was enabled to remain in any theatre of operation for a month without having recourse to its forward or rear bases.

Under the immediate command of Admiral Sir Bruce Fraser, the British Pacific Fleet was placed under the operational control of the American Commander-in-Chief, Admiral Nimitz, and he was soon able to make good use of it. By mid-March, the fleet was at Manus, in the Admiralty Islands, carrying out exercises after its stay at Sydney, and on the 15th it received instructions to prepare for operations in support of the assault on Okinawa, a stepping-stone on the way to Japan proper. Three days later the main fleet sailed for the American forward base of Ulithi. It consisted of two battleships, H.M.S. *King George V* and H.M.S. *Howe*, the four fleet carriers which had taken part in the operations against Palembang, one cruiser squadron, and three destroyer squadrons. In the Fleet Train were three escort carriers, the *Speaker*, *Striker*, and *Slinger*, and the big replenishment carrier *Unicorn*.

The task given to the British Fleet was to neutralize the Japanese airfields in the Sakishima Gunto and to prevent aircraft from them moving north to attack the Americans during their assault on Okinawa. In order to be of any real and permanent value, the attacks on these airfields would need to be carried out almost daily over a long period. It was for this purpose that the Fleet Train was assembled, in order to keep the fleet at sea in the operational area for long enough to carry out the required duty.

Operations began on March 26th, all the airfields within reach being subjected to continuous attacks. The main object was to destroy as many aircraft on the ground as possible, to put airfield installations out of action, and to crater the runways with 500-pound bombs. At the same time fighter patrols were flown over the airfields to prevent any Japanese aircraft from taking off.

Six days later, on July 1st, the fleet had its first taste of Japanese reaction when a Kamikaze, or suicide, plane dived into the base of H.M.S. *Indefatigable*'s island. For a short time the flight deck was put temporarily out of action, but repairs were soon in hand and, two or three hours later, she was able to operate her aircraft, although on a reduced scale. Later on the same day another Kamikaze attacked the *Victorious*, but by a rapid turn to starboard, the carrier avoided the full force of the impact and the Japanese plane spun along her flight deck and into the sea.

Equally unsuccessful was a Kamikaze attack on the *Illustrious* on April 6th, the machine being hit by the ship's guns during its dive and striking the island a glancing blow, to finish up in the sea alongside. It was notable that the British carriers, with their steel flight decks, stood up to this form of attack very much better than did the American carriers, in which the flying decks were of wood.

During these operations, which lasted nearly a month, H.M.S. *Formidable* arrived to join the fleet, in which she relieved H.M.S. *Illustrious*. When the second series of operations against Sakishima Gunto was begun on May 1st, the *Formidable* remained with the carrier force while the *Illustrious* returned to Sydney to refit.

It was during this second month of operations that Kamikaze aircraft made a dead set at the carriers. On May 7th, when the battleships and cruisers had steamed inshore to speed the damage to the airfields with their main armament, a suicide plane was seen diving from a great height. This first one made his attack on the *Formidable*, and although the ship was manœuvred at high speed under full helm, the Japanese pilot managed to fly into the flight deck near the island, starting a large fire, while a splinter penetrated the hangar deck and continued down to the centre boiler room, where it pierced one of the steam pipes.

Three minutes later another Kamikaze attacked the *Indomitable*. It was set on fire by the ship's anti-aircraft guns but at the last moment flattened out and landed at full speed on the flight deck, to go bounding over the side into the sea, where its bomb burst alongside. After another eight minutes a third machine again made a suicide attack on the same ship. It was repeatedly hit by the close-range weapons of the *Indomitable* and one of the escorting destroyers, H.M.S. *Quality*, and it dived, burning fiercely, into the sea about 10 yards from the *Indomitable*'s bows.

Both ships managed to make good the damage with remarkable speed and by mid-afternoon both were flying off and landing on aircraft as usual. One of the American liaison officers in the *Formidable* expressed the opinion that, had it been an American carrier with her wooden decks that had been hit as the *Formidable* had been hit, she would have sunk. The episode, too, had its lighter side. When the captain of the *Formidable* relieved his feelings in a signal to the admiral—" Little yellow bastard "— a reply was received from Admiral Vian inquiring whether the message were a personal one for him.

There were further attacks on May 9th, during which two Kamikazes hit the *Victorious*, one being a glancing blow, a third just missed H.M.S. *Howe*, and a fourth dived into the after deck park of H.M.S. *Formidable*. It started a considerable fire and destroyed a good many aircraft, both in the park and in the hangar below. As before, the damage was very speedily repaired and the ship continued to operate her aircraft. For another sixteen days, in spite of the Kamikaze attacks, the four carriers remained at sea and carried out their programmes of bomber and fighter attacks on the Japanese airfields. By preventing their use by the enemy, they played a notable, if indirect, part in the final capture of Okinawa by the Americans.

There remained one further large-scale operation for the British Pacific Fleet, the final attack on the Japanese home islands. But before that could take place the fleet returned to Sydney to make permanent the temporary repairs carried out on board. It was from that port that the carriers, with H.M.S. *King George V*, seven cruisers, and twelve destroyers, sailed on June 27th, with Admiral Vian flying his flag in the *Indomitable*.

The fleet reached the striking area on July 16th and, until the end of the war against Japan, operated off the coast of the main Japanese islands. The chief targets were again airfields on the Japanese mainland in an attempt to cripple the enemy's air force before shifting the raids to dockyards and other vital installations. The object was to prepare the way for an amphibious attack, followed by military operations in the islands. A prerequisite for this was, of course, command of the air above the theatre of operations.

The task of the carriers was made more difficult on this occasion by the weather, and especially by typhoons. Although it was high summer, and although Japan lies nearer the equator than Great Britain, fog is often prevalent during these months, sometimes shrouding the fleet, sometimes the shore. An average of four typhoons a month rage in this part of the Pacific, and on many occasions carrier strikes arranged on enemy targets had to be postponed or cancelled because of the approach of a typhoon with its wide area of tremendous winds and rough seas.

Nevertheless, the aircraft of the Fleet Air Arm managed to do a vast amount of damage in this preliminary bombardment of Japan. When the first atomic bomb was dropped on Hiroshima on August 7th, it became evident that the need for an invasion was unlikely and that the surrender of Japan could be achieved from the air. The second atomic bomb did the trick, and the war came to an end with the carriers, their task now completed, on the very doorstep of Japan.

Almost the last strike of the war brought to a pilot of the Fleet Air Arm the award of a Victoria Cross, the second to be won by a flying member of the Navy during the Second World War. He was Lieutenant R. H. Gray, of the Royal Canadian Naval Volunteer Reserve, serving as a pilot in H.M.S. *Formidable*. He was flying a Corsair in a strike on Shiogama, and had selected as his target a destroyer lying in the harbour of Onagawa Wan. He was leading the Corsairs of his squadron, No. 1841, in to the attack in the face of a very heavy concentration of fire from shore batteries and ships, and during its approach he was hit and his aircraft set on fire. In spite of the flames, he kept control of his machine and, by brilliant flying, obtained one direct hit on the destroyer before his aircraft plunged into the sea. The destroyer was sunk.

Gray was one of the best pilots in the ship and had always been an inspired leader. Shortly before his death he had been awarded the D.S.C. for his work in the operations against the Sakishima Gunto airfields.

Coastal Command

ALTHOUGH IN NO WAY A PART OF THE FLEET AIR ARM, no account of the activities of naval aviation between the years 1939 and 1945 would be complete without a reference to the work carried out by Coastal Command of the Royal Air Force. Although one of the three main Royal Air Force commands, it came during the war under naval operational control. Until shortly before the war, its headquarters were at Lee-on-Solent, with Group headquarters at Devonport, Lee, and Chatham. In the summer of 1939 the main headquarters was moved to Northwood, where it could be in closer contact with the Admiralty, and it set up a new group headquarters at Rosyth. Shortly after the outbreak of war, new group headquarters were established at every naval command where coastal air forces might be operating. Both in the main headquarters at Northwood, and in every group headquarters, naval officers worked alongside air officers, using the same rooms, the same operational charts and maps, and the same signal headquarters. Thus was built up an equal partnership and a mutual trust that was to pay very large dividends during the fighting.

As in the Navy, the outbreak of war found Coastal Command with very few and very indifferent aircraft. It remained a struggle throughout the war for Coastal Command to get the aircraft it needed, mainly because of the priority given to Bomber Command in the acquisition of all long-range, four-engine machines. It is true that Coastal Command had a few four-engined flying boats, but its main need was, and remained, for long-range land-based aircraft, an infinitely more efficient type of machine than the somewhat unwieldy flying boat.

The first commitment given to Coastal Command at the outbreak of war was the protection of coastal shipping. Every available machine was called into service, and even unarmed de Havilland Moths, known as " scarecrows ", were employed.

Though they were unable to attack a U-boat if they sighted one, they could force it to dive and report its position. A policy of close air escort over coastal convoys was established, which undoubtedly discouraged U-boat attacks in inshore waters.

As the war developed and the pattern of the enemy's attack against shipping evolved, the calls upon Coastal Command grew in number. The U-boats moved out into the Atlantic and the invasion of Norway and the occupation of France provided new bases from which they could operate at a greatly increased distance. The need for really long-range aircraft which could patrol far out to sea grew more pressing, only partly relieved in 1941 by the allocation of a few American Liberators which had been discarded by Bomber Command as unfit for night bombing because of the flames emitted by their exhaust pipes. It was not until a year later that Liberators began to arrive in reasonably satisfactory numbers.

Nevertheless, in spite of its lack of suitable aircraft, Coastal Command soon began to make its influence felt in the war against U-boats. It has been mentioned in an earlier chapter how it was through the use of aircraft over the convoys that the submarine threat was largely defeated. The presence of an aircraft with a convoy was sufficient at least to keep a submarine submerged, and under water its speed was not sufficient to enable it to keep up with the convoy it wished to shadow or attack.

New bases were soon established from which aircraft of Coastal Command could play their part in protecting the North Atlantic routes. Aircraft from Gibraltar could give protection for convoys bound to and from the South Atlantic, and the setting up of a base in Iceland moved the area of operational flying further out into the Atlantic. But even with these bases, there still remained a wide gap in mid-Atlantic which was outside the range of shore-based aircraft and which, until the supply of escort-carriers was sufficiently large to allow some to be used on the convoy routes, provided a profitable hunting ground for the U-boats.

But within the areas they could patrol, the aircraft of Coastal Command played a notable part in the war at sea. They provided air cover during daylight hours to convoys passing through those areas and they flew endless patrols across the grey wastes of the Atlantic Ocean in search of U-boats on passage. It was not until January, 1941, that Coastal Command was credited with its first U-boat destroyed. It had, it is true, assisted in the destruction of two in combination with surface forces during 1940. The one sunk on January 6th, 1941, fell a victim to a Sunderland of 210 Squadron, under the command of Flight-Lieutenant E. F. Baker. It was an Italian submarine, the *Marcello*, and was sunk some 150 miles west of Cape Wrath by two depth charges dropped across the boat's track.

It was during April, 1941, that the Admiralty assumed full operational control of Coastal Command, acting through its Commander-in-Chief, Air Chief Marshal Sir Frederick Bowhill. In that month the original policy of close air escort for convoys was dropped and a new one of air sweeps, searches, and convoy escorts by air striking forces in those areas where U-boats were known to be operating was substituted. This new policy soon began to pay handsome dividends, though it brought a large addition of work to the command. But it was at this time that the Liberators were allocated to Coastal Command, making it possible to extend the range of searching aircraft and so to enlarge the area of comparative immunity from U-boat attack.

Coupled with the arrival of the Liberators was the perfection of the airborne radar set known as ASV (Air to Surface Vessel). Early sets had been fitted in a squadron of Whitleys in 1940, but they had not been particularly successful. It was not until the arrival at Coastal Command of Air Chief Marshal Sir Philip Joubert de la Ferté as Commander-in-Chief in June, 1941, that the full possibilities of ASV were realized in the air war against U-boats. He had had considerable experience of radar work and was one of the first to exploit its great possibilities in the location of surfaced U-boats.

With the gradual fitting of ASV to Coastal Command aircraft, the war was carried to the U-boats and defence was turned into offence. A constant day and night patrol was carried out across the Bay of Biscay in search of submarines proceeding to, or returning from, their patrol areas, and a mounting toll was taken. It increased still further when another invention, by Squadron-Leader Leigh, was installed. This was a searchlight, which could be switched on a few moments before an attack and illuminate the target by night. Henceforward the U-boat could be harried night and day while on passage, and many of them fell to Coastal Command aircraft while crossing the Bay.

Perhaps, in the earlier days of the war, the most spectacular success achieved by Coastal Command was the surrender of a U-boat to a Hudson aircraft of 269 Squadron. In the morning of August 27th, 1941, the Hudson on patrol had sighted a U-boat off Iceland and had managed to drop four depth-charges before the submarine had time to dive. The swiftness of the attack and its accuracy caused something like a panic among the crew and, after a second attack from the Hudson's guns, a white flag, consisting of the commanding officer's shirt, was waved from the conning-tower.

The Hudson wirelessed for naval and air assistance. A Catalina of 209 Squadron arrived during the afternoon to take over watch on the U-boat and that night a naval trawler, the *Northern Chief*, reached the position. It was too rough then to take off the crew, but suitable threats of dire punishment were passed should the captain attempt to scuttle the U-boat. In the morning, other trawlers arrived on the scene, the crew of the U-boat was transferred, and the boat herself taken in tow to Iceland, where she was beached, repaired, and finally brought home to Britain. She was U.570 and in due course she served in the Royal Navy as H.M.S. *Graph*, incidentally sinking one of her U-boat sister ships during a patrol in the Bay of Biscay in the following year.

One result of the mounting successes of Coastal Command in the war against U-boats was to force the German submarines to operate still farther out to the westward, beyond the range of shore-based aircraft. The only reply to that was to find yet longer-range machines, and it was fortunate that at this stage Liberators began to come forward in fairly satisfactory numbers. Even with them there was still a gap of some 400 miles in mid-Atlantic beyond the range of Coastal Command machines, a gap that was to remain until, by arrangement with our oldest ally, Portugal, it became possible to establish a Coastal Command station in the Azores.

It was, however, not only in the war against the U-boat menace that Coastal Command proved so extremely valuable to the Navy. One of their major commitments was the provision of photographic reconnaissance of the enemy ports, harbours, and coastline, and a great wealth of information was compiled from this source. It entailed a continuous effort, requiring long flights at a great height over enemy-occupied territory by unarmed planes, and no praise can be too high for the pilots who undertook this arduous duty. Very frequently, a daily photograph of the same area was required, so that ship movements could be followed, a proceeding that often laid the photographic aircraft open to attack. Many good pilots were lost on this service, but throughout the war the provision of this valuable intelligence was continued in an increasing volume, frequently making it possible to plan naval or air operations with some degree of certainty in finding the target it was hoped to attack.

Another big task undertaken by Coastal Command was the attack on enemy shipping as it proceeded along the French, Belgian, Dutch, German, Danish, and Norwegian coasts. Almost the entire German trade carried by sea proceeded as close as possible to the enemy-held coastline where it could come under the protection of such coastal defences as were in operation and under fighter cover from German Air Force stations. This hugging of the coast offered few opportunities to the Navy for attack, since ships were too vulnerable to air attack unless provided with fighter cover, and fighter cover at sea meant the use of a carrier, all too scarce a ship in the early years of war.

So it was that the onus of attack on German seaborne trade fell upon Coastal Command, and at the start Hudson aircraft, the only ones available, were used. The first attacks, usually carried out on a night of full moon, resulted in the sinking of many ships until the enemy began to take counter-measures. Soon after the attacks started the ships were heavily armed with light anti-aircraft weapons and convoyed by armed trawlers. It was too much for the slow and cumbersome Hudson and as aircraft losses began to mount, another method of attack had to be evolved. High level bombing was far too inaccurate to hit a moving ship. In the end the Command was given Beauforts which, when adapted as torpedo-strike aircraft, proved most successful. The usual method of attack was, on the report of a German convoy, to send out a squadron of Torbeaus, as the torpedo-carrying Beauforts were called, escorted by one or more squadrons of Beaufighters, the long-range fighter version of the Beaufort. These machines had many successes, and later, as the supply situation became easier, Mosquitoes were attached to the striking force, to add considerably to its power, range, and speed.

Still later, airborne rockets were substituted for torpedoes in attacks on smaller ships, a more economical, more accurate, and equally deadly form of attack against shipping.

Coastal Command had, too, an important part to play in the passage of convoys to North Russia. For the first convoys air cover was limited to the range of aircraft flying from bases in the Orkney Islands and Iceland. Thus, as the convoys passed into the danger zone of attack by the German main units based in the north of Norway, they lost the protection of air cover by reason of the limiting range of the shore-based Coastal Command machines.

The most dangerous threat to these convoys came from the German heavy units, the *Tirpitz*, *Scharnhorst*, *Scheer*, and *Hipper*, all based on northern Norway. Any one of these could have overwhelmed any convoy that it succeeded in intercepting. As we have seen in a preceding chapter, it was not a practicable operation to take our own main units into these waters, because of the danger of U-boats and torpedo-carrying planes. So it was that covering support for the convoys by heavy units of the fleet had to be limited to the first half of the voyage unless it was established that the German heavy units were actually at sea and the fleet in a position to cut them off from their base. Only then was the risk a seamanlike one.

It therefore became important, first, to know whether the big German ships had left their harbours, and second, to have some alternative method of attacking them if they did put to sea. Once again it was Coastal Command that could supply the most economical answer. A photographic reconnaissance unit was sent to North Russia to keep a constant watch on the movements of the German ships. A squadron of Catalina flying boats was also based there to provide air cover from the other end of the journey, and finally two squadrons of Hampden torpedo bombers were sent north to operate from Russian airfields in the event of the big German ships putting to sea. These measures, allied to the fighter cover provided by carrier-borne aircraft of the Fleet Air Arm, solved the problem of these convoys and enabled them to reach their destination with only small losses.

The activities mentioned above are, of course, only a very brief sample of the duties that fell to the lot of Coastal Command. For the rest much of their work was unspectacular, entailing long patrols in search of shipping, endless anti-submarine patrols across the Bay of Biscay, out into the Atlantic, and up to Iceland, searches along the coasts of France, the low countries, and Norway, and the escorting of convoys to the limit of flying range. Yet their contribution to the victory at sea, especially in the victory over the U-boat, was a large and decisive one and they took over a great many duties that were far beyond the capacity of the Fleet Air Arm to accomplish. There were, it is true, occasional clashes of opinion between the Navy and the Royal Air Force as to the degree of control which the Admiralty could exercise, but on the whole the two Services worked in very close accord and the excellent results achieved were probably due as much to the integration of staffs at the various group head-quarters and the harmonious relations in which naval and air officers worked alongside each other, as to the individual and collective gallantry of the Coastal Command aircrews.

The Post-War Pattern

UNLIKE THE 1914–18 WAR, WHEN BY THE CESSATION of hostilities little coherent thought on the use of aircraft at sea had emerged out of the fighting, the war of 1939–45 at least produced a settled pattern of the tactical and strategical employment of the air arm. The lessons were clear-cut and decisive and left no room for doubt as to the profound effects on naval operations that carrier-borne aircraft could exercise.

It was demonstrated beyond all argument that naval aviation had become an integral part of the fleet, and that any attempt to operate ships in enemy waters without a strong air component was foredoomed to failure. The diversified activities of naval aircraft during the war, and the outstanding successes they had achieved, had held up in bold relief the ubiquity of their value at sea.

When the war came to an end, Britain had a strong fleet of carriers, manned for the most part by American machines. Most of the smaller escort carriers were American, too, obtained under the lend-lease programme. All these, of course, had to be returned when lend-lease came to an end, and as a result, in carriers at any rate, Britain was left only with ships of her own construction.

Not that there was any shortage of carriers. There were six fleet carriers—the *Implacable*, *Indefatigable*, *Indomitable*, *Formidable*, *Victorious*, and *Illustrious*—and five light fleet carriers, just completed or completing—the *Glory*, *Ocean*, *Theseus*, *Triumph*, and *Warrior*. Building were three very large carriers, which were cancelled, four large fleet carriers of 37,000 tons, of which two were cancelled, eight light fleet carriers of 18,000 tons, of which four were cancelled, and three 14,000-ton light fleet carriers, of which the work on two was, and at the time of writing still is, suspended, the third being completed for Canada. Since the end of the war H.M.S. *Indomitable* has been scrapped, the two new large fleet carriers, H.M.S. *Eagle* and H.M.S. *Ark Royal*, have been completed, as have three of the four 18,000-ton light fleet carriers, the *Albion*, *Bulwark*, and *Centaur*. In comparison with the remainder of the fleet, therefore, it will be seen that the Royal Navy has devoted a considerable proportion of her strength to the naval air arm.

The position in regard to aircraft was not so satisfactory. During the war the main priorities in aircraft construction were given to the Royal Air Force, leaving the Fleet Air Arm to exist as best it could on machines of American design and manufacture. Since the war the main priorities have still been allocated to the Royal Air Force, although the American source had largely dried up. The Fleet Air Arm had thus to rely on what was available after the appetite of the R.A.F. had been satisfied, and it was, on the whole, only with some difficulty that it managed to make its voice heard, and its requirements known, in the general allocation of aircraft-manufacturing facilities for defence.

This, however, was not the only problem that faced the Admiralty in respect to the Fleet Air Arm. Although, from experience of actual war, it could state its basic responsibilities in the fleet with some degree of certitude, new factors had appeared which were having a profound effect on aircraft generally. These were the many technical advances being made, the change-over from piston-engine to jet and gas turbine, the approach to sonic and supersonic speeds, and the development of new weapons of the atomic and guided missile type.

Before we take a look at the shape of the post-war Fleet Air Arm, it would be as well to lay down briefly the many lessons learned in the last war and to judge from those the essential requirements of naval aviation during any future conflict at sea. It is only when these requirements are fully appreciated and kept firmly in objective view that the present developments can be properly comprehended.

The first, and overriding, aspect of naval aviation that emerged from the war was that it was not a service apart, an air component of the Navy, but an integral part of it, extending the range and efficiency of sea power as exercised by the ships of the fleet. The two classic examples of this, of course, were the battle of Cape Matapan and the hunt of the *Bismarck*, although many more episodes could be picked out, such as the successful search for enemy raiders and blockade runners, in which aircraft co-operated with cruisers. This was direct work with the fleet, in which aircraft proved themselves to be an extension of the range of the guns and of visual search.

Equally important was the provision of close fighter support of fleets, squadrons, and convoys at sea. This lesson was most painfully and expensively learned off Malaya in the sinking of the *Prince of Wales* and the *Repulse*, in the naval losses off Crete in 1941, and in the many ships sunk in convoy before the Macships and the escort carriers made their appearance. The advent of the jet bomber has made this an even more vital commitment since the ending of the war, for the opportunities of surprise air attack on ships at sea are obviously greater with the new fast machines than with the older, slower ones.

We learned, too, that carrier-borne aircraft brought with them the ability to mount attacks on the enemy in places where he least expected it, and to cover assaults designed to further the land operations of the Army. As an example of the former can be taken the Fleet Air Arm attack on Taranto, where the main Italian Fleet was decimated in the security of its own defended base, of the latter were the invasion of Madagascar, the landing at Salerno, and the Allied assault on southern France in 1944. In these operations it was the presence of the carrier which made possible the assaults from the sea, since the chosen theatres of operation were beyond the range of shore-based fighters.

Finally there was the protection of trade. In order to maintain a major war, Great Britain must import munitions and supplies. Each week something like one million tons of supplies must arrive in British ports if the country is to be successfully defended. We have seen in earlier chapters the part played by the Fleet Air Arm and by Coastal Command in the protection of convoys, both from air and submarine attack, and how, as soon as air cover was provided, whether from carrier-borne or shore-based aircraft, the incidence of ship losses in convoy dropped decisively. Nor should it be forgotten that, of all the enemy U-boats sunk in the war, something like one-half of them fell victim to attack from the air. The success of air attack on the underwater menace during the 1939–45 war was something of a revelation to the Naval Staff.

It is, therefore, these main requirements that have to be borne in mind in any build-up of the Fleet Air Arm. They have, too, to be related to the growing power and speeds of the new machines and the technological advances in such ancillary services as directly concern the naval aircraft, such as development in radar, weapons of attack and defence, and so on.

It was within a few months of the end of the war in 1945 that the Navy had its first demonstration of the new techniques to which the Fleet Air Arm would have to be fashioned. The jet engine had made its appearance as the war was approaching its end, and its adoption had, at a single bound, raised the speed of aircraft by some 50 per cent. It was fairly obvious that to a jet attack would have to be matched a jet defence if the Fleet Air Arm was to be able to carry out its duty of providing fighter cover over the fleet, and that therefore some way must be found of operating jets from carriers.

The main problem was the high landing speed of a jet fighter. The flight deck of a carrier is, and always must be, limited in length, and so some method of reducing the stalling speed of such a machine had to be evolved. By the end of 1945 modifications had been made to a Vampire fighter which brought its stalling speed down to about 95 miles an hour, and it was thought that this would be low enough to attempt a deck landing.

The trial was carried out on 4th December, 1945. H.M.S. *Ocean* was at sea off the Isle of Wight, while ashore a modified Vampire, now known as a Sea Vampire, was drawn up on the runway at Lee-on-Solent. It was piloted by Lieut.-Commander E. M. Brown, and he took off as soon as signals had been received that the *Ocean* was ready for landing on.

In the ship the fire fighters were ready in their asbestos suits, and the crash crews standing by for any emergency. The Vampire circled the *Ocean* and came in over her stern to land. It was a tense moment, for this was a new development outside the experience of anyone on board. Brown, as he came in, picked up the first arrester wire and the Vampire came to a stop within 100 feet. It was the first time in history that a jet aircraft had landed successfully on the deck of a ship, and it opened up a new horizon in naval aviation. Later that day Brown demonstrated the reverse action and successfully took off in about half the length of the flight deck. For this he had an assisted take-off with rockets.

Once it had been demonstrated that the jet aircraft was a practical possibility as a carrier-borne machine, orders were placed for new types to fill the varied needs of the service—reconnaissance

machines; fighters, long and short range, day and night; torpedo-carrying aircraft and bombers; anti-submarine aircraft;
and so on. It is, of course, an extremely difficult task to look
ahead and try to foresee the future pattern of naval aviation in
days when the technological advances in design and performance
are extremely rapid, as is the case today, but the new aircraft that
are now coming into squadron service in the Fleet Air Arm are
fully capable of holding their own against any present-day opposition and of carrying out the offensive tasks for which they are
designed.

These new aircraft, however, are rapidly reaching the limit in
size and speed that can be efficiently handled in the carrier of today.
By modern standards, many of the carriers at present in the fleet
are approaching obsolescence and the handling of modern aircraft
on board them presents difficulties. Their conversion and modernization is an extremely costly business and, for some of the older
carriers, would be decidedly uneconomic. Sooner or later this
is a problem that will have to be faced and it is one that can only
be solved by the provision of new carriers to replace those that
are worn out and are not worth the cost of conversion.

Two modern developments in the carrier, designed to enable
them to handle the modern aircraft now coming forward, are
the angled deck and the steam catapult. The former, in which
the flight deck is offset by some eight to ten degrees from the
ship's centre line, gives in effect a longer runway, since the aircraft
park forward is now not a part of the flight deck proper. With
the conventional flying deck a crash barrier has to be erected
across the flight deck to protect the parked aircraft forward, and
this cuts down the effective landing length by nearly one-third.
With the angled deck, the whole length is available, and if a
machine lands on too fast, it can fly straight off again and come
round for a second attempt. The steam catapult, at the moment
not yet required with the present-day machines, will provide
additional launching power as naval aircraft increase in weight and
minimum take-off speed. Both these British inventions are being
incorporated in the new carriers just coming into service in the
fleet and will, no doubt, be fitted in those of the older carriers
that undertake full modernization.

Since 1945 the Royal Navy has had the opportunity in war
of testing out its carrier technique, though not under full naval

P

war-time conditions. Throughout the fighting in Korea, one
carrier was always on active service off the coast, though its tasks
in the main could hardly be considered as naval. There was, too,
no opposition from the sea and practically none from the air. It
is true that, during these operations, some purely naval flying was
done, such as the detailed reconnaissance of the enemy-held coasts
and strikes against enemy minelayers and local supply shipping,
but the majority of the flying was in support of the armies ashore,
the type of activity that would normally fall to a tactical air force
of land-based machines.

Yet the experience in Korea did provide the Fleet Air Arm with
valuable experience, especially in handling aircraft on board under
war, or semi-war, conditions. New techniques were worked out
to give greater efficiency on board and as the fighting in Korea
progressed it was found that substantially larger numbers of aircraft could be handled during a working day. At the start of
hostilities 60 to 70 sorties a day was an extremely good average
for a light fleet carrier ; by the time the fighting ceased, a light
fleet carrier could put up 120 a day. It was valuable training, too,
for pilots and aircrews, for much of the operational flying was
against heavy ground opposition and, occasionally, modern jet
fighters.

There is one aspect of modern aircraft development that may
well have a big influence on naval air warfare in defence of sea-
borne trade. This is the coming of the helicopter, a type of
machine which would appear to have a very big future in war.
For use at sea, its great advantage is that it can operate independently of a carrier, being able to take off and land on a small
platform such as could be erected on any merchant ship. There
would thus seem to be considerable possibilities for its use in anti-
submarine role, replacing the necessity of an escort carrier in many
of the ocean convoys.

Under the conditions of 1939–45, a convoy with air cover above
it could count on almost complete security from submarine
attack. The presence of an aircraft forced the submarine to
submerge to avoid attack, and their low underwater speed enabled
the convoys to get beyond, or keep beyond, torpedo range. The
helicopter can do this as efficiently as a conventional aircraft, and
with the added economy of not requiring a carrier for its operation and maintenance. It can also locate and attack submarines

by the same means as the conventional aircraft, the fitting of radar and the carrying of depth charges. It can even carry out some of the tasks of the escorting ships by lowering an Asdic set into the sea and hovering above it while it is being operated. Its drawback is its vulnerability to fighter attack and its inability to act as a fighter in the event of an attack by bombers, but for use beyond reasonable bomber range at sea it would appear to be an efficient and economical substitute for the carrier-borne machines. Helicopters are already in use in the Fleet Air Arm, and the first squadron formed for anti-submarine duties is, at the moment of writing, undergoing training.

But here again the technical advances made since the war may well overtake the intention and render necessary a new approach. Just as aircraft have been improving in design, so have submarines, and the new boats now coming forward are likely to be far more dangerous in attack than the old. They have already a higher submerged speed that can enable them to remain submerged and yet reach a convoy without disclosing their presence. In the United States there has recently been launched a submarine using nuclear reaction for its motive power, and official pronouncements give it a submerged speed of from 20 to 25 knots and a submerged endurance of as many weeks as its crew can stand. Such a vessel, if attacking a convoy, could produce a situation in which air cover would be only a very slight guarantee from attack. Equally dangerous is the new British submarine *Explorer*, driven by a closed cycle Diesel installation which gives similar speed and endurance under water.

These are the sort of problems which are continually facing the Fleet Air Arm and it is in their light that policy must be formed. The building of a new aircraft carrier takes some five or six years, or even longer ; two or more years will elapse before a newly designed aircraft reaches the production stage. Each new development, each technological advance, may render obsolete the carriers and aircraft not only of today but those under construction for tomorrow as well, and in no industry has technical advance been so rapid as in the aircraft industry.

Obviously, in the face of facts such as these, no finality can ever be reached, and no one can even be fully satisfied with the condition of things as they are. The Fleet Air Arm is no exception and it must always remain vulnerable to the speed of invention and the development of new types of aircraft and new techniques in operating them. The policy that has been adopted by the Naval Staff during these difficult years is to aim at qualitative, rather than quantitative, supremacy, and the production of limited numbers of those types of aircraft which, while embodying as much of the new invention as possible, were above all fitted for the tasks they would have to undertake in war. But that stage is passing and the new aircraft now coming forward for service in the Navy are the result not only of very considerable study during the years since the war but also of much experience in flying the various types that have been developed during these post-war years. These new machines, many of which are now in quantity production, are for their purpose the best that the country can produce.

Yet, even while the Fleet Air Arm is rearming with these new machines, the story is not ended. They, too, will have their day, to be replaced by others of still higher performance. Research is never-ending, and the modern Fleet Air Arm, if it is to remain modern, must always strive to keep abreast of every new development in the art of flying.

The Way Ahead

It has been the intention of this book to try to tell something of the story of the Fleet Air Arm, tracing it from its first beginnings to its present state, a force with all the knowledge and experience of two world wars behind it. The book has tried to show, too, how the growth and development of the Fleet Air Arm has depended on its complete integration with the surface ships of the Navy. Its rise has been rapid and, in something under half a century, it has brought about radical changes in naval thought and action. While the old principles of naval strategy still remain, the advent of naval aviation has enlarged their sphere and made possible a more ambitious conception of their execution.

It is a temptation, therefore, to attempt to look into the future and to try to forecast what lies ahead in the sphere of naval flying. The two factors that, at the present time and in the foreseeable future, are likely to have the most bearing on the employment of the Fleet Air Arm are those of national economy and the development of new weapons.

Since the end of the war the cost of ships has risen steeply to such a height that it is economically impossible in peacetime to provide a Navy of the size that we can remember before the war. We had, for instance, fifty cruisers before the war, and even that number was not considered sufficient to guard the trade routes of the Empire. Now the Navy's strength in cruisers is twenty-four, some of them approaching the end of their useful life. But today a cruiser costs some ten million pounds to build and it would be too great a burden on the country's economy to attempt to maintain cruiser strength at even the pre-war level. So, to some extent, the Fleet Air Arm must take the cruiser's place and be prepared to take a greater share of its traditional role in the protection of trade. In this respect one could foresee in any future war the Fleet Air Arm having to play a greater part in the work of intercepting and destroying enemy surface raiders.

The same story holds good for the battleship, too. The battleship of today is far too costly a ship to build on a peacetime budget, even though it is still the most powerful type of warship in the world. Through economic reasons the battleship is almost certainly a dying type, at least in its present form, though it may well later make a reappearance as the capital ship of the future in the form of a guided-missile ship. But until it does, one sees the carrier as the capital ship of the present day, with its strike aircraft largely taking the place of the battleship's heavy gun.

To some extent, therefore, economic factors today are playing into the hands of the Fleet Air Arm in making it a vastly important part, perhaps even a preponderately important part, of the Royal Navy. But it is as well to remember that, ubiquitous as the naval aircraft may be in the range of its activities, it cannot carry the whole weight of war at sea. There has on occasions been a tendency—happily not in the Navy itself—to assume that air power has replaced sea power, and that the warship, in all its categories, is obsolete. That doctrine has even been expressed in Parliament and solemnly debated. That it is a highly dangerous policy is not always easy to prove to the enthusiastic airman unless one studies the lessons of history and appreciates the vital dependence of this country in war upon its sea communications and the efficient guarding of the sea routes. Operations at sea form an integral part of overall strategy in war, and those operations at sea can only be carried out by ships, though nowadays with the co-operation, but not the substitution, of aircraft.

It was Admiral Sir John Fisher, when he was First Sea Lord, who said, in a memorable speech, that no soldier could fight unless he had a sailor to carry him on his back. It is a fundamental truth, and it applies directly today as much to the airman as it does to the soldier, for the airman is dependent on seaborne supplies even to get his aircraft into the air.

So it can be appreciated that, however much economic considerations may point towards a greatly increased Fleet Air Arm, a balance must be preserved between aircraft and ships ; that the Fleet Air Arm, while it has a very important role to play in the Navy, can never become the Navy itself, as some irresponsible people have been suggesting. Nor is it a naval service apart from the ships, for it depends on the ships, as much as the ships depend on its aircraft, for every branch of its activities at sea.

The other factor which must have a big influence on the Fleet Air Arm is the evolution of new weapons. If we carry to its logical conclusion the present development of the atomic bomb and the guided missile, and combinations of the two, one can see, perhaps far in the future, the time when the carrier becomes obsolete and must be discarded. Fighter cover for the fleet will then, presumably, be provided by the anti-aircraft guided missile, of which reports have already been made public. Similarly, strike aircraft will probably be replaced by guided missiles, either fired and controlled from ships at sea or, as their range increases, from firing stations ashore. This, of course, is the " push-button " warfare, towards which modern research appears to be heading, eliminating the human element from many of the present operations of war.

But whatever the final outcome of research in this direction, it is quite certain that it will be a great many years before such a type of warfare is perfected. And until it is we may expect to retain the conventional type of Fleet Air Arm that we have today, with aircraft carriers to perform the role of mobile airfield.

It would seem certain that, for many years ahead, the path to be trodden by the Fleet Air Arm must move steadily forward in the direction plotted by the experiences of the last two wars. Probably, in the end, that path will disappear in the mazes of atomic and guided missile warfare, but until it does its main direction looks fairly settled.

In the forty-five years of its existence the Fleet Air Arm has shown a surprising ability to weld itself into the traditional pattern of naval warfare, extending and diversifying it, and at the same time bringing together the sea and the air into a formidable partnership in war. In doing so it has achieved a notable record of gallantry and success. It is a record of which all who have been concerned with naval aviation can deservedly be immensely proud.

Index

224

Hertfordshire
COUNTY COUNCIL
Community Information

1 2 APR 2001

- 2 MAY 2001

2 7 SEP 2001   2 0 NOV 2006

- 5 OCT 2001   1 0 APR 2006

                    9/12

2 2 AUG 2006

Please renew/return this item by the last date shown.

So that your telephone call is charged at local rate,
please call the numbers as set out below:

	From Area codes 01923 or 020:	From the rest of Herts:
Renewals:	01923 471373	01438 737373
Enquiries:	01923 471333	01438 737333
Minicom:	01923 471599	01438 737599

L32

L.32

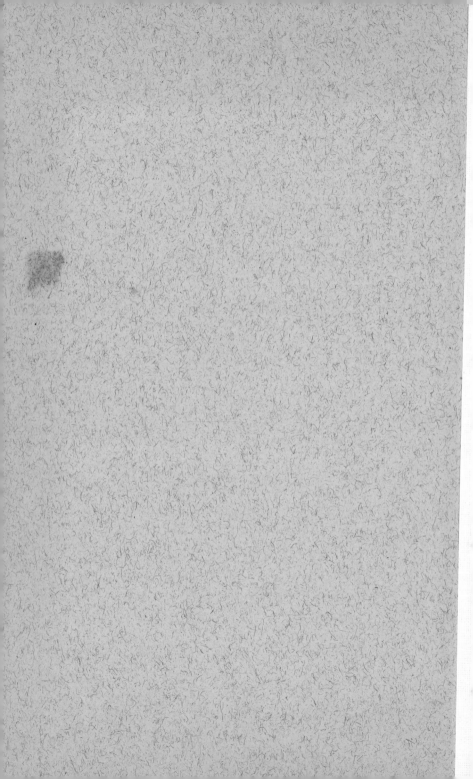